Religion in Strange Times:
The 1960s and 1970s

Religion in Strange Times:
The 1960s and 1970s

by
Ronald B. Flowers

Mercer University Press

ISBN 0-86554-127-2

All books published by Mercer University Press are produced
on acid-free paper that exceeds the minimum standards set by the
National Historical Publications and Records Commission.

Library of Congress Cataloging in Publication Data:

Flowers, Ronald B. (Ronald Bruce), 1935-
    Religion in strange times.

    Includes bibliography.
    Includes index.
  1. United States—Religion—1960-   . I. Title.
BL 2525.F56   1984   200'.973   84-1062
     ISBN 0-86554-127-2 (alk. paper)

CONTENTS

FOREWORD..ix

ACKNOWLEDGMENTS... xiii

CHAPTER ONE
The 1960s:
Trying to Remember and Trying to Forget 1

CHAPTER TWO
What Was So Strange About Jimmy Carter?
The Resurgence of Born-Again Christianity.............................. 31

CHAPTER THREE
"O for a Thousand Tongues to Sing":
Understanding the Charismatic Movement 61

CHAPTER FOUR
On Being "Moonstruck":
A Look at the "Cult" Movement...85

CHAPTER FIVE
On Living in Strange Times:
The Causes of It All... 113

CHAPTER SIX
Mrs. O'Hair, Where Were You When We Needed You?
Critical Issues in Church-State Relations 139

CHAPTER SEVEN
Is God Color-Conscious or Color-Blind?
Black Theology in the Church 177

CHAPTER EIGHT
All About Eve and the Goddess:
A Layperson's Guide to Feminist Theology 199

EPILOGUE 231

INDEX 233

DEDICATION

FOREWORD

Three concerns prompted me to write this book. First, I lived through the events I have described here. I was a pastor of several small churches and a graduate student during the first half of the 1960s. My college teaching career began in 1966. Throughout the 1960s and 1970s I was a fascinated observer of the religious phenomena of the times and, upon reflection, I became convinced that they were of major significance to the history of Americans as a people.

My second concern is the rather distressing ignorance of my students about those times. For many of them—in terms of their intellectual and emotional engagement with the period—the 1960s might just as well be the 1760s. Assuming that my students are typical of the majority of young adults, I believe that a book that attempts to pull together the major events of the two decades will be useful.

Third, I took up the task because I have received so many requests from church groups of various denominations, asking me to help them "make sense" of what they were reading in the papers and seeing on television. It seems likely, then, that other people might also want a better understanding of recent religious trends.

Therefore, this book is not aimed primarily at specialists in American religious history, but at a general audience of students, laypeople in church and synagogue, and all who are interested in the role that religion plays in American society. It also should be noted that this book is not a comprehensive treatment of the religious trends of those decades. Rather, it is an overview, an attempt to pull together the major events into a coherent whole. I have taken much of my agenda from the mass media, because it seemed that the events upon which the media had concentrated in the 1960s and 1970s would be the situations in which people might be most interested.

So the attempt here is to bring some analysis and interpretation to trends, rather than to describe every jot and tittle of the religious history of the period. In spite of the expectation of many moderns that religion will fade away and become only an artifact for antiquarian and nostalgic interest, just the contrary is true. Religion is very much a part of American life. It was very important in the 1960s and 1970s, strange times indeed. This book attempts to make sense out of what happened then and gives readers some clues about the way religion in the 1980s was greatly influenced by those decades.

As all authors know, and most admit, a project such as this is never a solo performance. In addition to those scholars and investigators whose previous work informs one's own, there are those people who render beneficial specific services. I owe a debt of gratitude to a number of co-laborers. Colleagues from the religion faculties of Texas Christian University and its seminary, Brite Divinity School, read the manuscript. Professors D. Newell Williams and D. James Atwood read the entire manuscript, Bryan Feille read chapters one through six and Nadia Lahutsky read chapters seven and eight. All of these scholars made invaluable comments.

In the preliminary stages of the work the secretary of the Department of Religion-Studies at TCU, Annice Ipser, and students in the department, Martha Jean Spleth and Linda Rosenstiel, contributed typing services. My enthusiastic gratitude goes to my student assistant for 1982-1983 and 1983-1984, Ann Watkins, who prepared the final copy of the manuscript and helped proofread the galleys and prepare the index. Ann not only learned word processing techniques in order to work on the project, but displayed perseverance, good humor, and a dedication to doing excellent work which are uncharacteristic of most people, much less undergraduates.

Finally, special appreciation must be expressed to my wife, Leah. She proofread the manuscript. But much more importantly, she endured this project for more than three years, from inception to completion. She shared with me and understood the elation, despair, and especially the fatigue I felt as the work progressed. For that I am grateful.

Book publishing is becoming increasingly expensive. For providing funds to help in this publication, my thanks go to the Christian Foundation of Corpus Christi, Texas, administered by the First Christian Church of that city; Michael McCracken, Dean of AddRan College of Arts and Sciences of Texas Christian University; and the donor of a substantial amount who preferred to remain anonymous. I also acknowledge with appreciation Gilbert Davis, Director of Church Relations at Texas Christian University, for his assiduous efforts in this matter.

ACKNOWLEDGMENTS

The following publishers have given permission to use quotations from copyrighted works: From the introduction of *Womanspirit Rising: A Feminist Reader in Religion*, edited by Carol P. Christ and Judith Plaskow. Copyright © 1979 by Carol P. Christ and Judith Plaskow. Reprinted by permission of Harper and Row, Inc. From *Issues of Theological Conflict* by Richard J. Coleman. Copyright © 1976 by Wm. B. Eerdmans Co. Reprinted by permission of Wm. B. Eerdmans Co. From "Women in Pulpits" by Lareta Finger, which appeared in *The Other Side* 15 (July 1979). Copyright © 1979 by Jubilee, Inc. Reprinted by permission of Jubilee, Inc. From *The Negro Church in America* by E. Franklin Frazier and *The Black Church Since Frazier* by C. Eric Lincoln (bound as one book). Copyright © 1963 by The University of Liverpool. Reprinted by permission of Schocken Press, Inc. From *The Work of a Common Woman* by Judy Grahn. Copyright © 1978 by Judy Grahn. Reprinted by permission of St. Martin's Press, Inc. From *Why We Can't Wait* by Martin Luther King, Jr. Copyright © 1963 by Martin Luther King, Jr. Reprinted by permission of New American Library, New York. From *Stride Toward Freedom* by Martin Luther King, Jr. Copyright © 1958 by Martin Luther King, Jr. Reprinted by permission of Harper and Row, Inc. From "The Christian Past: Does it Hold a Future for Women?" by Eleanor L. McLaughlin, which appeared in *The Anglican Theological Review* 57 (January 1975). Copyright © 1975 by the Anglican Theological Review. Re-

CHAPTER ONE

The 1960s:
Trying to Remember
and Trying to Forget

The 1960s: what a decade! The years 1961 through 1970 were years of excitement and stimulation, hope and promise, agony and despair, frustration and uncertainty, heroism and vision, pettiness and meanness, controversy and confrontation. Certainly they were not boring. Although those years may already seem like "ancient history" to some contemporary young people, they were of cataclysmic importance to American history. Many historians believe that decade was a time of national trauma, a turning point, a watershed for the course of American social and political life. A period of such significance should not be forgotten or ignored.

- *The Calm Before the Storm: 1945-1960*

Few forewarnings betrayed the turbulence that was to come. The 15 years after World War II were, in many ways, a time of tranquility and optimism. Although few citizens had thought of World War II as naively as an earlier generation had entered World War I—as "the war to end all wars"—nonetheless, there was a sense of confidence after 1945. Our enemies had been defeated by a combination of American ingenuity, industry, and spunk. For that reason, if for no other, there was a national sense of accomplishment. But the skills and energy that had won that victory now spilled over into peacetime.

Great days were ahead for America, now that it could go on about the business of living a "normal" life. G.I.s came home to rejoin wives or marry sweethearts and establish homes. There was a "baby boom" principally because people felt that the future held promise in which they could safely raise a family. Because of the beneficence of the government through the G.I. Bill of Rights, veterans invested in their promising future by going to college in unprecedented numbers. In the late 1940s and throughout the 1950s there was an "education boom." Because the veterans and those college students just out of high school were determined to learn the skills that would enable them to take their places in the expanding market place, they tended to devote their time to their studies. In spite of some of the usual college high jinks, historians have characterized the students of the 1950s as passive, bland, and uninteresting.

To be sure, in the midst of the optimism there were some fears; not everything was wonderful. The United States had dropped two atomic bombs on Japan—acts justified by the government with the argument that the use of this new power had shortened the war, saving American and even Japanese lives. But the appearance of this new and terrifying instrument of destruction cast a pall of apprehension over Americans. There was some questioning of both wartime and peacetime uses of atomic power. These anxieties were increased considerably when, in 1949, the Soviet Union revealed its own nuclear bomb and when, in 1952, the U.S. perfected the hydrogen bomb, a weapon that dramatically increased the efficiency of destruction.

Mention of the Soviet Union recalls another concern of the postwar years, the threat of Communism. There was, among some, a terrible fear that domestic "creeping Communism" was eating away at the vital organs of American cultural, intellectual, and political life, sapping the nation of its strength and resolve to be great. This attitude was personified and, indeed, promoted by Senator Joseph McCarthy of Wisconsin. McCarthy and some of his allies launched what many considered to be "witch hunts" to discover and root out Communists and "fellow-travelers," to purify the nation of those who would, it was said, destroy its internal security. Although it turned out that many of McCarthy's accusations were distorted, if not false, and that the reputations and careers of some innocent people were destroyed, the "red scare" dominated most of the first half of the 1950s. This fear of Communism was further provoked when, in 1950, Communist North Korea and later Communist China invaded South Korea. The United States played a major role in a United Nations "police action" to check the spread of Communist domination. In 1957 Russia demonstrated that a Communist regime could be innovative and technologically threatening to America by launching a space satellite, Sputnik I, into earth orbit; that one act shifted the emphasis of American education into more scientific pursuits for almost a generation.

Religion was characterized in those years by high levels of activity and interest. Indicators such as church membership, church and Sunday school attendance, new church construction, and the publication of religious books were all higher than in prewar years. Surveys indicated that a larger portion of the population was interested in religion; an increasing number thought of religious leaders as making a significant contribution to the good of the country. In 1954 the phrase "under God" was added to the pledge of allegiance to the flag.

In academic circles a theology known as "neo-orthodoxy" was still in vogue. Neo-orthodoxy had been formulated in the 1920s and 1930s as a corrective to the naive optimism of the religion of pre-World War I days. Although not literalistic in its interpretation of the Bible, it did emphasize classical theological themes such as the sovereignty of God, the strength and pervasiveness of sin, and the ambiguity of life. Neo-orthodoxy was a dominant theme in theological schools well into the late 1950s, although it was soon to give way to the radicalism of the 1960s. But even in the late 1940s and in the 1950s academic theology did not often filter down to the grass roots level. The surge of popular piety was largely uninformed by academic theology. Indeed, there were a number of critics who believed that popular religion was essentially empty of significant theological content. Rather, they perceived it to be a culture-religion in which the main articles of belief were not so much religious as political: free enterprise, "our country is God's chosen nation," opposition to atheistic Communism.

But in these years characterized by a sense of national well-being—an optimism tinctured with fears of global Communism and the evil potential of nuclear war—there were some specific problems in American life. Racial and ethnic prejudice continued to be part of our national character. Although blacks and other minorities had tried to gain a place as equals in American life for generations, that effort was intensified after

World War II. Black soldiers had gone to fight and die for "freedom." Yet they returned home to a segregated society that denied them basic rights that America claimed were due to all citizens. Nazi Germany, with its hideous campaign to exterminate the Jews, had shown what a society based on racism could become. Consequently, agitation for civil rights for blacks intensified after the war. In 1954 the Supreme Court declared, in *Brown v. Board of Education*, that educational institutions should not be segregated by race. The Court recommended "all deliberate speed" in implementing this decision. Some portions of the country understood that phrase to mean "never;" in virtually all cases, the process was agonizingly slow and painful, and is not yet complete. Black people recognized that there would be resistance to any kind of "speed" in desegregation, educational or otherwise, and thus began to take direct, although nonviolent, action. In 1955 and 1956 the black community of Montgomery, Alabama, boycotted the bus system of the city until the buses and some businesses in the community were desegregated. The Montgomery experience demonstrated that nonviolent direct action could be effective; it catapulted Martin Luther King, Jr. into a leadership position; and it emboldened blacks to try other strategies of direct action to integrate American society. What lay ahead for blacks and for the nation, however, was clearly demonstrated in 1957 when it was necessary for President Eisenhower to send federal troops to Little Rock, Arkansas, to enforce desegregation of the schools.

Another specific problem of the late 1950s that had great implications for the future was the disenchantment of a portion of the young population with the nature of American life and culture. Some youth, primarily those of college age, began to feel that American society was unexciting, devoid of meaning, and committed to a deadening materialism. They sensed that these features of society could lead to nothing but dreary, routine, meaningless lives. These people, inspired by writers such as Jack Kerouac and Allen Ginsberg who railed against virtually all "traditional American values," decided to pursue an alternative lifestyle, including use of consciousness-altering drugs, rebellion against sexual mores, and a refusal to get caught up in the "rat race" to "succeed." These young people became known as "beatniks."

As the 1950s came to a close, it seemed that the undercurrent of problems in the society had a force that unrelentingly drove them to the forefront of public consciousness. In the 1960s Americans focused on national problems. Whatever tranquility existed in the fifteen years after World War II was shattered in the 1960s, a decisive decade in American history.

• *The Search For Civil Rights*

The decade was dominated by the civil rights movement. That movement was based on the conviction of black people that American society was pervaded by a racist mentality, a conviction that was derived directly from the observations and everyday experiences of blacks all over the land. The civil rights movement was also based on the belief that the consciousness of the white power structure needed to be sensitized to the plight of blacks and other minority groups; that whites generally needed to be enlightened about the prejudice, discrimination, and overt cruelty that black people continued to endure. The civil rights movement was also rooted in the awareness that whites would not voluntarily give up positions of privilege and power. Clear illustrations were available that the movement for equality would face hate and strong resistance. Since the *Brown* decision little progress had been made in the integration of schools; the conflict at Little Rock illustrated that the schools would be a battleground against unyielding prejudice. Montgomery had been another case in point. It was obvious to increasing numbers of black people that since the majority community would not voluntarily relinquish "Jim Crow" laws and customs that enabled them to lord it over the minority, equality would have to be wrested from them. The civil rights movement in the 1960s embodied strategies of direct action to confront and destroy the structures of prejudice and segregation.

On 1 February 1960, four black college students in Greensboro, North Carolina, walked into a Woolworth's store, sat down at the lunch counter, and asked for coffee. When they were denied service, as they knew they would be, based on the prevailing racial customs, they refused to move away from the counter until it was closed for the day. Thus was born the "sit-in," a strategy of confrontation that brought black expectations for equal treatment to the awareness of the white community. The procedure caught on quickly among black students and became a primary characteristic of the movement for the first few years of the decade. All across the South, blacks and their white sympathizers, often in large numbers, would enter lunch counters and restaurants and request service. When it was denied, they refused to leave, either forcing the establishment to close or to call the police to "quell the disturbance." Whites in power could not help but take notice, so the sit-in was an effective method of agitating for change in America's social patterns.

Sit-ins were often accompanied by an economic boycott. Until the lunch counter would be desegregated, blacks might refuse to patronize the rest of the store as well. Soon the boycott was separated from the sit-in, as blacks realized that to desegregate eating facilities was to deal with only a small part of the discrimination they faced. Discrimination was pervasive in society and the economic boycott of the businesses in a community gave blacks more visibility and leverage than did attacking eating facilities only.

A variation on the sit-in was the "freedom ride." Blacks would ride intercity buses and trains, integrating the vehicles themselves and the lunch counters, waiting rooms, and rest rooms of the terminals, all of which continued to be segregated in the South.

Another strategy to call attention to the plight of black people in a segregated society was the organized march. The largest and most famous of these was the March on Washington in 1963, when, before the eyes of the nation, thousands of blacks and their sympathizers of other races illustrated the need for a change in the racial patterns of American society. It was at the end of that march, in front of the Lincoln Memorial, that Martin Luther King, Jr. made his "I have a dream" speech, clearly articulating the yearning of blacks to take their rightful place in society and their resolve to continue to work until they accomplished that goal. Many other, less spectacular, marches in local communities all across the South brought blacks into the streets to bring pressure on local power and economic structures to grant justice and equality to all citizens.

Voter registration became yet another extremely important weapon in the battle for racial justice. Civil rights leaders soon realized that, as important as integrating eating places, terminals, and stores could be, it was even more imperative for blacks to become a part of the ruling power itself. In a democratic society, this goal was naturally to be accomplished through the ballot, so voter registration became a high priority in the civil rights movement. It was not an easy task, however, since through both legislation and intimidation Southern whites had prevented most blacks from taking part in the democratic process; many of them were intimidated enough to be terrified of trying to change the status quo. Civil rights workers labored with determination to get blacks properly enrolled on voter lists, eventually achieving considerable success with the help of the federal Voting Rights Act of 1965.

In all these things—sit-ins, freedom rides, marches, and voter registration activities—blacks drew the wrath of the traditional South upon themselves. As they labored to confront the institutions of racial ostracism, they were often met with insults, hostility, and overt violence. It was a dangerous business, this challenging of the patterns of racism and discrimination that had been entrenched for generations, and many blacks were not only verbally abused but sustained serious physical injury at the hands of whites. They responded with a disciplined nonviolence, behavior that was characteristic of the civil rights movement until at least 1965.

Not all blacks who wanted to protest their plight were trained in the discipline of nonviolence. Multitudes of these people took to the streets to riot. Riots can hardly be called a planned strategy of the civil rights movement, but they did happen and they contributed considerably to the victories the movement finally did achieve in the 1960s. Riots were born of anger, frustration, and a feeling of helplessness from being dominated by a racially prejudiced society. Many black people just could not take it any more and they vented their rage in destructive ways. Racial confrontation was no longer confined to the South, but was manifest in California, New Jersey, New York, Michigan and wherever a large black population existed. Discrimination was perhaps most blatant and overt in the South, but it had never been restricted to the South. Consequently black people in Northern cities began to express their grievances through riots as well as nonviolent action.

The civil rights movement was not created by the mass media, but it was certainly sustained and given momentum by the media, particularly television. As Americans watched in their homes while protesting blacks were beset by policemen with dogs and swinging nightsticks or were knocked over and swept along by water from powerful fire hoses, as in the famous Birmingham demonstration of 1963, many began to develop an understanding and sympathy for what blacks faced. Although there was never as much overt white cooperation in the movement as blacks hoped for, it can certainly be argued that federal legislation such as the Civil Rights Act of 1964 and the Voting Rights Act of 1965 was largely possible because of some sympathy created in whites by media coverage of blacks laboring heroically in search of justice.

• *The Agony of Vietnam*

The war in Vietnam emerged as a second public issue of major importance for the last half of the decade. Although the civil rights movement was still active, from around 1965 on it had to share media time and public attention with the war. The war was extremely controversial and it aroused great passions in American society. The only thing that seemed clear about the war was that no one could ignore it.

There were many things not to like about the war in Vietnam. Congress had never formally declared war and so many citizens opposed the war because they considered it to be illegal. The United States had become involved in the conflict by sending military observers/advisers to help the South Vietnamese defend themselves against North Vietnamese Communists. Gradually the entanglement of the United States with the South Vietnamese war effort increased. When, in August of 1964, it appeared that some American ships had been attacked in the Gulf of Tonkin (in retrospect, the evidence that such an attack took place is dubious), Congress voted overwhelmingly to give the President power to defend American armed forces from attack. From that time on, our involvement in the war was escalated essentially by executive order. That resolution was the closest Congress ever came to declaring war formally, and many people continued to consider the war illegal.

Many people also opposed the war because they felt it was based on an incorrect view of the Communist presence in Southeast Asia. The prevailing view, firmly espoused by President Lyndon Johnson, was often called the "domino theory;" it assumed that the various countries of the area were so interrelated that if one were to fall to Communist insurrection, then the other nations would be subject to the same fate: they could be "picked off" one by one. Vietnam was seen as the first domino of the series. It was the first line of defense against Communist aggression; the whole of Southeast Asia was at stake. Most opponents of the war thought that this argument was all wrong; that there was not that much linkage among the nations of the area. Furthermore, these opponents argued, there was insufficient evidence of Communist resolve to push on to capture other nations even if Vietnam should fall. The domino theory was thought to be an improper premise on which to pursue a war. In the long run, Vietnam just did not mean that much to America or to the "free world."

Sensitivity to racial matters stimulated by the civil rights movement created another argument against the war. Many opponents interpreted American activities in Vietnam as an expression of racism. It was a war of white people against people of color. The President, members of Congress, and those in the bureaucracy and the military charged with conducting the war were white men and women either consciously or unconsciously asserting their feelings of superiority over the people of color in Vietnam. Even worse, this white people's war appeared to be fought primarily by people of color. The military draft in the United States had been structured so that college students were excused from serving in the military—an exemption that siphoned off many middle and upper class men who were able to enter college. It turned out that the bulk of these people were white, so that a large portion of draftee/ foot soldiers serving in Vietnam were black or Hispanic. The argument was, then, that the conduct of the war was doubly racist: people of color fighting a "white man's war" against people of color.

Some people complained that the war was being fought primarily for the benefit of that portion of American industry that could be contractors or subcontractors for machinery, munitions, uniforms, and other supplies necessary for the war effort. These opponents contended that to put the lives of Americans in jeopardy and to devastate another country was not a proper way to stimulate the American economy or even a portion of it. Even if it were proper, it was not working. President Johnson, in a legitimate concern for the plight of the poor and minorities, had characterized his administration as the "Great Society," an attempt to make the good life available to all Americans. But, as he escalated the war, more and more resources were being diverted to the conflict, much to the detriment of domestic programs. Although the president insisted that it was possible to have both "guns and butter," it was not. So the impact of the war, in the minds of many, was to inflict physical suffering on American military personnel and the entire nation of Vietnam and to inflict economic suffering on people at home, particularly the poor and helpless.

The opinions summarized here were not unanimously held. A large segment of the population supported the war, although even some of those began to fall away by the end of the decade. They rejected these reasons for opposing the war or believed that if there were any truth to them at all, they were vastly exaggerated. They supported the war primarily because it was a "fight against communism." They believed that Communism anywhere in the world was a threat to America and the rest of the "free world." Communism had to be eradicated and it was best to stop it in Vietnam before the rest of Southeast Asia succumbed to it, as well. Some people even couched this argument in religious terms: America had a divine mission to crush the advance of "godless Communism." America was God's instrument in this time to prevent still more nations from coming under the influence of an atheistic ideology. What greater rationale could there be for the war than that? In the minds of many, the only thing wrong with the war effort was that the United States was not "fighting to win." Somehow, they said, those in charge had been intimidated by the antiwar movement and so did not pursue the war aggressively enough to gain a complete victory. Some even felt that nuclear weapons should be used if it took that to bring the war to a successful conclusion.

• *Being Young in Those Times*

There is no doubt that both the civil rights movement, as it came to be perceived as riotous and violent, and the Vietnam war, as it dragged on with no obvious solution in sight, polarized the American population. Both of these crises in the 1960s excited the passions of Americans, either pro or con. Perhaps no one group was more affected by the events than young people. Not all young people were affected, but both the civil rights movement and, later, Vietnam protest drew young people into activism in significant numbers.

The sit-ins, which galvanized the civil rights movement in the 1960s, were apparently conceived and certainly carried on by black college students. College-age black people constituted a very high proportion of civil rights activists in that decade. Although the media emphasized the leadership roles of older people like Martin Luther King, Jr., A. Philip Randolph, and Bayard Rustin, many leadership positions in the movement were filled capably by people in their early twenties. Indeed, around 1964, the Student Nonviolent Coordinating Committee (SNCC) became one of the principal groups agitating for social change in America. Some white people of all ages joined the blacks in their efforts to achieve equality. But most white civil rights workers were also of college age, idealistic youth identifying with the suffering of blacks and wanting to change society for the better.

Around the middle of the decade black leaders began to assert the idea of "black power." This concept involved, among other things, the inclination of blacks to work out their own problems in relation to a racist society without the help of white co-workers. For all practical purposes, an increasing number of black civil rights leaders had decided to go it alone, changing the character of the movement and forcing many white students out. Meanwhile, the escalation of the war had become an issue transcending other concerns; those idealistic white youth who still wanted to try to promote change through direct action turned their attention to antiwar activities. But their attention was not focused on the war alone. Many young people, and some of their elders, felt that society as a whole needed changing. As one historian has described the social situation of youth in the 1960s, their generation was:

> the first to grow up in persistent affluence, with divorce commonplace in the family, experiencing incredible geographic mobility. It was the first to be given an inoculation against virtually every disease and, perhaps more important, a pill against the contingency of pregnancy. It was the first to be raised on television. It was the first to be influenced by Dr. Spock's liberal notions of child raising, and to consider itself entitled in adolescence to an extended retreat in college. It was a generation diapered in throwaways, nursed with plastic bottles, strengthened on a diet of protein and weakened by endless snacks of sugar-coated cereals. It was the first dressed in synthetic fibers and freed of household chores by laborsaving devices. The inventory is long, and one can add to it or subtract from it at will.[1]

In spite—or because of—having been reared in such a way, many young people began to believe that "respectable society" was a facade covering a multitude of evils needing correction. The government, institutions of society such as the university, and the middle class life-style itself were all labeled with the word "establishment." "Establishment" became a dirty word in the minds of a multitude of disillusioned youth because they regarded it as not only racist and militaristic, but as excessively ma-

---

[1]Milton Viorst, *Fire in the Streets: America in the 1960s* (New York: Simon and Schuster, 1979) 59.

terialistic, devoid of meaning, stifling of individuality and personal freedom. To many of them, the "good life" was not to have a split-level
home, two cars in the garage and a chicken in the pot, as their parents
had seemingly thought. They, rather, wanted to experience new things,
to be "in touch with nature," to identify with the poor and the oppressed, and to have "good vibes" about the persons around them. The
more radical of these students, such as those who worked in Students for
a Democratic Society, felt that there was no hope for America as long as
the "establishment" was in place; they tried to bring it down.

Some of these alienated youth turned to the streets to try to recreate
the society. In protesting what they saw as the faults of society, particularly in their antiwar discontent, they were activist, given to confrontation, and often violent. This tendency to confrontation reached its
height in 1968 as young people demonstrated at the Democratic National Convention in Chicago. In those few days there was virtual warfare
as students and other radical youth violently challenged authority in the
streets and the police responded in kind. On campuses students occu-
pied buildings, particularly administrative offices, as a means of protesting the war, demanding the removal of rules and regulations that had
made the colleges seem too much like substitute parents, and insisting
on a modification and radicalization of curriculum to make it more "relevant" to young people living in the modern world. Sometimes buildings were bombed or burned and, on at least one occasion, at Cornell
University in 1969, students used firearms in the taking and occupying
of a building.

At the very least, the activities of student radicals and other youth
in the 1960s could be said to be "teenage rebellion" with a vengeance.
And the rebellion had results: it brought down a president. Lyndon
Johnson chose not to run for another term in 1968 primarily because it
was clear that the antiwar movement would be so disruptive as to prevent
his reelection. This rebellion also startled a nation. Parents and adults
in general were alternately confused, enraged, and deeply grieved when
they saw young people burn draft cards and even the American flag in
the name of remaking the country.

Yet, not all youth were in the vanguard of political radicalism. Some
"countercultural" young people just preferred to drop out of establishment society. No less disenchanted with mainstream society than their
radical counterparts, these young adults chose to turn their backs on the

"American dream" and walk away from it. They often left home, with or without telling their parents where they were going (often they did not know), and went to join other young people in their quest for authentic, meaningful, exciting, or "groovy" lives. Many communes and collective "crash pads" came into existence as places where these wandering young people could stay while they tried to find themselves—or lose themselves, as the case might be.

Although they engaged in different activities, the radical young people and the dropouts shared some common characteristics. Both the peaceniks and the flower children loved to show their disdain for "straight," establishment culture by dressing in sloppy, dirty, and/or outlandish clothes, altering consciousness with various kinds of drugs, engaging in free and promiscuous sexual relationships, cultivating styles of music calculated to offend the adult ear, and developing a jargon all their own. In addition, young men wore long hair, which, curiously, seemed to disturb their elders as much as anything else.

• Lost Heroes and Tough Decisions

These trends were compounded by some specific events that made the decade even more traumatic. Any society, and particularly its youth, needs hero figures, persons who can personify the spirit and direction of a time. But in the 1960s American society was deprived of three of its principal hero figures by assassins' bullets. The assassination that had perhaps the most profound importance was that of President John F. Kennedy in 1963. Although not all Americans supported his programs and views, Kennedy was young, handsome, articulate, and vigorous; he projected an image of promise for the future of the country. The nation was profoundly shocked when he was killed. Five years later Kennedy's brother, Robert, was assassinated. Formerly Attorney General during his brother's administration and publicly committed to civil rights for all, Robert Kennedy was conducting a campaign for the presidency at the time of his death. In that same year, Martin Luther King, Jr., was killed by a sniper as he was trying to help the sanitation workers of Memphis, Tennessee, gain a fair labor settlement. At the news of King's death, black people all across the country vented their frustrations and anger by rioting, the very kind of reaction King had labored so long to avoid in the struggle for civil liberties. These assassinations led to deepening despair, particularly among young people; even the most indifferent and unaware individuals began to ponder what was to become of America.

Certain decisions of the Supreme Court also contributed to the radical nature of the decade. The court, under the leadership of Chief Justice Earl Warren, was known for its judicial activism, much to the consternation of those who believed that the role of the court was to "interpret law, not make law." In 1962 the court handed down *Baker v. Carr*, a decision with far-reaching implications. The decision reapportioned state and federal legislatures so that rural areas would not have legislative dominance over the bulk of the population, living in cities. From now on, the rule was to be "one person, one vote," a concept that had great potential for changing American society.

In 1962 the court handed down *Engel v. Vitale* and, in 1963 *Abington Township School District v. Schempp*, decisions that together had the effect of removing any kind of religious devotional exercises from public schools. Since those cases will be examined more closely in chapter six, it is sufficient here to mention that they caused a storm of protest to roll across the country. Indeed, it was these two religion cases that initiated the clamor among "conservatives" to impeach Chief Justice Earl Warren.

One other area of great controversy in the court's opinions was that of criminal rights and procedure. In a series of decisions, *Gideon v. Wainwright* (1963), *Escobedo v. Illinois* (1964), and *Miranda v. Arizona* (1966), the court held that law officers must inform arrested individuals of their constitutional right to remain silent and grant them access to an attorney at any pretrial interrogation. In addition, states were obligated to provide legal counsel for defendants who could not employ their own. There was a great outcry against these decisions because they were perceived by many to shift the authority and the rights away from the police and the victims of crimes to the perpetrators. With as much lawlessness and rioting in the streets as there then seemed to be, many people—and not just staunch conservatives—felt that these procedures would contribute to an increase in criminal behavior. Reaction to these decisions contributed significantly to the popularity of the strident "law and order" emphasis in the presidential campaigns of Governor George Wallace of Alabama. The same emphasis, presented in a somewhat less blatant way, also characterized Richard Nixon in the campaign of 1968.

Turning from judicial decisions to legislation, the Civil Rights Act of 1964 and the Voting Rights Act of 1965 had significant impact in the decade. Even though the resistance to implementation was stiff, these laws spelled the beginning of the end for the overt, official racism that had been so much a part of American culture.

• *Radical Religion*

In the 1960s religion also exhibited its share of radical and startling features. Religion both reflected and contributed to the turmoil and activism of the decade. The theological currents of the time found much of their inspiration in the work of the German theologian, Dietrich Bonhoeffer. Bonhoeffer had done his theological work just prior to and during World War II. Although he had the opportunity to stay in the United States as Hitler was preparing for war (he was in America giving some lectures), he chose to return to Germany to oppose the Nazi regime and to be in a position to help rebuild his country after the war was over. Because of his anti-Nazi activity he was arrested and spent two years in prisons and concentration camps. He was finally executed just two days before American troops liberated the camp in which he was imprisoned. Some of his most powerful theological work was done while he was in prison and smuggled out page by page to friends who later compiled and published it.

In his work, Bonhoeffer coined some phrases that caught people's attention, and laid solid theological foundations to support his winsome wording. Bonhoeffer advocated "religionless Christianity." He defined religion as a person's attempt to separate the sacred and the secular realms of life. Religion is what one does in acts of piety in the church. The problem with this is that it tends to separate religion from the real world; religion is separated from the bulk of a person's life. There is the realm of the sacred, where religion is practiced, and the realm of the secular, where people devote most of their time and energies but do not pay much attention to God.

But the Bible indicates that God, in the person of Jesus Christ, is revealed in the real world where persons live. By coming into the world in the person of Jesus, God bridged the gap between the sacred and the secular; in fact, God eliminated the difference between the two. Furthermore, Jesus went to the cross to identify with and to communicate

God's love to suffering humanity. Bonhoeffer felt that God's action in Christ was a model for living the Christian life. He believed that the Christian must not be involved in religion, but rather should be active in the world. The Christian must not stay within the sacred but should be involved in the secular. Bonhoeffer believed in the church, but he said that the church, as well as individual Christians, should be in the world, working for the salvation of the world and reminding everybody that God loves the world. The task of Christians, then, is not to live a pious life, but to witness to Christ in the world through Christian action. That is what Bonhoeffer, and many of his subsequent followers, meant by the phrase "religionless Christianity."

Bonhoeffer also said that "man has come of age." That is, modern people tend to find most of the answers to their questions of existence through science and modern culture, whereas people used to answer those questions by reference to divine imperatives and supernatural intervention. Because they have a world view informed by science, modern persons explain all questions and try to solve all problems without reference to God. But it was not God's purpose to be an "answer man" for our questions of existence. Rather, God's purpose was and is to liberate human beings from sin and suffering through divine love. Jesus was the instrument of this activity. In Bonhoeffer's terms, Jesus was the "man for others." Again, Jesus was the model for the sincere Christian's work in the world and the phrase "man for others" was the slogan that encapsulated the imperative for the religionless Christian in the 1960s.

These themes of Bonhoeffer's, plus the severe problems of the time, set the agenda for the most visible style of religion in the 1960s. Because of Bonhoeffer's untimely death, he was not able to see his ideas implemented. But other theologians adopted his concepts and expanded them as being just the kind of religion that was necessary for the 1960s. Many held that one may not only serve one's fellow human beings by working in the world, but that one literally finds God through social activism. One finds God by working in the world, rather than in the church's tradition, or even in devotional activity. One establishes a relationship with God in the streets, by being a person for others. One finds God in another person as he or she tries to alleviate that person's hurts.

As the result of that kind of thinking, a surge of social activism was initiated from religious motivations. Harvey Cox, then a professor at Andover Newton Theological School and later at Harvard Divinity

School, wrote a book entitled *The Secular City* in which he argued that the city was a place where great strides could be made in improving the condition of people and, in that service, encountering God. The nature of God, as it is revealed in the Bible, is that of an active and caring deity. Many people shared that view, and, consequently, the decade of the 1960s became an era of intense social and political activism among a significant minority of the religious community. The agenda was obvious; justice for blacks, the poor, and others among the disinherited, and antiwar protest. Others might get involved in these great causes for other reasons, but for some the motivations were clearly religious.

There was a kind of antiecclesiastical emphasis in all of this. "Religionless Christianity" could be interpreted to be indifferent or even hostile to the church. One found and served God in the world, rather than in "playing church." Furthermore, some of the more radical of the religious in those days tended to see the church, in its various national and local manifestations, as "part of the problem" of the society. The churches had tended to perpetuate a racially and economically segregated society, rather than trying to break down those barriers. In short, some perceived the church to be part of the "establishment." They believed that the church would have to be ignored because it was hopelessly a part of the status quo or it would have to be radicalized, that is, to be transformed into an agent for the reformation of society.

A component of this radical theology and social activism was the "new morality." Questions of morality or ethics are extremely complex and many different perspectives have been developed about how a person may live a good life. One response is "legalism," living the moral life by being obedient to a set of rules or laws. One may live a religiously correct life by doing what the law commands and avoiding what the law prohibits. One problem with legalism is that in times of shifting standards of conduct, legalism simply cannot keep pace with the changes; it cannot give adequate guidance on how to live the good life. An additional problem is that legalism often becomes sterile, that is, people obey the laws without any understanding of their meaning or purpose.

The "new morality" was a rejection of legalism and, for that matter, any other preconceived pattern of moral behavior. This approach argued that there is only one principle for moral guidance: love. Rather than follow a set of laws that may be outdated and of obscure meaning, one is simply to make his or her life one that exhibits love. In every situation arising in life, one must determine what is the loving thing to do in that situation, in that moment, and then do it. (The new morality was also called "situation ethics.") Whatever action is loving and actualizes and enhances the personhood of others is the proper action in that situation.

One can see how this viewpoint might have been a factor in stimulating social ethics in the 1960s, especially since the social situation seemed to cry out for the application of love. But the new morality had implications for personal behavior as well as social ethics. With its rejection of traditional ways of ordering the moral life in favor of more freedom and flexibility, the new morality was willing to consider even formerly prohibited behavior as legitimate in certain circumstances. The classic example is sexual relationships outside marriage. Whereas traditional views of morality had condemned sex outside of marriage as being categorically wrong and unacceptable, the new morality disagreed. This view argued that the important thing was not the formality of marriage, but rather the quality of the relationship between a man and a woman. If sexual activity was part of and an enhancement of what was a generally compassionate and caring relationship based on mutual concern, then it was acceptable, even if the couple were not married. (This kind of reasoning caused some critics to say that the "new morality" sounded much like the "old immorality.") This idea appealed to multitudes of youth in the counterculture, although one wonders if many of them really understood the dimensions of love, concern, and responsibility that the theorists of the new morality presumed would be part of a proper sexual relationship.

Certainly the idea that encapsulated the nature of radical religion in the 1960s better than any other was the "death of God theology." Incredible as it seemed, not long after the decade began several Christian theologians wrote books and articles proclaiming the death of God. Here, also, the underlying assumption was the secularity of the times. Particularly because of the advances of science and technology, increasing numbers of people found that the problems of mankind were being solved by humans. In this perspective, what did it mean to speak of God? Why did humanity need to rely on God? The death of God theology was thought by its advocates to be a theology suited for this kind of age. If it were a break with mainstream Christianity, that was justified, for the times were out of joint. There was a need for a "with it" style of religion to be compatible with the style of the decade. Radical, death of God, theology met that need.

Five theologians wrote major works about the death of God theology: Gabriel Vahanian, Harvey Cox, William Hamilton, Paul Van Buren, and Thomas Altizer. Their thought is complicated and they did not agree among themselves, but the concept may be summarized in the following way. The traditional ways of thinking and speaking about God are obsolete and meaningless. Since modern people work in the realm of empirical verification, as secular/scientific humans, God has become dead to us because there is no way to verify empirically a supernatural, miraculous deity. Furthermore, language about God has no meaning because language must refer to experience. Modern, scientific, secular people really do not experience the transcendent. If we say we do, we are just remembering the bygone days of another theological era. Consequently, all "God talk" is meaningless and has to be abandoned. Furthermore, most people live their lives as if God did not exist. Bonhoeffer had shown that "man come of age" thought of God only when there were questions that he or she could not answer, what Bonhoeffer called a "God of the gaps." But, since those gaps in persons' lives over which they had no control were becoming increasingly infrequent for moderns, God was becoming progressively irrelevant. But, argued these theologians, even if people lived as if God did not exist, that was all right because they could still be Christians. God was dead, but the example of Jesus lives.

These Christian atheists, as they were sometimes called, clearly recognized the social problems of their times. Their theology fit in with the political and social activism of the era and was designed to be a justification for it. Now that humans were able to give up their immature dependence on a transcendent God, they were able to solve their own problems in the world. Persons could learn how to confront the world through conformity with Jesus, who is the pattern or model for responsible service to the neighbor in a profane world. Jesus shows us what it means to be truly human. Being human means to enter into the affairs of the world on behalf of our fellow humans, just as Jesus did. Jesus calls us to authentic, responsible, free human existence. God is dead. God, for us, is simply Jesus. Faith in Jesus is essentially an ethical stance: living as a "man for others."

To no one's surprise, the media widely popularized this theological phenomenon. Christian theologians proclaiming the death of God were an oddity, to say the least. This media attention probably reached its zenith when *Time*, in the issue for 8 April 1966 (its issue for Easter week), had a completely black cover emblazoned with the scarlet words "Is God Dead?" Of course, the feature story attempted to explain the theology and the reasons for it. That the idea received so much media attention was just one more sign of the secularization of the times.

Since there was so much media coverage of the death of God concept, few people were unaware of it. Responses were diverse: confusion, anger, dismay, and, as I remember from my own pastoral experience, no few tears. As a theological position, it probably attracted more attention than it merited. The number of professional theologians who actually embraced it was very small. It declined as a recognizable phenomenon almost as soon as it had arisen, within three or four years. It was a theological fad. (A colleague of mine called it "a theological hula hoop.") But it may have had some lasting influence in that such a radical and extreme position surely was one of the causes that triggered a resurgence of conservatism in the 1970s.

• *Conservative Religion*

It would be a mistake to think that all Protestant religion in the 1960s was of the liberal/radical sort described so far. There is no doubt that much of it was and that it attracted a good deal of attention, but conservatism was well represented, too. Although the nature of conservatism will be explored more fully in chapter two, it can be said here that conservatism rejected the themes and emphases of radical religion in the 1960s. Conservatism as a movement was not nearly as visible or attractive to the media as radical theology in that decade, but it was not without at least one well-known spokesman. Billy Graham had emerged on the national scene in 1949 and throughout the 1950s and 1960s he was the best-known voice of conservatism. His emphasis was on a traditional, literalistic interpretation of the Bible. He emphasized that the main function of religion is not social action, but to save people's souls from sin in order to prepare them for eternal life. The idea that God was dead was incredible and anathema to him and his coreligionists. The latter were legion, for Billy Graham was the first mass evangelist to employ television efficiently in his presentation of the gospel. By the 1960s he was internationally known and respected. Although many advocates of radical religion considered Graham's message old fashioned and quaint, public opinion polls consistently named him as one of the most admired public figures in America.

There was one other rather visible manifestation of conservative religion toward the end of the decade; what the press labeled the "Jesus movement." Some young people, of both high school and college ages, became disillusioned with the activities in which they were engaged. Although some progress had been made in the area of race, their political activism had not ended racism and the war was being fought with as much intensity as ever. This was very discouraging to them. Furthermore, some of these same youth began to see that drugs did not provide permanent ecstasy and were potentially dangerous. In the light of these disappointments and disillusionments they turned to emotional, conservative religion. It was not that the Jesus movement was any less countercultural than the previous life style of these young people, for long hair, outlandish clothes, and youth jargon (without the profanity) were still acceptable. Furthermore, many of the Jesus people groups tended to regard the established churches with contempt and refused to join. But now, rather than getting high on drugs and trying to build meaningful relationships with promiscuous sexual activity, they achieved their "high" by accepting Jesus into their hearts and gained warm, personal relationships by participating in close-knit groups which had definite conceptions of their purpose and meaning. Rather than spending their time trying to achieve racial equality or end the war, they devoted their energies to witnessing about Jesus to all whom they met or doing other activities imposed on them by the group. The Jesus movement attracted considerable attention at the end of the 1960s and early years of the 1970s.

• *Roman Catholicism*

The 1960s was a very important time for the Roman Catholic Church in America. At the beginning of the decade Catholics were flushed with pride because one of their own, John F. Kennedy, had been elected President of the United States. Prior to that time, particularly for the preceding century, Catholics had been regarded by many as second-class citizens. Since most Catholics were immigrants or children of immigrants and because Catholics were suspected of giving their highest loyalty to the Vatican rather than to America, most non-Catholic Americans had regarded them with suspicion. But, with Kennedy's election, Catholics felt that their Americanness had at last been recognized and that they were finally regarded as being equal with others in the American body politic.

In addition, it seemed to many Catholics that things could only get better when Pope John XXIII called for a council of the bishops of the church to convene in 1962. The purpose of the council, according to the Pope, was *aggiornamento*, an updating or modernization of the church. The Pope said he intended to open the window of the church and let the breezes of modernity blow through. But by the end of the decade, many Catholics were convinced the breezes had actually been a tornado.

Although the bishops at the Second Vatican Council articulated new church policy on a number of issues, three issues seemed to attract the most attention. The first of these had to do with the liturgy, that is, the conduct of public worship in the church. For centuries the universal language of the liturgy in the Roman Catholic church had been Latin. The advantage of Latin was principally its "universality;" one could go to any church and hear a familiar Mass. Latin also symbolized for many Catholics the mystery of God's grace and will. But the unintelligibility that suggested mystery was also a liability; the people could not understand it. So Vatican II provided for the liturgy to be conducted in the vernacular, the language of the parish.

A second major change was in the council's decree on the governance of the church. For centuries the church had been a hierarchical church in the truest sense of the word; power and authority flowed from the top down: from the Vatican to the bishops, then to the priests, then to the laypeople. Vatican II articulated the idea of "collegiality," the concept that the governing of the church is a shared responsibility, with authority and opportunity for counsel distributed more widely among church members. The church would be governed through more participatory rather than autocratic means, although the traditional officers and levels of authority would continue to exist.

Third, for centuries the Catholic church had regarded itself as the only true church and had proclaimed that there was no salvation outside the church. But Vatican II recognized that other varieties of Christians have legitimacy and declared that even non-Christian religions have the right to exist and to conduct worship as their adherents see fit, within the framework of proper morality.

In the United States the practical results that flowed from these concepts were immediate and, in some cases, startling. Promptly after the council gave its approval there was fraternization and cooperation between Catholics and Protestants in social action projects and even in worship, with Protestant ministers and Catholic priests exchanging pulpits. These developments represented a new departure after centuries of suspicion and recrimination between Catholics and Protestants.

The greatest problems for the church resulted from the new views of authority. Conflicts developed over authority between priests, particularly younger priests, and bishops, who tended to adhere to the more traditional concept of church governance. Priests wanted to participate more in the decision-making process and to have their opinions taken more seriously by the hierarchy of the church. Furthermore, young priests, nuns, and laypeople were impatient that the modernization of the church was not proceeding rapidly enough. An example is the conduct of worship. Although the council had made significant modifications in the liturgy, some wanted to go farther. An "underground church" developed in which priests would go to people's homes or other locations outside a church to conduct Mass, often with laypeople taking a much larger role than would be allowed in a church and with the bread and wine being placed in the hands of the recipients, a practice officially forbidden by the church.

Although the council had permitted orders of nuns to modernize their habits and to redefine their ministries, many nuns did not think these reforms went far enough. Some were upset that all of the church authorities who made these kinds of decisions for nuns were men. Like many young priests, after the council many orders of nuns began to assert themselves, making decisions for themselves as to their garb and the style of ministry they should pursue. Many dressed in secular clothing and took jobs in the world, exercising their ministry in secular contexts, going far beyond the traditional roles of being nurses in Catholic hospitals or teachers in parochial schools.

For priests, a burning issue was the requirement of celibacy. In the Western rite, the rule for centuries had been that clergy were not to marry. Few priests wanted to do away with that custom altogether, but very many thought that the tradition was too strict and that celibacy should be optional. Many thought they would be more complete human beings and better pastors to their congregations if they were married. However, the church hierarchy remained steadfastly opposed to the possibility of marriage for priests and nuns.

Perhaps the most serious challenge to the authority of the Pope and to the hierarchy of the church as a whole was the issue of birth control. For some time the church had taken the position that artificial means of conception control were against God's natural law and thus contrary to the church's teaching. However, there was increasing pressure from Catholic laypeople and some priests, particularly those serving local parishes, for the church to change its rule. A papal commission was convened concurrently with the council to study the issue. The commission recommended a liberalization of the church's policy in the matter. However, Pope Paul VI, in 1968, issued the statement *Humanae Vitae* in which he reaffirmed the church's prohibition against birth control devices. Over the world there was an outcry of protest. It was very loud in this country. Some theologians composed a document arguing the contrary. Some priests openly spoke out against the papal decree from their pulpits. Others more discreetly simply advised Catholic couples to ignore the prohibition, and apparently many of them did. One Catholic historian has remarked that never again could a Pope expect reverential deference to a decree from American Catholics; from now on the church would have to persuade them through reason.[2]

As a result of their frustration over the church's reluctance to follow through on the program of modernization initiated by Vatican II, many priests and nuns left their vocations, some to get married (sometimes to each other), some to pursue a more secular vocation such as social work, some simply to leave a church that they felt was badly antiquated, to fade into the general population. Further, fewer decided to enter the vocations of priest or nun so that there developed, by the end of the decade, a shortage of professionals in the church. All this turmoil precipitated by the council affected laypeople as well, so that attendance at Mass and at the confessional had declined dramatically at the end of the decade.

Finally, although there is not clear evidence that many Catholics adopted the radical "secular theology" described above, many, both cler-

---

[2]John Cogley, *Catholic America* (Garden City NY: Doubleday, 1974) 107.

ical and lay, participated in the civil rights movement and in antiwar protest. The most visible but, by no means, the only examples were the priests Philip and Daniel Berrigan, who led some spectacular protests against the war.

The Jewish community was not spared the trauma of the 1960s, either. In the early part of this century large numbers of Jewish immigrants had come to this country, people fleeing from hostile environments to the country that they perceived to be a haven of freedom and opportunity. In spite of some persistent anti-Semitism, America had, in fact, proven to be a land of freedom and opportunity. Consequently, by the late 1950s and early 1960s the grandchildren of those immigrants had attained the economic status to move to the suburbs, an act that they saw as the finishing touch to the process of assimilation into American society. During this process Jews developed an ambivalent attitude toward their religious tradition. They wanted to be regarded as full-fledged Americans, having put off every vestige of foreignness, yet they did not want to forget completely their Jewish heritage. Although there were some exceptions, the majority of Jews tended to attend synagogue and even to send their children to Jewish schools to keep alive the fond memory that they were Jewish. But they were not terribly strict in the Jewish life or understanding the major theological characteristics of Judaism.

As the 1960s developed into the radical decade that it was, neither leaders nor laypeople adopted a Jewish version of the kind of radical, secular theology that was found among some highly visible Protestant theologians. But that is not to say that Jews were not involved in the social struggles of the time. Very many Jews, particularly young adults, were sympathetic with the plight of blacks and were deeply involved in the civil rights movement. The Jewish people had a centuries-long experience of being persecuted. Most recent in their minds was the Holocaust, the devastation of European Jews at the hands of the Nazis. Consequently, the majority of Jews had an affection for the underdog—in this case, the blacks—and wanted to help them gain a rightful place in society. This social liberalism was part of the cultural Jewishness referred to above. To some, to be Jewish was to be liberal. They had to adopt no radical theology of social involvement, for the very fact of being Jewish led them to participate in the civil rights movement.

But problems developed. When, around 1964 or 1965, many blacks decided that they no longer wanted the help of white people in their quest for liberation, they turned their backs on their Jewish supporters. Furthermore, many blacks began to blame Jews for some of their problems; they saw that Jewish merchants and landlords in heavily black areas of the North and East contributed to the misery of blacks by charging high prices and exorbitant rents while withholding services. In some quarters "black anti-Semitism" developed and relationships between the two peoples cooled considerably.

The real crisis for American Jews came in 1967. In June of that year Israel fought its famous "six-day war" against Egypt, Syria, Jordan, and Lebanon. Israel was victorious, and American Jews were delighted, but the war also had a serious negative psychological impact on them. Many American Christians did not take an unequivocal stand in favor of Israel, but rather saw some merit in the Arab positions. Those blacks who tended to feel an attraction to Islam—and many did—also saw Israel as the aggressor. In short, Jews felt more isolated in the American community. Furthermore, the Arabs had declared their intention to destroy the nation of Israel. This raised the specter of genocide, which had also been the goal of Hitler. Although the Holocaust had never been absent from the Jewish memory, after 1967 it became something of an obsession.

These events—the alienation from blacks in the civil rights struggle and the results of the 1967 war—caused many American Jews to reaffirm Jewish religion. No longer was cultural Jewishness enough. It was not enough to be liberal socially and politically, it was necessary to study Jewish Scripture and tradition. Jews realized that they ran the risk of extinction as a result of the twin threats of assimilation and the hostility of others. Consequently, they had to work to guarantee their continued existence. They increased financial support for Israel and also began emigrating in unprecedented numbers. They began to articulate their views more assertively. For some time after the six-day war, Jewish-Christian dialogue in America declined markedly. Jews increasingly called attention to the Holocaust, a study stimulated by the hostile environment of Israel and the hostile attitude of other groups at home. The motto "never again" was on their lips. Many began to see that if Jews did not assert themselves as Jews, including a devotion to the religious tradition, then their own indifference would accomplish what Hitler had tried, but failed, to do. Hitler, or any other opponent of Judaism and the Jewish people, must not be allowed to win. Consequently, the 1960s ended with a significant portion of the American Jewish community taking its religion and the obligation to live a Jewish life more seriously.

• *Summary*

The 1960s began with some black college students sitting in at a segregated lunch counter. The decade ended in 1970 when four students were killed and several wounded at Kent State University in Ohio as National Guardsmen attempted to put down an antiwar protest. In between those events was a time that some Americans are still trying to forget. There is much about the 1960s that ought to be remembered because it was good. There was the attempt to make religion relevant to the world, rather than just an exercise in personal piety. This, of course, was part of a larger effort to demonstrate concern for the poor, helpless, and minority groups: a good thing. There are other phenomena on which Americans have turned their backs, mainly the disorder in the streets and also the public "craziness" of many young people. In religion, those days are in many ways gone and forgotten, except that what happened in religion in the 1970s was in large measure a reaction to what took place in the 1960s.

• *Suggestions for Further Reading
for Context and Perspective*

Bell, Daniel. "Religion in the Sixties." *Social Research* 38 (Autumn 1971): 447-497.

Berger, Peter. *The Noise of Solemn Assemblies*. Garden City NY: Doubleday, 1961.

Cox, Harvey. *The Secular City*. New York: Macmillan, 1965.

Deedy, John. *'Apologies, Good Friends': An Interim Biography of Daniel Berrigan, S.J.* Chicago: Fides/Claretian, 1981.

Devine, George. *American Catholicism: Where Do We Go From Here?* Englewood Cliffs NJ: Prentice-Hall, 1975.

Glazer, Nathan. *American Judaism*. 2nd ed., revised. Chicago: University of Chicago Press, 1972. Chapter IX.

Gustafson, James M. ed. "The Sixties: Radical Change in American Religion," *The Annals of the American Academy of Political And Social Science* 387 (January 1970).

Hamilton, Kenneth. *God is Dead: The Anatomy of a Slogan*. Grand Rapids MI: Wm. B. Eerdmans, 1966.

_____. *What's New in Religion?* Grand Rapids MI: Wm. B. Eerdmans, 1968.

Robinson, John A. T. *Honest to God*. Philadelphia: Westminster Press, 1963.

Viorst, Milton. *Fire in the Streets: America in the 1960s*. New York: Simon and Schuster, 1979.

CHAPTER TWO

What Was So Strange About Jimmy Carter? The Resurgence of Born-Again Christianity

When Jimmy Carter ran for President in 1976, one of the interesting features of the campaign was the emphasis on religion. Because Mr. Carter is a "born-again" Christian and during the campaign he acknowledged that his faith played a significant role in his life, his religion was a curiosity to many media reporters and to people in the general population. The campaign raised "conservative" religion to levels of visibility it had not enjoyed for a long time.

Mr. Carter was identified as an "evangelical." A definition of that word was proposed by George Gallup, Jr., the pollster, and it was widely used in print. An evangelical is one who "has had a born again conversion, accepts Jesus as his or her personal Savior, believes the Scriptures are the authority for all doctrine, and feels an urgency to spread the faith." The evangelical also believes that his or her relationship with God is intensely personal and he or she tries to live in obedience to a strict moral code.[1] In the midst of its reporting of the campaign, *Newsweek* called 1976 "the year of the evangelicals."[2] While it might have been surprising to hear a politician be so candid about his faith, Jimmy Carter

---

[1] Quoted in Albert Menendez, "Who are the Evangelicals?" *Christianity Today* 22 (27 January 1978): 42.

[2] "Born Again," *Newsweek* 88 (25 October 1976): 68-78.

was not so strange. He was just the most public manifestation of a major feature of the 1970s: the resurgence of conservative Christianity.

The words "liberal" and "conservative" are labels that lack precision and are subject to misunderstanding. Although this entire chapter will be devoted to explaining and analyzing these concepts, particularly conservatism, a preliminary definition may be helpful. In general, "conservative" designates a theological style based on a literalistic interpretation of the Bible—that is, an interpretation that takes the words of Scripture in their ordinary meaning, rather than recognizing a figurative or symbolic meaning. Related to that is the conservative emphasis on trying to protect historic Christianity from being spoiled by influences of modern, scientific, secular, culture. Rather than borrowing insights from the nonreligious "world" for the formation of theology, conservatism tends to be suspicious of it and tries to protect the faith from it.

"Liberalism," on the other hand, has been characterized by a much more open attitude toward the world. It is willing to accept "truth" from many sources and incorporate it into theology. A corollary of this openness is the willingness to interpret the text of the Bible in a nonliteral way, interpretation based on the assumption that the Biblical text is conditioned by the humanity of its authors—that is, that their writing reflects the historical events and the ways of thinking of the ancient world. Liberalism's use of the Bible is also based on the belief that modern interpretation needs to take account of contemporary culture. Liberalism, then, historically has not been so much interested in preserving the faith from the world as in making it relevant to the world.

• *Background of Contemporary Conservatism*

One can speak of a resurgence in the 1970s because conservative Protestant Christianity is certainly not a new thing in America. To go back just as far as the beginning of the nineteenth century, there was a kind of theology that adhered to the basic Biblical and Reformation doctrines of the trinitarian nature of God, the divinity and lordship of Jesus Christ, the freely-given grace of God, salvation through accepting that grace by faith, and the authority of the Bible as the literal word of God. As had happened so many other times in church history, these ideas were sharpened against the hard stones of what the orthodox considered to be heresy, Deism and Unitarianism.

Deism was a child of the rationalism of the Enlightenment. Its adherents held that there were five essentials in religion: the existence of a transcendent, impersonal God, the worship of that divine being, the imperative of a virtuous life, life after death, and that virtue is rewarded and evil living is punished, both in this life and the next. Jesus was regarded as, at most, a great moral teacher and the Bible as a book of moral teachings alongside fantastic, irrational, and unreliable miracle stories. Unitarianism was closer to the mainstream of Christian thought. It rejected the Trinity, thinking of Jesus as a great teacher and example of God's love, but not as divine and equal with God. The Bible was considered to be the Word of God, but subject to the interpretation of human reason. The creeds and confessions of orthodox Christianity, especially those clauses relating to one-God-in-three-persons, were rejected as without foundation in the Bible. Orthodox preachers leaped to the defense of more conventional beliefs with eloquence, and the opposition to Deism and Unitarianism became a convenient way of articulating the traditional faith with power and persuasion.

Nineteenth century America also harbored multitudes of unconverted people who were even more the object of orthodox preaching. The message was often taken to these people through the medium of revivalism. In the early part of the century revival meetings invaded the frontier and, toward the middle of the century, they began to be conducted in urban areas of the East, primarily through the work of Charles G. Finney. There were variations in some of the details of theology among the various denominations engaged in revivals, but in the main this kind of preaching was strongly Christocentric and Biblically oriented. Its message was that humanity languishes in sin, unable to accomplish its own salvation. God has taken the initiative to save human beings by sending Jesus as the clearest expression of divine love. Through faith in Christ one could be saved. This good news is contained in the Bible, which must be understood as the literal truth of God. Revival preachers often added to the basic message of salvation another element, namely, that America is God's elect nation. The colonial leader John Winthrop had written that because of God's choice, ". . .we must consider that we shall be as a city upon a hill, the eyes of all people are upon us. . . ." Nineteenth-century revival preachers believed that for America to fulfill its vocation, to be God's beacon of truth in the world, it was necessary for America to be a Christian nation. Not only was the salvation of individual souls at stake, but also the future of the nation and, indeed, the world.

After the Civil War orthodox Protestant Christianity had to contend with new problems, principally the challenges presented by science. The challenge of scientific thinking was epitomized in the concept of biological evolution articulated by Charles Darwin in his *Origin of the Species*, published in 1859. The concept of evolution called into question God's creation of humankind as it is described in the Bible. That challenged the authority of the Bible itself that, in turn, endangered the credibility of a wide range of Church doctrines. Many Christians were convinced that science and religion were incompatible and that religion had to defend itself against the secular influences of the time. Again, not only was individual salvation at stake, but also the health and the future of the nation. Orthodox religion became more defensive and conservative as the nineteenth century came to a close.

That process was accelerated by the progress of theological liberalism. In the late nineteenth and early twentieth centuries many leaders in Protestantism made peace with science and even began using the concept of evolution to shape their theology. Liberalism "baptized" evolution—because liberalism was open to new ideas from wherever they might come—and people began to say that evolution was "God's way of doing things." To people who held traditional views, that was bad enough, since it meant that liberalism was not willing to "take the Bible literally" on the issue of creation. But when liberalism began to use the same kind of critical methods to interpret the Bible as were used to interpret other kinds of literature, the entire Bible was seen as literature that reflected the culture-bound viewpoints of its ancient authors rather than as the divinely inspired word of God. To the liberals, the Bible was a source of religious principles and insights, but it was far from being the infallible source of divinely-given truth.

The conservative reaction to this double-edged challenge to orthodox Christianity was to become more conservative. Many people felt that a strong defense should be made against attacks on the certainty of the Christian faith, and they became aggressive in mounting a counteroffensive against those who were willing to compromise with the secular world. A series of books under the general title *The Fundamentals* was published to make the case for strictly-held orthodox Christianity, and this brand of conservatism became known as "fundamentalism." Although fundamentalism was never so simplistic, it is often said to concentrate on five points of theology: (1) the inerrancy of the Bible (the Bible is without error and is to be interpreted literally), (2) the divinity of Jesus Christ (he was divine by nature and thus much more than a good man or a great moral teacher), (3) the virgin birth of Christ, (4) the substitutionary atonement (Jesus suffered for human sin, taking upon himself the punishment due guilty humanity, although he was innocent), (5) the physical resurrection and imminent physical return of Jesus. Fundamentalists believed that if liberalism were allowed free reign, not only would entire denominations be lost to orthodox Christianity, but the salvation of multitudes would be imperiled. In the first three decades of the twentieth century, a fierce battle waged between modernist and militantly orthodox Christianity; a battle for people's minds and for control of the leadership of several Protestant denominations. This conflict is known to historians as "the fundamentalist-modernist controversy."

The issue came to a climax in 1925 at the famous Scopes trial in Dayton, Tennessee. Fundamentalism had gained such influence in several Southern states that it was able to have laws passed prohibiting the teaching of evolution in public schools. Tennessee was one of those states. John Thomas Scopes taught the concept of evolution in his high school biology class and was brought to trial. It was a confrontation of monumental proportions between the famous trial lawyer, Clarence Darrow, who represented Scopes, and the equally famous politician, orator, and spokesman for fundamentalism, William Jennings Bryan, who was part of the prosecution team. Although Scopes was convicted, Darrow and the national press were able to subject Bryan and fundamentalism to ridicule, making them appear old fashioned and anachronistic in a scientific era. For approximately fifty years after the Scopes trial many people thought that fundamentalism had been killed in Dayton, Tennessee. Even professional historians of American religion, who should have known better, gave fundamentalism short shrift in their works.

But fundamentalism was not dead; rather it was a sleeping giant. In the early 1940s the giant stirred. In 1941 Carl McIntire, a vocal and vitriolic fundamentalist, organized the American Council of Christian Churches (ACC) to oppose the mainstream liberal National Council of Churches of Christ in the United States and to be a rallying point for American fundamentalists. Although it has always had a relatively small membership, the ACC has done its best to keep extreme right wing

Christianity in the public eye. In 1942 the National Association of Evangelicals (NAE) was organized to represent those denominations that did not want to join the National Council of Churches. NAE leaders believed that liberalism was compromising orthodox Christianity by identifying too much with worldly culture. But they did not want to be a part of the American Council of Churches either, for they did not identify with its militant, "against everything" conservatism. Although significant differences among conservatives had existed throughout the century, now they were institutionalized in two kinds of councils: the militant, aggressive, fundamentalism of the ACC and the moderate conservatism of the NAE. We will return to the differences between various kinds of conservatism later in this chapter.

Conservative religious sentiment grew apace in the 1950s, but it did not attract a great deal of attention in American society. In the 1960s it was overwhelmed by the radicalism and the countercultural trends of the times. But it was the very radicalism of that decade that roused the sleeping giant to begin to play a meaningful role in society, convinced that America desperately needed to return to those traditional values taught by old-time, Biblically-oriented, conservative religion. Conservatives were convinced that the transformation of America could be accomplished. By 1976 it was estimated that 40 million Americans considered themselves to be conservative, born-again Christians. In his religion, Jimmy Carter was not so strange at all; he was simply the most visible symbol of a dynamic force in American society.

• *Liberal Decline,
Conservative Growth*

A helpful way of perceiving the fortunes of conservatism and its liberal counterpart in Protestant Christianity is to look at church membership trends and other indicators of church growth and/or decline. Such statistics are not a perfect method of analysis because there are inaccuracies and discrepancies in the figures themselves; the differences among denominations in the ways they define church membership, for example, make it difficult to make absolute comparisons between groups. But the figures are helpful in revealing tendencies and trends among various groups and viewpoints.

The period from 1940 until 1960-1965 was a time of growth in church membership, attendance, and other indicators of interest in religion. There are two sources of statistics on church membership, the Gallup poll and the reports of churches. These do not produce the same figures because, in response to poll questions, more people acknowledge church membership than the churches themselves report to data-gathering agencies. The survey figures on church membership show that in 1940, 72 percent of the people interviewed claimed membership in a religious communion. By 1947, this figure had increased to 76 percent, and in the period from 1952 to 1965 the poll results of church membership stabilized at 73 percent.[3]

By contrast, the churches themselves reported a far smaller percentage of the population as members, but they also indicated a sustained and dramatic growth. In 1940, the churches could boast of 49 percent of the American people. Ten years later, church membership had climbed to 57 percent of the population. By 1964 the churches could claim 64.4 percent of the people as members.[4]

Figures for church attendance are lower than those for church membership because many people who identify themselves as members of a denomination may not maintain membership in a local parish or congregation or attend services regularly. Yet attendance statistics also reflected a growing interest in religion among Americans from 1940 to the mid-1960s. While 37 percent of the population was reported to be attending church in 1940, 49 percent was attending in 1955. That peak was touched again in 1958. Attendance remained at 46 percent or above through 1963.[5] Attendance in Sunday schools also quickened in this period. In 1947-1948 enrollment in Sunday schools increased by 7.3 percent, leading the gains in church membership by 1.5 percent for the same years.[6] In a survey of nine "mainstream" denominations—includ-

---

[3] "Church or Synagogue Membership," *Religion in America 1981* (Princeton, NJ: The Princeton Religion Research Center, 1981) 25.

[4] Benson Y. Landis, ed., *Yearbook of American Churches 1966* (New York: National Council of Churches of Christ, 1966) 218.

[5] "40% Attend Church in a Typical Week," *Emerging Trends* 3 (February 1981): 1.

[6] Cited in Will Herberg, *Protestant, Catholic, Jew* (Garden City NY: Doubleday Anchor Books, 1960) 50.

ing such groups as Methodists, Presbyterians, and Episcopalians—Sunday school enrollment increased by 25.6 percent from 1950 to 1955, and by 10.2 percent from 1955 to 1960, before entering a slight decline in the first half of the 1960s.[7]

Among the more interesting indicators of increasing American participation in religion after 1940 is the amount of money spent in constructing church buildings. Wartime shortages dropped the total expenditure from $59 million in 1940 to $26 million in 1945, but the years following witnessed an exponential growth in church building development. Construction costs passed the billion-dollar mark in 1960, and reached a peak of $1,035,000,000 in 1962. Although these statistics are not corrected for inflation, they still reflect a growing American concern with organized religion.[8] At a more abstract level this favorable sentiment was demonstrated in polls taken in 1947 and 1957 showing that religious leaders were highly regarded as persons contributing to the good of the country.[9]

Yet as healthy as organized religion seemed to be in the 1950s, after 1960 the leading indicators began to slide downward. For many people, the figures were ominous, an alarming reversal of familiar trends in religious life. Sunday school enrollment provided the first warning signs. After the sustained, even dramatic, increases we have previously noted, enrollment dipped slightly from 1960 to 1965, then plunged 13.8 percent from 1965 to 1970 and another 10.1 percent from 1970 to 1975. This drop far exceeded the decreases in the population for persons under 18 years of age.[10]

Sunday school attendance proved its worth as a predictor of church attendance and membership statistics, as church attendance soon began to decline. Gallup pollsters reported a sustained steady drop from 1961 to 1971 in the percentage of Americans who would claim attendance at

---

[7] Ruth T. Doyle and Sheila M. Kelly, "Comparison of Trends in Ten Denominations 1950-1975," in Dean R. Hoge and David A. Roozen, eds., *Understanding Church Growth and Decline, 1950-1978* (New York: Pilgrim Press, 1979) 154.

[8] Figures compiled from various volumes of the *Yearbook of American Churches*.

[9] Herberg, *Protestant, Catholic, Jew*, 51.

[10] Doyle and Kelly, "Comparison of Trends. . . ." 154.

a church or synagogue in the past week. From 1971 to 1975, these attendance reports continued at 40 percent, rose two points to 42 percent in 1976, and dropped back to 40 percent in 1979-1980.[11] That percentage of Americans who would acknowledge church membership also declined after 1965, from a high of 73 percent to a low of 68 percent in 1978-1979.[12] When the churches themselves reported their memberships, their figures also told of a decline: in terms of percent of the nation's population, church attendance declined 3.9 percent in 16 years, from 64.4 percent in 1964 to 60.5 percent in 1980.[13] There is clear evidence that those who were most disenchanted with the church were young adults, those under the age of 30.[14]

Since the mid-1950s the Gallup poll workers have been asking people how important religion is in their lives and whether or not they think that religion is gaining or losing influence in American life. The number of people who said that religion is important in their personal lives began to decline as early as 1952, especially among Jews, but the decline became especially precipitous from 1965 until 1978, except among Jews, who were at the same level of disinterest from 1965 until 1978. Americans were even less confident about the influence of religion in the life of the nation. From 1957 until 1970 those who responded to the poll were convinced that religion was definitely losing influence in American life. This decline persisted in spite of all that the liberals were trying to do to make religion relevant in the 1960s. Then in 1970 the public began to believe that the influence of religion on American life was increasing.[15]

Finally, another indicator of religious interest that rose during the 1950s declined in the late 1960s and particularly in the 1970s; the amount of money spent on church buildings. Although inflation increased building costs in the 1970s, by using constant 1972 dollars, it

---

[11] "40% Attend Church. . . ." 1.

[12] "Church or Synagogue Membership," 25.

[13] Figures compiled from various volumes of the *Yearbook of American Churches.*

[14] "Church or Synagogue Attendance," *Religion in America 1982* (Princeton NJ: The Princeton Religion Research Center, 1982) 45.

[15] *Religion in America 1981*, 40, 48-49.

can be shown that, until late in the decade, money spent on church construction decreased from more than one billion dollars in 1970 to a low of $627 million in 1975. By the end of the decade construction expenditures had risen almost to the $800 million mark. [16]

None of the data for religious interest and church attendance in the 1960s was broken down by theological perspective. However, in the early 1970s observers noticed differences in the data between the "mainstream" denominations and the more conservative groups. Their initial impression was later confirmed: while the major and more "liberal" denominations were declining in attendance and membership, the "conservative" groups were growing. Those groups that were on the fundamentalist/evangelical end of the theological spectrum, groups that also seemed to make rather strict demands on their members, were growing while the liberal, less demanding, groups were declining in membership, sometimes rather dramatically. To be more specific, while denominations like the United Methodist Church, the Christian Church (Disciples of Christ), the Episcopal Church, the Presbyterian Church in the United States, the United Presbyterian Church in the USA, and the United Church of Christ were not only declining in reference to the population growth of the country but were losing members in absolute numbers, groups like the Assemblies of God, the Salvation Army, the Jehovah's Witnesses, the Church of Jesus Christ of Latter-day Saints (Mormons), Seventh-day Adventists, the Mennonite Church, the Churches of Christ, and the Southern Baptist Convention were gaining members. This development created great consternation among members of those denominations that were declining, since, in most cases, the decline represented a reversal of more than a century of growth, while it caused great glee among the growing groups, some of which were coming to public notice for the first time. This phenomenon was a major topic of conversation in church circles during the 1970s.

One must realize that the generalization that conservatively-oriented churches are growing while mainstream churches are declining refers to percentages rather than absolute numbers. That is, the conservative/strict churches have had a rate of increase that has exceeded that of the

---

[16] Constant H. Jacquet, Jr., ed., *Yearbook of American and Canadian Churches 1981* (Nashville: Abingdon Press, 1981) 268.

mainstream churches. However, with the exception of the Southern Baptist Convention, the Churches of Christ, the Lutheran Church (Missouri Synod), and the Assemblies of God, most of the churches growing rapidly are still much smaller than many of the mainstream denominations. Although evangelical and fundamentalist churches seem to be growing more, the mainstream denominations still number many more people. Yet the strength of conservatism in the 1970s was enhanced by the growth of fundamentalist-oriented radio and television ministries and because even the mainstream denominations included significant portions of people who were willing to identify themselves as evangelicals. There has been a shift to the conservative end of the theological spectrum even in mainstream denominations and, in some of these denominations, conservatives organized themselves into pressure groups to try to move the entire denomination to a more orthodox position. Perhaps the most noticeable of these groups are the Presbyterian Lay Committee and the Presbyterians United for Biblical Concerns in the Presbyterian Church in the USA, Good News (sometimes called the Forum for Spiritual Christianity) in the United Methodist Church, and the Fellowship of Witness in the Episcopal Church. With the growth of conservative denominations and the rise of the number of conservatives who have chosen to remain within mainstream denominations, it is not difficult to see why even the secular press took notice of this phenomenon in the 1970s. On the basis of many surveys, which have failed to distinguish between evangelicals and fundamentalists but have asked people if they considered themselves to be "born-again" Christians, it has been estimated that there are between 35 and 40 million evangelicals in America.

What was the character of this growing conservatism? Although it will be necessary to make some finer distinctions later in this chapter, a general characterization can be made now by comparing the conservatism of the 1970s with the dominant religion of the 1960s. One way to compare the two is to contrast their central theological methods. As it was noted in chapter one, in the 1960s the "secular theology" set its agenda from the Christian answers to the questions raised by the society, questions of race, the war, poverty, etc. It was necessary for religion to respond to the stimulus of the broader society. In contrast, conservatives in the 1970s continued their traditional practice of deriving theology from the Bible and/or traditional creedal statements. Evangelical and fundamentalist theology insists upon beginning its theological task with the Bible. The Bible is the norm for religion. The task of theology is first and foremost to elucidate the Bible. The religious life is to live out the truths found in the Bible.

An illustration of the primacy of the Bible for conservative theology is the "Chicago Call." In May 1977 a group of evangelical leaders and scholars assembled to issue a call for modern evangelicalism to reappropriate its heritage. Recognizing that there was an increasing dynamism in the evangelical/fundamentalist sector in American religion, these individuals met to point out where conservatism was in danger of misappropriating its heritage and to issue a call for fidelity to that heritage. The full title of the document they issued is: "The Chicago Call: An Appeal to Evangelicals." One section of the document reaffirms the centrality of the Bible for religion:

> We deplore our tendency toward individualistic interpretation of Scripture. This undercuts the objective character of Biblical truth, and denies the guidance of the Holy Spirit among his people through the ages.
> Therefore we affirm that the Bible is to be interpreted in keeping with the best insights of historical and literary study, under the guidance of the Holy Spirit, with respect for the historic understanding of the church.
> We affirm that the Scriptures, as the infallible Word of God, are the basis of authority in the church. We acknowledge that God uses the Scriptures to judge and to purify his Body. The church, illumined and guided by the Holy Spirit, must in every age interpret, proclaim and live out the Scriptures.[17]

Another convenient method by which to compare the religious temper of the 1970s to that of the 1960s is to compare the seminary students of the two decades. In the 1960s college and seminary students who were preparing themselves for careers in ministry were very interested in social action. They were much aware of both domestic and foreign social problems and they were convinced that they, in the name of Christian compassion, wanted to help solve those problems. In the most radical of student groups it was commonly said that "the establishment," the framework of power in society, was responsible for the plight of the poor, the minorities, and the powerless. The radicals wanted to bring down the establishment and create a new, more equitable, government. A milder

---

[17] Quoted in Richard J. Coleman, *Issues of Theological Conflict* (Grand Rapids MI: Wm. B. Eerdmans Co., 1980) 263.

form of such sentiments was held by many ministerial students, who believed the church was part of the establishment. They saw the church as, at best, a status quo oriented institution impeding progress toward a more humane society. Consequently, many of these students abandoned their loyalty to the church and resolved to pursue their ministries in noncongregational forms such as councils of churches, inner city projects, or even secular agencies. There was a serious questioning of the parish church throughout much of the decade on the part of those preparing themselves for religious leadership roles. They did not see themselves in careers as local pastors; their careers were to be worked out in the secular city, solving the social ills they found there. These students often gathered to discuss the faults of the church and the opportunities to serve God in the streets or in social agencies, but rarely did one find students gathering for prayer and Bible study.

In the 1970s that picture changed considerably. Students preparing for ministerial careers were more conservative theologically and less interested in social action. That is not to say that they ignored or rejected the concept of Christian social action, but rather that it was not an imperative item on their ministerial agenda. One heard much less talk about inner city ministries, taking to the streets, or antiestablishment strategies. Indeed, in the 1970s ministerial students seemed to have a much greater appreciation for the local church. Many more of them wanted to be pastors of local congregations. Furthermore, the majority of these students were very much more self-centered in their religious experience. That is, they emphasized personal piety, the "Jesus in *my* heart" style of religious life. In the 1970s it was not at all uncommon to find ministerial students (and nonministerial students) gathered together for the study of the Bible (usually literally interpreted) and prayer meetings in their college residence halls or married student housing facilities. Their piety was not outward looking, taking its cues from the surrounding society, but much more individualized and inward looking. This was true of students at seminaries that traditionally had espoused liberal or moderate theologies. But, because of their more conservative attitudes, increasing numbers of students enrolled in seminaries that were clearly identified as fundamentalist or evangelical. In the 1970s very conservative seminaries had a population explosion, whereas more liberal seminaries saw their enrollments decline and had to conduct increasingly active recruitment programs to have viable student bodies.

• *Diversity in Conservatism*

Although it is possible to generalize about the nature of conservatism, not all conservatives are the same. The distinction between evangelicals and fundamentalists has already been mentioned, but it is necessary to fill in the details of that distinction and to notice that further subdivisions may be made. One scheme for recognizing the differences among conservatives has been proposed by Richard Quebedeaux in his book *The Young Evangelicals: Revolution in Orthodoxy*.[18] Although some reviewers have suggested that Quebedeaux's categories are oversimplified, they may serve adequately for this overview. Quebedeaux posits four categories of conservatives, starting with the most rigid and moving to the more flexible.

(1) *Separatist Fundamentalism*. This is the least flexible of all conservative theological viewpoints. These fundamentalists believe that God virtually dictated to the Biblical authors what they were to write, even to the choice of words. Therefore, the words on the pages of the Bible are the words of God, completely true, without any error or cultural conditioning, and the Bible is consequently an infallible source of truth for faith. This is the most absolutist form of belief in the verbal inspiration and inerrancy of the Bible.

As the name Quebedeaux has given this category implies, these people are both offended and alarmed at the evil ways of American culture and at the lack of orthodoxy of theological liberalism; even evangelicalism is suspect. Consequently, strict fundamentalists try to maintain separation from "ungodliness." Since in their view, ungodliness is rampant in American life, they see themselves as the true believers set upon by the forces of evil and corruption. They perceive that their mission is to maintain the true faith, thereby defending themselves and the faith from the reprobate and apostate world.

In the past separatist fundamentalism has had little use for social ethics. "This present world" is so evil there is little use to try to change it. There has been a fairly strong anti-Communist, pro-America element

---

[18] Richard Quebedeaux, *The Young Evangelicals: Revolution In Orthodoxy* (New York: Harper and Row, 1974). The categories cited are discussed on pp. 19-41.

among some adherents of this style of fundamentalism, but, for the most part ethical activity has concentrated on personal piety. Furthermore, because of fear of contamination by the corrupt society, the personal piety of separatist fundamentalism has had a strong negative component in it. To be a Christian, one must not do what the world does. No drinking, no smoking, no dancing, no gambling, no attendance at the theater or most movies are permitted.

Another reason why social ethics has usually been lacking in separatist fundamentalism is the conviction that the end of the world is soon to come. The second coming of Jesus Christ will inaugurate the Kingdom of God and only that event will eliminate evil and establish righteousness. Social and political activity will not bring in the Kingdom, indeed, the existence of evil in the world is a sign that God is ready to intervene and establish his rule on earth. As examples of this style of theology, Quebedeaux lists Bob Jones University and Carl McIntire's Twentieth Century Reformation movement. Examples even better known in the late 1970s were the television ministries of Jerry Falwell and James Robison.

(2) *Open Fundamentalism.* This style of conservatism is somewhat less easily defined. In general, it has all the characteristics of separatist fundamentalism: the literalistic approach to Scripture, the emphasis on personal as opposed to social ethics, and the expectation that Christ will soon return to establish God's Kingdom. America is less often identified as God's chosen nation, although this position is also zealous in its opposition to communism. It opposes the "apostate" liberal and moderate theologies of mainstream denominations, but, unlike separatist fundamentalism, it is willing to discuss issues with other orthodox schools of thought. It is less militant in its separatism from the rest of the world, while at the same time trying to preserve the purity of faith. Its schools, such as Dallas Theological Seminary, have made strong efforts to place a solid academic base under the faith by publishing scholarly materials in several areas of theology and by giving students a thorough training in the traditional subjects of theological education. This approach is fundamentalism with a measure of self-criticism and a somewhat greater openness to what is happening outside its own boundaries. Another example of this style of theology was Hal Lindsey's *The Late Great Planet Earth,* published in 1974 and enormously popular throughout the rest of the 1970s.

(3) *Establishment Evangelicalism*. Establishment evangelicalism represents the main thrust of the evangelical viewpoint. This is the style of theology of the founders of the National Association of Evangelicals, and the NAE continues to be a principal symbol of what might be called "mainstream evangelicalism." This viewpoint continues to adhere to the verbal inspiration and authority of the Bible, but it does not limit itself to a literal interpretation of the text. It recognizes the possibility of symbolic language in the Bible. Furthermore, the question of the nature of the inspiration of the Bible has been reopened for scholarly debate. The concept that there might be different views on that crucially important topic is in itself an illustration of how different this position is from either kind of fundamentalism. Although there are many in this category who continue to think of the second coming of Christ as an imminent and highly desired possibility, some have abandoned the understanding that the entire Bible must be interpreted with this in mind (a view known as Dispensationalism).

Establishment evangelicalism is not nearly so anticultural as either kind of fundamentalism, being much more accepting of the tendencies of modern life, although still being on guard not to surrender to the wiles of secularism and the pitfalls of immorality. Some within this camp have seen the need for the application of the Christian gospel to the needs of society through political strategies and other activities of social concern. But the vast majority still understands Christian morality in terms of personal piety.

Perhaps the principal characteristic that distinguishes this mainstream evangelicalism from fundamentalism is its willingness to discuss issues with others who hold different theological perspectives. Although most denominations that are predominantly evangelical have not participated in the ecumenical, or church unity, movement (the NAE was formed at least in part in protest against the National Council of Churches), they often are willing to take other groups and theological views seriously and not write them off as heretics. (An exception to that generalization was their attitude toward the "secular theology" of the 1960s.) Perhaps the most visible example of this theological stance is Billy Graham.

(4) *New Evangelicalism*. The most "liberal" of the conservatives, the new evangelicalism has abandoned the idea of the verbal inspiration of the Scriptures; that is, that God virtually dictated what the Biblical au-

thors wrote. Rather these evangelicals are willing to concede that the text of the Bible is a product of historical situations, that the choice of words, the style of expression, and, indeed, the theology of the Bible were influenced by the historical and cultural contexts of the authors and by the limitations of their very humanness. The Bible is the word of God in the words of humans. Thus they are willing to use a method of interpretation that takes all these assumptions into account, a method commonly known as the historical-critical method. This is not to say that these evangelicals consider the Bible to be just one more piece of literature. They believe that it is crucially important for faith. But many of them are willing to say that it is the *teachings* of the Bible on faith and the Christian life that are without error, not the text of the Bible. They are still interested in talking about the inspiration of Scripture, but not in any mechanical sense that would detract from the humanity of the Biblical authors. The new evangelicals have largely abandoned the pessimistic view of history held by other segments of the conservative spectrum. This means that although they certainly believe that God will end history by the second coming of Jesus and that God certainly can do so whenever God wants, they are not so dominated by that idea that it prevents them from working in the world. One of the principal characteristics of the new evangelicals is their involvement in social activism in the name of the Christian gospel. Although they have not ceased to believe in the necessity of conversion or spiritual rebirth for individuals, they give an equal amount of emphasis to the social dimension of the Christian faith. Because of the imperative of Christian social sensitivity, the new evangelicalism warns against an uncritical identification with middle class values, a kind of status quo mentality that it views as having been characteristic of conservatives.

Finally, this left-wing evangelicalism is open to dialogue with virtually anybody—not only with other conservatives (an invitation that separatist and most open fundamentalists refuse, since they think the new evangelicals have sold out to the "world"), but also with liberals and even Marxists. New evangelicals are also open to dialogue with science, rather than just automatically regarding it to be an enemy of the faith. Some are even willing to grant the possibility of some kind of theistic evolution, virtually unheard of among other conservatives. The magazines *Sojourners* and *The Other Side*, which will be discussed later in this chapter, represent this point of view.

In the analysis of church membership and attendance figures showing conservative churches grew faster than liberal churches in the 1970s, it is not clear if any particular type of "conservatism" has grown more rapidly than any other. Part of the problem is that the categories cannot easily be correlated with specific denominations, particularly the "new evangelicals." One can speculate on the basis of the theory that the denominations that are growing most rapidly are those that are most efficient in conveying meaning and in expecting the most of their members (a concept that will be examined in depth in chapter five), that open fundamentalist or establishment evangelical groups are those that are growing most rapidly.

• *The Jesus Movement*

Another way to notice the variety of conservatism is to look at the "Jesus movement" of the late 1960s. The Jesus movement was perhaps the first sign of the end of radicalism in religion and the beginning of the conservative tendencies of the 1970s. An object of considerable interest by the media, for a while, the Jesus movement was predominantly made up of young people of high school and college age. Many of these had formerly been radicalized people who had been involved in the civil rights/political protest activities of the mid-1960s. Some of them had not been political radicals, however. In either case they had become completely disillusioned with American materialism and middle-class life and had joined the drug-oriented counterculture. As the 1960s waned, these youth became increasingly disenchanted with their style of life. In spite of their efforts, racism did not disappear from American society (although it began to diminish) and the Vietnam war raged on. The establishment was still firmly in control and materialism/capitalism seemed to be just as insensitive as ever to the needs of individuals, especially minorities and the poor. For those who had dropped out of society to adopt alternative life styles and those seeking a heightened consciousness through use of drugs (this category included both activists and dropouts), things had not gone the way they had wanted. In many cases the counterculture life style led to misery: loneliness, hunger, disillusionment with the dishonesty of many peers, boredom, and a growing awareness of the lack of any goal in life or any reason for living. Some of these young people began to realize that the "chemical heaven" of the

drug culture was not so wonderful after all. The heightened consciousness was temporary, lasting only as long as the effects of one's latest fix
(except for the recurring and unpredictable "bad trips" resulting from
LSD), and the continued use of drugs sometimes produced an addiction
or dependence that was debilitating. For many, political activism and/
or the drug culture had turned out to be a dead-end street.

It was in this context that the Jesus movement was born. It offered
a meaningful life, a reason for living, some emotional and psychological
structure; it was the ultimate trip. For some young people it provided a
satisfactory alternative to what had become the sterile youth culture of
the mid-to-late 1960s and it grew rapidly. Each one of the groups within
the Jesus movement represented some form of conservatism.

The most fundamentalist of the Jesus people groups were the Children of God, the Christian Foundation of Tony and Susan Alamo, and
The Way. The Children of God, renamed The Love Family in 1978, was
begun in 1968 under the leadership of David Berg, who is known in the
movement as Moses David. The Children of God have been characterized
by extreme authoritarianism; Moses David's word is absolute. The group
clearly thinks of itself as Christian. It proclaims the lordship of Jesus
Christ and gives large amounts of time to intense study of the Bible. It
allows no deviation from the group's interpretation of the Bible and from
its fundamentalist theology. However, if Moses David wants to give the
traditional faith any new interpretations, the members of the group have
recognized his authority to do so. The Children have been characterized
by a strong belief that the world is completely evil, that it is coming to
an end soon, with a special destruction reserved for America, and that
only the Children of God are properly prepared for the end.

The Christian Foundation of Tony and Susan Alamo was started in
1966 by a movie impresario and his wife, a Pentecostal evangelist. The
Christian Foundation specialized in recruiting young people off the
streets and into an authoritarian Christian movement. Located originally in Hollywood, California, the Christian Foundation represented
the separatism of strict fundamentalism because the Alamos believed
that the world is totally evil and that one needs to be taken out of the
evil world to be saved. Consequently, as did the Children of God, the
Christian Foundation formed a Christian commune where its converts
could live and be protected by a controlled Christian environment.

The Way is a movement begun by Victor Paul Wierwille that emerged into public view in the late 1960s. Wierwille claims that he has the correct way of interpreting the Bible and that only his way will lead to meaningful Christian life. The Way has appealed to youth through Bible courses called Power for Abundant Living. One can advance through classes of increasing depth and intensity, all the while becoming more deeply enmeshed in the movement. The group is very authoritarian and fundamentalist in the sense that it preaches that The Way alone has the true faith.

Most fundamentalist Christians, however, would not welcome these three groups, particularly the Children of God and The Way, into their ranks. The reason is not that they are too "worldly," since these groups have tried to present young people a viable alternative to the world, but rather that they have teachings that most fundamentalist Christians would regard as false and heretical. Both Moses David and V. P. Wierwille have interpreted the Bible in ways that are far from the norm of Christian belief. Because of the authoritarian nature of the groups they head, their followers believe their teachings, regardless of how unique they may be. For that reason, many conservative Christians, especially fundamentalists, have labeled those groups "cults," a charge that will be discussed in chapter four. However, because they were widely recognized as being a part of the Jesus movement in the late 1960s and early 1970s and because they defined themselves as Christian groups, it is proper to include them in a discussion of the varieties of conservatism as seen through the Jesus movement.

Conforming more closely to the views of establishment evangelicalism are such groups as the Campus Crusade for Christ and the Fellowship of Christian Athletes. Campus Crusade has historically concentrated its ministry on American college campuses, although in the mid-1970s it broadened its work to include many age levels, in this country and abroad. The Crusade has been characterized by aggressive evangelism centered on the "Four Spiritual Laws" formulated by Bill Bright, the founder of the movement. These laws stress that human beings are sinful, that God loves us in spite of our sin and has demonstrated that love through Jesus Christ, and that people need to accept that love of God through Christ by faith. Only in that way will people be saved. The Campus Crusade organizes Bible study groups for those youth involved in its ministry, in which the Bible is interpreted in a lit-eralistic way.

The Fellowship of Christian Athletes (FCA) is, as its name implies, an evangelical ministry focused on athletes, coaches and trainers, and those who financially support athletic programs. The FCA sponsors groups for Bible study, prayer, and discussion. Those for junior and senior high school athletes are called "Huddles," those for college athletes are "Fellowships." The theology and methods of the FCA's work with youth appears to be similar to that of the Campus Crusade, except that the gos-pel is couched in athletic jargon: the plan of salvation is "God's Game Plan," the Bible is God's "scouting report" on how to win the game of life, to sin is to be on the losing side, to gain salvation is to win, Jesus Christ is "your team captain," and so on. The FCA also extends its min-istry to professional athletes and athletic staffs.

Roughly equivalent to the new evangelicals are such groups as the Christian World Liberation Front (CWLF), the Inter-Varsity Christian Fellowship, Youth for Christ, and Young Life. The Christian World Lib-eration Front was born in 1968 in the city synonymous with student rad-icalism, Berkeley, California. It ministered to the street people, taking in hippies and others who had no place to lay their heads and giving them food, lodging, rehabilitation from drugs, and the Christian mes-sage. CWLF published a Christian underground newspaper, *Right On!*, the best of several such papers in those years. In the light of its left-wing evangelical theology, it addressed issues of the day in a sensitive, intel-ligent, and provocative way. Members of CWLF dressed and spoke like the street people and "hip" college students to whom they ministered and they presented the gospel in very creative ways; for example, through street drama and classes at a "free university." This group has been, through the years, one of the more intellectually-oriented groups of the Jesus movement. Late in 1975 the CWLF changed its name to the Berkeley Christian Coalition. Throughout most of the 1970s this group gave much of its attention to its Spiritual Counterfeits Project, designed to expose and combat so-called "cults."

Another movement that became much more visible during the Jesus movement days, focusing on college students, is the Inter-Varsity Chris-tian Fellowship (IVCF). Although it does not pursue the aggressive evangelism of the Campus Crusade, IVCF is active on campuses in pro-moting the Christian nurture of students from a relatively nondogmatic theological position. Through its campus study groups, its magazine *His*, and its publishing house, which publishes works on the Bible and other aspects of religion, the IVCF encourages young people to think about their religion. Although it is far from "liberal" in its theological orientation, the IVCF encourages a rational approach to the Bible and the doctrines of Christianity. It is famous for its missionary conventions held triennially, during which students have the opportunity to hear evangelical speakers and consider the need of doing both domestic and foreign missionary work. IVCF workers have also tried to keep the necessity of social action in the consciousness of the students with whom they work.

Two organizations that aim their activities primarily at high school age people are Youth for Christ International and The Young Life Campaign. Although these are separate ministries, they represent attempts to bring young people to a saving knowledge of Jesus Christ through fellowship groups and nondogmatic, fairly low-key Christian influence and teaching. Both groups have developed ministries that are nondenominational and that cross racial, cultural, and economic boundaries with a willingness to love and work for and with teenagers, offering to them a rather flexible evangelical theology.

Many of the groups listed here as being part of the Jesus movement of the late 1960s and early 1970s were organized long before that time. The Inter-Varsity Christian Fellowship began its ministry in America in 1941, the Campus Crusade was founded in 1951, Youth for Christ and Young Life were both created in the 1940s, and the Fellowship of Christian Athletes was organized in the mid-1950s. All these groups took advantage of the temper of the times in the late 1960s and early 1970s and capitalized on the Jesus movement. They had the ability and the creativity to expand their ministries and take advantage of the developing spiritual hunger among high school and college youth.

The Jesus People movement no longer exists, as such. One can argue that, in some ways, it was a media event. As has been shown, most of the groups that were active in it had existed long before. There were, however, some groups and ministries organized in the late 1960s to deal with and appeal to what seemed to be a revitalization of religious interest among youth. Furthermore, even if the movement itself were a media event, there had to be something initially to attract the attention of the media. What attracted its attention was the numbers of youth leaving the counterculture and "getting religion" in a rather noticeable, emotional, and theologically "conservative" way. But if the attention of the mass media helped to create the Jesus movement, it also contributed to its demise simply by withdrawing its attention. The media concentrates on new, unusual, and interest-arousing phenomena. When the newness wears off and a movement or series of events becomes routinely accepted, the media moves on to something else. Thus it did with the Jesus movement. Another factor in the decline of the Jesus movement was that those young people who were so much in the public eye grew older; they began to pursue more education, get married and start families, and "settle down." Many of them have moved into more established evangelical or fundamentalist churches. The leakage out of the Jesus movement has surely contributed to the increasing attendance figures for conservative denominations. But the Jesus movement still continues, in spite of the lack of media attention that it once had, because every one of the groups mentioned above still exists and continues to promote its cause.

• *Views on Social Action*

In the preceding pages some reference has been made to social action among conservatives. In this century one of the clearest differences between liberal and conservative religion has been the degree of interest and involvement in social action. In this century liberalism has been deeply involved in social action, in two distinct phases. The first of these was prior to World War I. In that time many liberals saw the need to apply the moral teachings of Christianity, as they understood them, to the problems of society. These problems included increasing industrialization, involving starvation-level wages and poor working conditions, and the accompanying problem of urbanization, involving miserable living conditions for workers. The liberals believed that they could solve those problems through Christian social action, and they actually believed that within the near future a just and equitable society—which they equated with the Kingdom of God—could be created. This belief, and the activity it spawned, was known as the Social Gospel.

The second phase of Christian liberal social action took place in the 1960s, as reviewed in chapter one.

In both periods, social action was understood to be motivated by Christian concerns but was, nonetheless, based to some extent on extra-Biblical assumptions about society. For the Social Gospel, the assumption was that evolution was true and that God used this method to accomplish godly purposes in the world. The concept of evolution suggested progress in history, progress toward the climax of an ideal society. Social Gospel adherents believed they could cooperate with God's method of historical evolution and accelerate the progress toward that religious utopia, the Kingdom of God. It is unlikely that the Social Gospel would have been the major effort it was if liberals had not so thoroughly adopted the concept of evolution and incorporated it into their view of history. In the 1960s, the extra-Biblical assumptions that underlay social action were the ideas of humanity come of age and the pervasiveness (and positive nature) of secularism.

In both of these periods the liberals labored for social rather than for personal salvation. Liberals subordinated the "saving of souls" to the redemption of society from collective sin. This has always been one of the principal objections of conservatism to liberalism. Fundamentalist and evangelical religion has emphasized rescuing individuals from sin by persuading them to accept Jesus Christ as their personal savior. For conservatives, the redemption of individuals has received highest priority. The mandate for this is not only that God sent Jesus for the salvation of each individual, but also the imperative of the "Great Commission" (Matthew 28:19-20), in which Jesus told his followers to go into all the world and make disciples. Many conservatives have argued that the liberal emphasis was misplaced. The necessary Christian activity is saving souls.

This emphasis on personal salvation has caused twentieth century conservatism to avoid the kind of social action that has been characteristic of liberalism. When the issue has been raised, both fundamentalists and evangelicals have said that they are just as interested in promoting a moral society as liberalism, but that the way to accomplish that goal is through personal evangelism. That is, the moral quality of society will be changed only when the individuals who make up the society are each changed by being born again. The activity of personal evangelism has social implications. As men and women are saved from sin they will put away their evil and live moral, Christian lives. That will make society better. So, the way to transform society is to save as many individuals as possible.

The dispensational theology characteristic of most of conservatism plays a role in this neglect of direct social action. Premillennialism, the belief that the second coming of Christ will inaugurate the Kingdom of God (that the return of Christ will precede and begin the millennium), sees human social action as unnecessary and ineffective. That is, only the coming of Christ will right the wrongs of the world. The proper role for the Christian is to win people to Christ to enable them to be ready for his coming, not to tinker with political structures or lobby for social legislation.

Consequently, social action has not been characteristic of conservatism in this century and indeed, especially for fundamentalists, "Social Gospel" has been a dirty word. Conservatism has self-consciously rejected social action because it was so closely tied with liberal theology prior to World War I, when the Social Gospel adopted evolution as a part of its theological method, and in the 1960s because it allied itself so closely with secularism.

In the 1970s, however, a renaissance of social action began in conservatism. "Renaissance" is the proper word, because recently some historians have shown that in the nineteenth century efforts to transform society from a Christian perspective were very much a part of conservative or orthodox Protestantism. Conservatism has, as it turns out, a long tradition of social activism. In the nineteenth century, the energies of socially aware conservatives were directed toward three major targets: slavery, the oppression of women, and alcohol. While not all those in the North who worked for the abolition of slavery did so for religious reasons, many of them did. (However, it must be acknowledged that many in the South used religion to defend the institution of slavery.) Orthodox Christian women (and some men) were in the fore of the effort to improve the conditions of women and many churches expressed themselves as supporting feminist goals. Many denominations, concerned individuals, and Christian-oriented special interest groups labored diligently to stamp out the evil of alcoholism from American society. The fact that they were less successful on that project or feminism than were those working on abolition is not because they did not try.

In the very late nineteenth and early twentieth centuries conservatives largely abandoned efforts at social action. The reasons for this change are complex, but seemed to stem primarily from a reaction against liberalism and the Social Gospel and from discouragement and disorientation that emerged among conservatives in the wake of the Sco-

pes trial. The result was the aversion to social action that has characterized conservatives in much of the twentieth century.

In the 1970s, however, social action concerns surfaced powerfully in
that segment of the conservative community often described as the
"new" or "young evangelicals." Indeed, willingness to be involved in social action is one of the principal characteristics distinguishing new
evangelicals from other conservatives. These socially concerned evangelicals are deeply disturbed by the passive and indifferent attitude toward
the problems of society that has been characteristic of twentieth-century
conservatism. They believe that authentic Christianity demands social
action and society desperately needs it.

"A Declaration of Evangelical Social Concern" is an example of this
style of thinking. Signed by 50 evangelicals from a number of denominations and backgrounds, the document acknowledges that evangelicalism has been a captive of American culture and, because of that, has
failed to exert a Christian witness to the society. The gospel demands
justice, but evangelicals have not been sensitive enough to that requirement. Evangelicalism has condoned racism and the inequitable distribution of resources, both here and abroad. The signers of the paper call
upon themselves and other evangelicals to work to combat the effects of
racism and to labor for the alleviation of the sufferings of the poor and
hungry. The dangers of economic imperialism and an excessive reliance
on military strength are mentioned, along with a warning against making the economic and military powers of the country virtually objects of
worship. Also included is the recognition of the equality of men and
women in all aspects of life. The purpose of the document seems to be
to raise the consciousness of evangelicals and to stimulate them to Christian action in the world. Although this document was issued late in
1973, there does not seem to have been any specific implementation of
it. Of course, there is no way to know if any individuals may have been
challenged by it to engage in social action.

A more radical example of left-wing evangelical social concern is the
People's Christian Coalition. Founded as a kind of Christian commune
in 1971, this group was very different from most Jesus People communes
founded in the late 1960s and early 1970s. Whereas virtually all of those
were founded to escape the world, this one was founded to try to serve
the world, first from Chicago and, since 1975, from Washington, D.C.
Although the community is putting Christian concern into action in the

Washington ghetto where it is located, its ideas are disseminated much more widely by the magazine *Sojourners* (originally called *The Post-American*), edited by Jim Wallis. *Sojourners* reminds one of a radical publication of the 1960s, except that its social views are all argued from a Biblical, theological basis. A bold publication, *Sojourners* seeks to bring racism, multi-national corporations and the abuses of capitalism, violence, militarism, sexism, and the narrowness of vision of both liberal and conservative Christianity under the judgment of Scripture. Clearly a journal of advocacy, *Sojourners* challenges its readers to live with only God as lord of their lives and to refuse ultimate allegiance to anything else, especially a nation, any type of prejudice, or anything that would exploit human beings or deny them justice and opportunity.

Another example of the new evangelical social concern is the magazine, *The Other Side*. This journal is not quite so outspoken as *Sojourners*, but leaves no doubt that it sees the world as exploitive of human beings. Founded in 1965 to bring the evils of racial segregation to the consciences of fundamentalist and evangelical Christians, the magazine now addresses a wide range of issues. The conviction in this publication, as of the new evangelicals as a whole, is that society's problems will not be solved and the oppressed (and one can be oppressed in a number of ways, even by having too much power or money) freed until people are willing to surrender their lives to Jesus Christ and are bold enough to implement his values in daily life. It is to that end that evangelical social activists work.

In the months leading up to the elections of 1980 (a presidential year) fundamentalists rather suddenly also became outspoken on social issues. Although the description of that phenomenon will be presented in chapter six, it is worth observing here again that this social/political activity on the part of fundamentalists was totally out of character for them. But as uncharacteristic as it was, through the leadership of some articulate spokesmen, fundamentalism exploded onto the social/political scene with very definite ideas and attracted national attention.

In the light of all this activity on the part of conservative Christians in the 1970s, what *was* so strange about Jimmy Carter that the media went to such lengths to pay attention to the fact that he was a born-again Christian?

• *Suggestions for Further Reading*
for Context and Perspective

Bloesch, Donald. *The Evangelical Renaissance*. Grand Rapids MI: Wm. B. Eerdmans Co., 1973.

Dayton, Donald W. *Discovering an Evangelical Heritage*. New York: Harper and Row, 1976.

Dollar, George W. *A History of Fundamentalism in America*. Greenville SC: Bob Jones University Press, 1973.

Ellwood, Robert S., Jr. *One Way: The Jesus Movement and its Meaning*. Englewood Cliffs NJ: Prentice-Hall, 1973.

Enroth, Ronald M., Ericson, Edward E., Jr. and Peters, C. Breckinridge. *The Jesus People: Old-time Religion in the Age of Aquarius*. Grand Rapids MI: Wm. B. Eerdmans Co., 1972.

Henry, Carl F. H. *Evangelicals in Search of Identity*. Waco TX: Word Books, 1976.

Johnston, Robert K. *Evangelicals at an Impasse: Biblical Authority in Practice*. Atlanta: John Knox Press, 1979.

Kelley, Dean M. *Why Conservative Churches are Growing*, 2d ed. New York: Harper and Row, 1977.

Moberg, David O. *The Great Reversal: Evangelism and Social Concern*. Rev. ed. Philadelphia: J. B. Lippincott Co., 1977.

Quebedeaux, Richard. *The Young Evangelicals: Revolution in Orthodoxy*. New York: Harper and Row, 1974.

_____. *The Worldly Evangelicals*. New York: Harper and Row, 1978.

Wells, David R. and Woodbridge, John D., eds. *The Evangelicals: What They Believe, Who They Are, Where They Are Changing*. Nashville: Abingdon Press, 1975.

CHAPTER THREE

"O for a Thousand Tongues to Sing": Understanding the Charismatic Movement

"O for a thousand tongues to sing my great Redeemer's praise. . . ." Charles Wesley did not write this line to his great hymn with the Pentecostal experience in mind, but rather to commemorate his conversion in 1738. However, the line communicates very well a major emphasis of Pentecostalism, the gift from the Holy Spirit of diverse languages to praise God. The purpose of this chapter is to look at a major phenomenon of the 1960s and the 1970s, the rise of Neo-Pentecostalism. But in order to understand that phenomenon rather extensive background information is needed.

• *Roots and Origin*
of Modern Pentecostalism

Pentecostals insist that they are seeking and finding a recovery of the experiences of the early Christian church, especially those described in the New Testament in Acts 2 and 1 Corinthians 12-14. Acts 2 tells of the beginning of the Christian movement, an event caused and energized by the Holy Spirit. The apostles were empowered to witness to Christ and him crucified by an infusion of the Holy Spirit; the Spirit gave them language other than their own. Pentecostalism claims that in these latter times the Holy Spirit is again moving among God's people, and a sign of the Spirit is the ability to speak in unknown tongues.

In Acts 2 there are two clues as to the nature of the tongues. In Acts 2:5-12, there is the clear indication that the languages spoken by the apostles were intelligible languages, easily understood by those people from foreign lands who were in Jerusalem for the feast of Pentecost. They were tongues unknown to the speakers, but easily understood by their auditors. However, there is also the indication, in Acts 2:13-16, that some perceived these languages as being unintelligible. Indeed, they accused the apostles of being drunk. But Peter, the spokesman for the apostles, attributed these unintelligible tongues to the power of God, one of the signs and wonders of God in a crucial moment in history. Modern Pentecostalism also sees tongues to be manifestations of both intelligible and unintelligible languages.

In I Corinthians 12 and 14 Paul describes gifts of the Spirit other than tongues and also exhorts the church on the proper use of unknown tongues in worship. Paul enumerates a series of gifts (1 Corinthians 12:8-10): the utterance of wisdom, the utterance of knowledge, faith, healing, the working of miracles, prophecy, the ability to distinguish between the spirits, tongues, and the interpretation of tongues. Of these, Paul seems to have thought that prophecy was the most important. When tongues were spoken in public worship, there were to be only two or three speakers at a time, each one in turn, and there was to be interpretation. In 1 Corinthians 14 Paul emphasizes the necessity for good order in the worship setting and for the need for interpretation. Good order was seemly for the people of God; interpretation was necessary for the edification of the congregation, to inform the people of what God was saying, for the building up of the church.

These are the principal passages upon which Pentecostals base their modern-day religious practices. They are totally convinced that they are a restoration of New Testament practices; that, unlike nonPentecostal Christians who have forgotten many of the gifts of the Spirit, they adhere to the "full gospel."

The claim that Pentecostalism is a recovery of these features of New Testament Christianity acknowledges that the practice of the gifts seems to have been experienced less frequently after New Testament times. Although there seem to have been some incidences of tongues in the centuries immediately after the New Testament period, by the fifth century this kind of ecstatic experience was virtually nonexistent in Christianity. This was perhaps because the structure or organization of the church was becoming more rigid and patterns of worship were becoming more formal and ritualized. With the development of Catholicism and its formal liturgy, there was no place for the kind of spontaneous behavior that tongues and interpretation represented. Since the Protestant Reformation in the sixteenth century there have been isolated outbreaks of Pentecostal activity from time to time. But it is clear that there was no coherence or organization to these varied manifestations of the Spirit-filled experience. It was not until the twentieth century that Pentecostalism became a movement.

Yet Pentecostalism did not originate by spontaneous combustion; it did not "tangibilitate," to use Father Divine's wonderful word. Rather it grew out of Wesleyan theology. In the late eighteenth century, John Wesley, the founder of Methodism, argued that the experience of God in salvation is a twofold process. The first experience Wesley called "justification." Justification is the result of one's having accepted the Lordship of Jesus Christ, acknowledged that Christ is the surest expression of God's love, and been forgiven of sin. In justification one repents of sin and is forgiven for all those sins which one has committed up until that time. But, Wesley believed, after justification one still possesses a "residue of sin within." That is, although all prior sins have been forgiven, the inclination to sin is still within the individual. This inclination to sin is dealt with by a "second blessing" that Wesley labeled "sanctification." Sanctification purifies the believer of inward sin, the inclination to sin, and gives him or her perfect love toward God and fellow humans. This concept of the second blessing was a part of the Methodist theology that was transported to this country and it became a significant factor in frontier and urban revivalism. This emphasis on the importance of the second blessing was known as "holiness," and in the middle and late nineteenth century the holiness branch of Methodism became increasingly vocal and visible. A breach in the relationship between holiness and regular Methodists developed because holiness folk, with their concept of the sanctified life, began to think that regular Methodists loved "the world" as much as, if not more than, God. By the 1890s the two viewpoints had dissolved their relationship and the holiness people became a separate movement, the Holiness denominations.

In some Holiness groups the idea developed that there was a third blessing in the Christian experience, the baptism of the Holy Spirit. It was out of this view that the baptism of the Holy Spirit was a separate and distinct experience that Pentecostalism arose.

The person usually associated with the birth of the Pentecostal movement is Charles Fox Parham, a Holiness preacher of the three-experience belief. Early in 1900 Parham opened a Bible school in Topeka, Kansas, to teach the doctrines of his church to interested ministry and missionary students. With about 40 students Parham worked through the Biblical bases of various Holiness beliefs and practices. Toward the end of the year they came to the concept of the baptism of the Holy Spirit. It was necessary for Parham to be away for a few days for a preaching mission and, to cover the time of his absence, he gave his students the assignment to look for the Biblical evidences for the baptism of the Holy Spirit. When he returned, the students reported that they had, indeed, found the signs of the Holy Spirit's anointing: unknown tongues.

That intellectual idea became an existential experience on the evening of 31 December 1900. Parham and his students were gathered for a "watch night service," welcoming the new year with prayer and Bible study. During the course of that worship activity, one of the students, Agnes Ozman, asked her teacher if he would place his hands on her head, bless her, and pray that she might receive the baptism of the Holy Spirit with the sign of unknown tongues. He did and Miss Ozman began to speak with a language unknown to her, but which was believed by her and the others at the school to be Chinese. With this manifestation of the power of the Holy Spirit, the Pentecostal movement had begun. Within a short time the other students and Parham himself also received the gift of tongues.

Parham soon closed his school and began a series of revival meetings in Kansas and Missouri in which he enthusiastically preached the baptism of the Spirit accompanied by tongues. In 1905 Parham opened another Bible school, this time in Houston, Texas. One of his students there was a black man named William J. Seymour. A Baptist with strong Holiness inclinations, Seymour accepted his teacher's message of Pentecostal manifestations with enthusiasm and the concept soon became a part of his own preaching.

In 1906 Seymour was called to be the preacher for a small group of Holiness people in Los Angeles, California. Before long a revival began and it attracted so many people that Seymour had to move his meetings from the home in which he had been holding services to a ramshackle,

abandoned Methodist church on Azusa street. There the revival intensified and, when news stories about it were printed across the country,
Holiness and other conservative Christians from all across the United
States and Canada began to visit the services. The revival meeting lasted
three years with almost continuous preaching by Seymour and other
ministers. The main feature of the services, in addition to heartfelt
expressions of praise to God, was the baptism of the Holy Spirit, evi-
denced by unknown tongues, interpretations, and divine healings. Although there were some scoffers and critics, the majority of the people
who came were convinced that they had seen and experienced the activity
of God. As they went home, they took the Pentecostal message and experience with them. Pentecostal historians sometimes refer to the Azusa
street revival as the "American Jerusalem," since it was that revival
which provided the impetus for the spread of the Pentecostal movement
all across America.

As Pentecostalism developed, however, it did not remain one ho-
mogeneous group. Rather, the movement divided into a number of denominations, each with a distinctive theology. It may be said that a
"family" of denominations was the result of the great Azusa street revival. The common feature holding the family together is the experience
of the Holy Spirit baptism, with evidences in tongues, interpretation,
healing, and other gifts described in the New Testament. It is this family
of denominations, growing out of the manifestations of the Holy Spirit
at the beginning of this century, which historians often refer to as "Classical Pentecostalism."

• *The Nature and Value of Tongues*

The nonPentecostal person who learns of the distinctive features of
Pentecostalism is often skeptical and curious about them. What are "unknown tongues?" What is the nature of the experience of tongues? Pentecostals reply that, as indicated in the New Testament, the gift of
tongues is evidence that one's life has been invaded in a dynamic way by
the Holy Spirit of God. Although the other gifts already mentioned are
also manifestations of the Holy Spirit, most Classical Pentecostal groups
believe that tongues is the initial and the essential gift. Some believe
that once one has spoken in tongues, God may give that person another
of the gifts so that one might not speak in tongues again, or only infre-

quently. On the other hand, one may actively speak in tongues regularly for the remainder of one's life. It may be that one will enjoy more than one of the gifts. It is difficult to generalize about the distribution or frequency of the gifts.

Unknown tongues become a vehicle of prayer and devotion. Not only is the ability to speak in tongues the sign that God has come into one's life in a special way, that there is now an intimacy and closeness between the believer and God that did not exist before the baptism of the Holy Spirit, but also one now possesses a special language with which to express the devotion and praise that is due to God. A "tongue" is first and foremost a language, given by God, to facilitate the most intimate expressions of praise and love for God through prayer.

There is one generalization which is true for all manifestations of tongues: the language is unknown to the speaker. However, Pentecostals believe that it may be a language spoken somewhere in the world. Just as some of those in the streets of Jerusalem at the first Pentecost were able to understand the apostles as speaking their language, so now. Although linguists and philologists have not been able to find any hard evidence of this phenomenon, Pentecostal literature is full of examples of persons from foreign countries who attended an American Pentecostal worship service, heard a person speak in tongues, and were able to recognize the language as his or her native tongue, even though the speaker, in normal circumstances, had no ability to speak that language.

However, "glossolalia" (the word scholars use to designate tongues speaking) does not always take the form of an intelligible language; there are many instances of the unintelligible language tradition, also. Sometimes the tongue spoken is recognized as no known language. Unfortunately for defenders of the intelligible language tradition, the examples which linguists and philologists have recorded for study have been of the unintelligible type. They have noticed languagelike qualities such as phrasing and inflection of the voice, but they have not been able to identify their examples as any existing language. Whether or not the language spoken under the influence of the Spirit is an existing human language does not matter, since the language and the thoughts it contains are directed to God, anyway. Whether the language is understood by others is immaterial, since God understands.

Still, it is of considerable importance whether or not the people in a worshiping congregation understand what is said in a tongue. Paul wrote in 1 Corinthians 14 that tongues should be for the edification of the congregation. The ability to interpret tongues is just as much a gift of the Spirit as is the ability to speak in tongues. So, although the prayer language provided by God can be understood by God, it cannot be understood by the speaker's fellow worshipers without interpretation. God has provided the means for interpretation through an additional gift of the Holy Spirit. When one speaks in tongues, another is to interpret, although it sometimes happens that the speaker also has the gift of interpretation. The purpose of the interpretation is the uplifting and informing of the congregation. Pentecostals usually understand the interpretation to be a paraphrase of the utterance in tongues, rather than necessarily a direct, literal translation.

But sometimes a tongue is not interpreted. Paul speaks of the necessity of interpretation in the context of a worshiping congregation. But often Pentecostals speak in tongues when they are alone, in their private devotions. Pentecostals believe that once one has received the initial gift of tongues, then one can speak in tongues at will; it is a volitional rather than a spontaneous act. Consequently, one can choose to pray in the tongue(s) one has been given in one's private moments with God. In such circumstances, unless the same person also has the gift of interpretation, then the individual virtually never knows what he or she is saying in the moments of praying in tongues.

The principal question the nonPentecostal person may raise about all this is, "So what?" Put somewhat more elegantly, the question about tongues is, "What good is it?" One can perhaps see some value in tongues when they are interpreted, but if there is interpretation in the language of the people, why not just speak the language of the people in the first place? This is especially true since another of the gifts of the Spirit is prophecy. (Prophecy is the speaking of words from God, not in a tongue, but in the language of the people. It is highly regarded by Paul in 1 Corinthians 14:1-5.) More to the point, what good is tongues if one is alone, without any interpretation, so that the words are totally meaningless?

Pentecostalism has answered these objections in a number of ways. Tongues, and the other gifts of the Spirit, are signs that the Holy Spirit has become an integral part of one's life, enabling one to draw closer to God and to better live the life of the committed Christian. The Holy

Spirit empowers and enables the individual to live the more devout and Godly life in the face of these wicked times.

More specifically, tongues enable one to establish a fellowship with God which is not inhibited by the limitations of the mind. As great as our minds are, they are limited—by finite intelligence and by finite abilities to conceptualize and articulate our ideas. So long as our prayers are dependent upon normal speech, they are constrained by our finitude. But in tongues God has made available a way of communicating and sharing with the divine which bypasses the mind and its limitations. In tongues, one is able to express the unexpressible.

Think of it this way: Have you ever had an experience which was so moving, so profound, that in describing it to someone you finally had to say, "I cannot put that into words"? Pentecostalism says that the experience of God in one's life is like that. To be a Christian; to be the beneficiary of God's unmerited grace is so magnificent an experience that, no matter how much we might talk about it in ordinary language, finally words fail us as we attempt to communicate to God our thanks and praise for the love given to us. But God, as another dimension of grace, supplies us with a language for prayer and praise. That the speaker cannot understand it is not only beside the point, it is the advantage, the glory of the language. It enables one to bypass the limitations of the mind and allow the feelings of gratitude, of unworthiness, of praise to bubble up from the deepest recesses of the soul and be expressed to God. Its analog is that mysterious and inarticulate communication which is possessed by those who deeply love each other. It is God's gift to someone God deeply loves, to enable that person's most interior religious feelings to come to the surface.

There are other gifts of the Spirit, most of them much less spectacular than tongues and interpretation. Healing has been rather noticeable as the principal characteristic of the ministries of some Pentecostal ministers and evangelists, but it can be and is done much more unobtrusively by individual Pentecostals, both within and outside the context of public worship. Words of wisdom and knowledge often come when they are least expected but most valuable, as when one is witnessing to one's faith or counseling with another about a problem. Paul lists faith itself as a gift of the Spirit and Pentecostal people often speak of a sudden infusion of faith in moments of doubt or temptation. Miracles are often small things, changes in circumstances brought about by God's intervention, answers to prayer. Finally, discernment of spirits means sensing, by the Holy Spirit, what spiritual influences are at work in an individual or at a worship service.

• *Sociological Characteristics*
of Classical Pentecostalism

Classical Pentecostalism has traditionally had a particular sociological characteristic, namely, that it has been made up of people at the lower end of the socioeconomic scale: the poor, the underskilled, the undereducated, the people who are sometimes described as the "disinherited" of society. Although there have been people in this category who practiced nonPentecostal religion, Classical Pentecostalism, through most of its history, has been populated by this kind of persons.

Churches of this type have historically had certain identifiable characteristics. One of these is theological conservatism. To say this is not to suggest that all conservatives are Pentecostals of the disinherited class, but it is to assert that churches of the disinherited have been conservative. This conservatism consists of several features. One of these is a Biblical literalism such as that described in the previous chapter as characteristic of fundamentalism. These churches tend to be dogmatic in theology: "We know exactly what the Bible means, we know the doctrines which are derived from the Bible, and we hold these as being absolutely true." Consequently, these congregations tend to think of themselves as the only true believers. Any group that disagrees with the interpretation of the Bible and the general theology of the group is wrong. As a result, these groups have tended to have rigid membership standards: "In order to become a part of our group, you must believe exactly as we do."

In addition to this conservatism, churches of the disinherited historically have had emotional worship services. In Pentecostal churches tongues and interpretation have been components of this emotionalism, but frequently it has also consisted of shouting, dancing, crying and moaning (in distress for the unsaved or perhaps in fear of one's own damnation), and fainting. Such behavior has caused critics to give the dreadful term "holy rollers" to such people. These congregations have typically worshiped in plain, simple, austere church buildings. Sometimes, in fact, they have not had church buildings at all, but have utilized old houses or store fronts adapted for the purpose of worship. They have tended to have an untrained clergy, ministers without higher or theological education, preferring leaders called by God to those with college education. The impression may prevail that those two conditions are mutually exclusive. In addition, insisting that church leaders should be without higher education reinforces a desire to be isolated from "worldly" society and its ways. Finally, churches populated by the disinherited have consistently believed that the end of the world is coming—soon. The sooner it comes the better that will be.

In trying to understand why these characteristics have been consistently found among the churches of those at the lower end of the socioeconomic scale, including nearly all Classical Pentecostal churches, and are generally not found in the churches of the middle and upper social classes, scholars have argued that these characteristics are ways the poor have for compensating for and coping with their lower class status. Conservative theology, including its "true believer" dimension, is a way the poor have of saying to themselves and to anyone else who might pay attention: "Other people may have good jobs, fine homes, clothes and cars and other things that the world values, but we have the truth; we are God's people. It is much more important to be God's people than to possess worldly things."

Although it would not be true to say that the poor have no means of recreation and emotional outlet, observers point out that they have far fewer resources for these things than do middle and upper class people. When life is essentially a struggle for survival, when all resources gained have to be used for necessities, there is little if any money to be spent for recreation and entertainment, as important as these are for relieving the stress produced by our times. Consequently, the emotional worship of the churches of the disinherited, especially the emotionalism attendant on speaking in tongues and other manifestations of the Holy Spirit, has provided the emotional outlet for the poor that middle- and upper-class people find in the secular world. Emotional worship is a way of coping with the unrelieved drudgery brought on by life at the bottom of the socioeconomic scale.

Austere worship settings and untrained clergy are obvious results of living far down the socioeconomic ladder: there simply are not any resources to provide better. Funds to provide higher education or pew cushions are virtually nonexistent for the poor.

When this world does not offer one much in terms of creature comforts or opportunities to improve one's condition, it is not surprising that the possibility of the end of this world is very attractive. People who are fairly comfortable socioeconomically may not be all that interested in the coming of the end of the world, but people for whom this world does not offer much eagerly await it, especially if they consider themselves to be God's people and believe that they will reap the rewards God has for them in the final judgment.

While Classical Pentecostal churches usually have had as members people from the lower economic strata of society, some denominations within Classical Pentecostalism began to change their character after World War II. Although the expanding postwar economy certainly did not eliminate poverty from the United States, many poor people did begin to move up the socioeconomic scale. For some Classical Pentecostal churches this new affluence meant that their buildings became more elaborate and comfortable. They began to expect their clergy to have a college education. They became less dogmatic and began to think of themselves less as the only true believers (although most of them continued to interpret the Bible literally). Their emotionalism began to cool down and become less undisciplined, that is, their worship became more orderly. Although the second coming of Christ remained part of their doctrine (since it is a New Testament concept), they tended to talk about it less and not to be so eager for its coming. This process has continued into the present for some, but not all, Pentecostal denominations.

• *Origins of Neo-Pentecostalism*

Against the backdrop of this extensive examination of the background of contemporary Pentecostalism, we now turn to the subject of this chapter, the events of the 1960s and 1970s. In those years a new dimension developed within the Pentecostal tradition, Neo-Pentecostalism, also sometimes called the Charismatic Movement or the Charismatic Renewal of the church. Neo-Pentecostalism may be defined as traditional Pentecostal behavior now being practiced in middle and upper class churches. Neo-Pentecostalism is Pentecostal procedure, particularly tongues and interpretation, breaking the bounds of its traditional lower class environment and manifesting itself in churches of the middle and upper socioeconomic strata.

The origins of this remarkable phenomenon are diverse. The earliest beginnings of this movement lie with the organization in 1951 of the Full Gospel Business Men's Fellowship International (FGBMFI). This organization was begun by Demos Shakarian, the son of an Armenian immigrant family that had witnessed the Azusa street revival and had been Pentecostal ever since. Shakarian, who by the 1950s had become a wealthy dairyman in California, felt the need to conduct some kind of lay ministry among other Pentecostal businessmen. He invited them to join him in breakfast and luncheon meetings for the purpose of prayer, Bible reading, and discussions of religious topics.

Even though the group was not restricted to any particular Pentecostal denomination but drew from several, in the early years it was very small, primarily because there were not many Pentecostal businessmen in those days. But, as more and more Pentecostals moved up the socio-economic scale, there were more businessmen whom the FGBMFI could attract. However, in addition to the purposes of prayer and Bible study, the group also resolved to evangelize and to present Pentecostal Christianity to others. Through their business contacts they inevitably witnessed to people who were members of "mainstream," nonPentecostal churches. Some of these people responded and then spread the good news of Pentecostalism to others in their middle- or upper-class congregations. In the late 1960s and the 1970s the FGBMFI was an expression of and vehicle for Neo-Pentecostalism as much or more than it was a Classical Pentecostal group. Through the group's magazine, *Full Gospel Business Men's Voice*, later its television program, and international travel for evangelistic purposes, the FGBMFI had indeed become international by the end of the 1970s, having chapters in at least fifty countries. A vigorous organization which now allows women and young people to participate, FGBMFI was a prime mover in the development of Neo-Pentecostalism and, throughout the 1970s, as it recruited people from all across the denominational spectrum, was one of the principal forces in its growth.

One of the principal names in the story of the development and growth of Neo-Pentecostalism is Dennis Bennett. In 1959 Bennett was the rector of St. Mark's Episcopal Church in Van Nuys, California, an Anglo-Catholic ("high church") congregation. In the fall of that year he was asked by a fellow Episcopal clergyman for some advice concerning what to do about a couple in his church who were Pentecostal. It seems that this couple, John and Joan Baker, had been evangelized by some Pentecostal friends of theirs, but rather than leaving the Episcopal church after having been baptized by the Holy Spirit, they threw themselves into it more enthusiastically. Their minister was afraid that they would ruin his congregation. When he asked Bennett for advice Bennett did not know what to say because he was ignorant of Pentecostalism; but he became intrigued. He met with the Bakers in November 1959, and, after they had witnessed to him about their own Pentecostal experience, he claimed a baptism of the Holy Spirit.

By the middle of 1960 about 70 members of Bennett's own congregation had received the Pentecostal experience, having been influenced by the Bakers and encouraged by their pastor. These Pentecostals did not speak in tongues or do any other thing out of the ordinary in the worship services at their church, but it soon became an open secret in the congregation that there was a Pentecostal cell holding separate meetings for prayer and Bible study, meetings which sometimes lasted until the early hours of the morning. In the morning worship the second Sunday before Easter, 1960, Bennett informed his congregation that he and a significant group from their number had, indeed, been baptized by the Holy Spirit and that they had experienced the accompanying signs: tongues, interpretation, etc. This announcement was received with much displeasure by many in the church, including some in the ministerial staff. In order to calm the passions, both pro and con, within the congregation, Bennett soon resigned his post.

Although he was generally regarded by Episcopalians as some kind of religious crank, Bennett was not unemployed for long. A bishop in Washington invited him to become the pastor of a small church in Seattle that was in disarray and showed few signs of life. What some ministers might have considered to be banishment Bennett saw as an opportunity and he ministered to St. Luke's church with all his ability, energized and emboldened by the Holy Spirit. Soon the congregation was thriving. Many within the church were Pentecostal and many were not. But they learned that they could coexist in the same congregation with Christian love.

Bennett's revival of St. Luke's in Seattle, an accomplishment he and others attributed to the power of the Holy Spirit with Pentecostal manifestations, catapulted him into the fore of the Neo-Pentecostal movement. He traveled, spoke, and wrote extensively as an advocate for Charismatic Renewal and was one of the primary reasons that it grew so rapidly in America in the late 1960s and throughout the 1970s.

Bennett's experience of the Spirit and his leadership within the context of the Episcopal church illustrates what a radical departure Neo-Pentecostalism is from Classical Pentecostalism. The Episcopal church is largely made up of people from the upper strata of the socioeconomic scale. Although there is some variation in style among Episcopalians, their worship services tend to be well ordered, conducted by established ritual, and not given to extremes of emotion. This type of worship conforms to middle- and upper-class standards of dignity and is rooted in the tradition of the Episcopal church, the worship of which has historically been closer to Roman Catholic Mass than that of any other Protestant denomination. Few would have anticipated that Pentecostal manifestations would emerge in this denomination. But they did and they have persisted to the present. Furthermore, it soon came to the attention to observers of American religion that Neo-Pentecostalism was to be found in most other "mainstream" denominations; that it was a movement of sizable proportions. Dennis Bennett was a driving force in the spread of the Charismatic movement into denominations other than his own, particularly Lutherans and Presbyterians.

Another factor in the growth of Neo-Pentecostalism has been the work of David Du Plesis, known to some as "Mr. Pentecost." Born in South Africa in 1905, Du Plesis received the baptism of the Holy Spirit in 1918. Since that time he has worked tirelessly to promote Pentecostal Christianity. What makes him so important for Neo-Pentecostalism is that he early felt that the separation between Pentecostals and non-Pentecostals was a scandal. For that reason he began to try to bridge the gap by making overtures to the World Council of Churches, an organization perceived as liberal by fundamentalists and evangelicals and therefore considered anathema. He was well received by officials in that organization. In fact, he was of such an irenic spirit and so effective a spokesman for Pentecostalism that since 1951, when he first approached the World Council of Churches, he regularly has been invited to participate in ecumenical gatherings. He spoke to international missionary conferences, to several assemblies of the World Council, and to the students at such schools as Union Theological Seminary in New York, Yale Divinity School, and Princeton Theological Seminary. He was an observer at the Second Vatican Council and, in the 1970s, functioned as the co-chair of a conversation among Roman Catholics, Classical Pentecostals, and Neo-Pentecostals. He traveled the world and became perhaps the most articulate spokesman for Pentecostalism.

The importance of Du Plesis for the development of Neo-Pentecostalism is that he helped to make Pentecostalism respectable to people in the mainstream churches. Because of its primarily lower-class status and the emotional excesses to which it was often given, Classical Pentecostalism had often been either derided or ignored by the mainline churches. Du Plesis was able to present a better face for Classical Pentecostalism. In the process he made it more appealing for those in the mainstream and some even responded to his witness by opening themselves to the work of the Holy Spirit, thus becoming part of Neo-Pentecostalism. In addition to building a bridge between Pentecostalism and nonPentecostals, Du Plesis was also able to facilitate relationships between Classical Pentecostals and Neo-Pentecostals. This was important for the latter because it helped them to understand the characteristics and the strengths of the tradition of which they were becoming a part. Although Du Plesis received his share of criticism from some Classical Pentecostals and other conservatives because he fraternized with "liberals," he did a great service within Pentecostalism by giving visibility, respectability, and strength to the tradition, especially to the new Pentecostalism of the mainstream churches.

For purposes of this brief overview, a final striking development in the rise of Neo-Pentecostalism is Catholic Pentecostalism. Flying in the face of the fact that Classical Pentecostalism, at least through World War II, was essentially anti-intellectual, Catholic Pentecostalism began and thrived in a university environment. It began in late 1966 and early 1967 among faculty members at Duquesne University in Pittsburgh. These persons were concerned about the vitality of their spiritual lives. They prayed and examined spiritual literature in the attempt to add depth to their spirituality. One of the books which made an impact on this small group was *The Cross and the Switchblade*, by David Wilkerson. That book is the story of a young pastor who went into one of the toughest areas of New York City to minister to teenage gangs and youth on drugs. Wilkerson was successful in converting and changing the direction of the lives of many young people. He testified that it was the power of God through the Holy Spirit which enabled him to launch and sustain that ministry. The people at Duquesne learned from that that the Pentecostal experience gives power to life. They also read *They Speak With Other Tongues* by John Sherrill, a journalist's account of how an experience of the Spirit could change lives and how this was happening to men and women in settings far removed from traditional Pentecostalism.

Intrigued by this reading and all the more interested in improving their spiritual lives, these teachers went to meet some Pentecostal people to find out whether what they had been reading was really true. They became a part of a prayer group made up of both Classical and Neo-Pentecostal people. It was not long before these Roman Catholics had received the baptism of the Holy Spirit with evidence of tongues. They discovered that the intervention of the Holy Spirit in their lives made them appreciate the Mass more and, in general, made them better Catholics. By their witness and example more Catholics in and around Duquesne became interested in this deepened form of spirituality and soon there was a rather significant number who had received the Pentecostal experience.

A Catholic Pentecostal group evolved in January and February 1967. By March, through the witness of visiting friends, Pentecostal groups had sprung up at Michigan State and Notre Dame universities. From that time, Notre Dame served as a focal point for Roman Catholic Pentecostalism. Some of the movement's principal apologists taught or studied at Notre Dame; the major national and, more recently, international Charismatic conferences were held at Notre Dame. Of course, Catholic Pentecostalism was not restricted to these colleges. The movement spread into a multitude of parishes throughout the 1970s. But the campus, especially Notre Dame, has been the locus of much of the dynamism of Catholic Pentecostalism in America.

In the very earliest days of this surprising development within the Catholic church, the leadership of the church was wary and apprehensive about what seemed to be a very unCatholic style of spiritual behavior. But virtually from the outset of the phenomenon, the people involved were not only undergraduate and graduate students, but also professors, priests, nuns, theologians, and even some bishops. When these more influential persons were anointed with the Holy Spirit, they provided an aura of respectability for the movement which prevented it from being ignored or condemned by the leadership of the church. The swelling numbers of people involved, both in this country and abroad, also forestalled hasty action by the hierarchy. Finally, in 1975, there was an international Catholic Pentecostal Conference in Rome, attended by 10,000 people from 50 nations. Pope Paul VI addressed the conference and expressed his appreciation for the movement. Pope John Paul II gave his attention to other matters in the church through 1980 and neither endorsed nor tried to hinder the Pentecostal movement within his church. However, the movement gained a momentum of its own and, throughout the 1970s, Neo-Pentecostalism grew more rapidly in Roman Catholicism than in any other denomination.

• *Characteristics of Neo-Pentecostalism*

The manifestations of the Spirit in Neo-Pentecostalism are essentially those found in Classical Pentecostalism. The emphasis is on tongues, interpretation (when tongues are spoken within the context of public worship), and healing. Prophecy, the word of wisdom, and the other gifts mentioned earlier are certainly part of the concept of valid, intensified spirituality promoted by Neo-Pentecostalism. A principal difference between Classical and Neo-Pentecostalism is the lack of undisciplined emotionalism in the latter. Although some Classical Pentecostal denominations have moved up the socioeconomic scale and have cooled their emotionalism considerably, some have not. One can still find instances of unrestrained emotionalism in some Classical Pentecostal churches. However, it has been the rule in Neo-Pentecostalism that Paul's admonition that everything must be done in good order has been a paramount consideration. The "holy roller" style of worship has simply been avoided in most of Neo-Pentecostalism.

Ordinarily the worship of the Neo-Pentecostal individual was not offered in the context of the regular worship service of his or her denominational church, but rather was conducted in private or in the context of a Pentecostal fellowship group. It may be said that the fellowship group has been one of the principal organizational features of Neo-Pentecostalism. People come together for prayer, Bible study, singing, and testimony. Interspersed with these are the manifestations of the Spirit. Leaders in the Neo-Pentecostal movement have encouraged Neo-Pentecostals to stay in the churches of which they were members before they received the Spirit. Many have done so. They have tended not to practice the spiritual gifts in their churches. That is why the extra-congregational fellowship was so important; to give the Neo-Pentecostals the opportunity to share with each other the praises which are due to God. The small group was the center of the life of the Charismatic movement.

A few Neo-Pentecostal congregations have developed. Some of these were congregations which remained within the fellowship of their denomination. But there also developed some Neo-Pentecostal churches which were nondenominational. These churches were often called "Christian centers." The prototype and perhaps best known of these is Melodyland Christian Center in Anaheim, California. Founded in 1960, this Christian Center has expanded so that it is able to provide a wide range of services for the international Neo-Pentecostal community. It holds several worship services a week, provides a Bible school for laypeople and a School of Theology for the training of clergy, a telephone "hotline" drug counseling service, the distribution of Neo-Pentecostal literature and cassette tapes, and Charismatic conferences. The variety of programs offered by Melodyland is probably broader than that of most Neo-Pentecostal Christian Centers, but it is a good example of the kind of ecclesiastical developments which grew out of the Charismatic movement during the 1960s and 1970s. Neo-Pentecostals were encouraged not to leave their traditional churches, but because many of them desired the kind of spirit-filled worship and fellowship the Christian Center and/or the small group provides, many Neo-Pentecostals have had a kind of dual citizenship, holding membership both in their traditional church and in a Neo-Pentecostal group of some kind.

Another difference between Neo-Pentecostals and their Classical counterparts, in addition to the middle- and upper-class origin of most Neo-Pentecostals, is that they are usually evangelical in theology rather than fundamentalist. Indeed, to utilize a category introduced in the previous chapter, very many Neo-Pentecostals could probably be called "young evangelicals," for their theology of the work of the Spirit seems to repudiate a literalistic view of the Biblical text. Neo-Pentecostalism seems to believe that because God continues to be revealed through tongues, interpretation and/or through prophecy, the text of the Bible cannot be the final source of truth; it cannot be God's infallible word. This is well expressed by one observer of Neo-Pentecostalism:

> In Charismatic Renewal, . . . it is felt that the truth of Scripture is available to the reader or hearer *only* through the power (action) of the Holy Spirit,

who himself is understood as the (experiential) source of all Christian unity. Neo-Pentecostals maintain that biblical authority (the word written) must always be subservient to the authority of the *living*, "dynamic" word of God made known through the present activity of the Spirit himself. . . . This open stance, whereby the Holy Spirit is seen to lead people to theological truth *following* (rather than prerequisite to) a common experience, is clearly ascendant throughout Neo-Pentecostalism. . . . In Neo-Pentecostalism, then, spiritual authority rests ultimately in the present activity and teaching of the Holy Spirit at least as much in the Bible itself, whose essential truth is made known to individuals only by the power of the Spirit. Thus Charismatic Renewal rejects "bibliolatry."[1]

Interestingly, in the seventeenth century Quakers were accused by their detractors of having the same view, which they did, and many of them were executed for heresy because of it. Consequently, although Neo-Pentecostalism falls to the right of center theologically and is part of the conservative revival of the 1970s, it represents a leftward-leaning conservatism. For that reason, some Classical Pentecostals and other fundamentalists have been very antagonistic toward it.

Having disagreements with others in the conservative theological camp is not the only way that Neo-Pentecostalism has divided the contemporary church. It is a matter of concern both to people within the movement and to those outside it that Neo-Pentecostalism sometimes generates a spiritual elitism among its adherents. Although their leaders have counseled against it, Charismatics have sometimes considered those Christians who have not had the baptism of the Holy Spirit to be rather inferior Christians. The idea is: "God has come into my life in a special way and obviously has not come into yours, since you do not exhibit the signs, so I am more spiritual than you." Such an attitude is not found in all Neo-Pentecostals, but it is found in enough to become a problem.

Divisiveness has also worked from the other end. NonPentecostals have been hostile to Neo-Pentecostals, too. Mainstream Christians have always been wary of manifestations of Pentecostalism; now that such manifestations have appeared right in their midst, apprehensions have intensified. No matter who initiated the alienation, Neo-Pentecostalism

---

[1]Richard Quebedeaux, *The New Charismatics: The Origin, Development, and Significance of Neo-Pentecostalism* (Garden City NY: Doubleday & Co., 1976) 110-111, 113. (All italics in original.)

has sometimes caused a rupture in the relationships between Christians within a particular congregation and/or denomination. This divisiveness has been one reason that Neo-Pentecostals have sometimes formed their own congregations. It has also been the case that some Neo-Pentecostals who no longer feel at home in their own churches have begun to worship with Classical Pentecostal congregations. However, one cannot generalize too broadly about this development. Neo-Pentecostals have not joined with just any Classical Pentecostal church or denomination because many of those still are populated by people at the lower end of the socioeconomic scale. People who are accustomed to associating with those of middle or upper social status are not eager to become participants in churches with a much different sociological character. But, as noted above, some Classical Pentecostal denominations have moved into the middle socioeconomic bracket from below as the majority of their members have improved their status. It is those congregations which have been ready receptacles for Neo-Pentecostals who have wanted to participate in a more traditional Pentecostal worship experience. There is evidence that many of the Assemblies of God churches are a good example of this process. Since the very late 1940s, the Assemblies of God have taken on many characteristics normally associated with mainstream, middle class denominations. In the 1970s many Assemblies churches received a large number of people from nonPentecostal backgrounds. In my home city of Fort Worth, Texas, there is a large Assemblies of God church in an obviously middle-class section of town. The minister of that church has told me that around 70 percent of his congregation are people who were raised in nonPentecostal churches. The vast majority of them are Neo-Pentecostals who have left the non-Pentecostal churches of which they were formerly members.

If there has been a divisive element in Neo-Pentecostalism, there has also been a unifying or ecumenical dimension. The Charismatic movement has brought people together in new and creative ways. The Holy Spirit is no respecter of persons and has manifested itself in these recent years to a much broader spectrum of people than was true for the first six decades of this century. If some Neo-Pentecostals have left their traditional churches, they have come together in new alignments with Classical Pentecostals or other Neo-Pentecostals in Charismatic churches. Since the Holy Spirit has invaded the so-called mainstream churches, Protestants of all kinds have come together for Christian fellowship. Into that marvelous mix have been added Pentecostal Catholics and even some people from the Jewish tradition, people who call themselves Jewish Christians or Messianic Jews.

An important example of this Pentecostal ecumenism is the Conference of Charismatic Renewal in the Christian Churches, held in 1977 in Arrowhead Stadium in Kansas City, Missouri. There were forty thousand people registered at that four-day conference, which was dedicated to the praise of God and the instruction of the people in spiritual disciplines. Of those people in attendance, about 45 percent were Catholic, but there was a liberal sprinkling of Lutherans, Episcopalians, Baptists, Methodists, Presbyterians, United Church of Christ, Classical Pentecostal, Messianic Jews, and Disciples of Christ. There seems to have been true Christian fellowship in the Spirit with virtually no attention paid to denominational differences. Some speakers acknowledged that, up until that time, the unity enjoyed by Neo-Pentecostals was principally at the emotional level, that they had not yet come to grips with the real doctrinal differences that do exist between people who come from various backgrounds. But in spite of that, there was and is a strong feeling that the work of the Holy Spirit through Pentecostal signs will do what numerous ecumenical negotiations have not yet been able to do: bring divided Christians together again.

Neo-Pentecostalism is part of the larger picture of the expansion of conservatism in the 1970s. One reason that Neo-Pentecostalism has grown is that most of the people involved are evangelistic. They truly believe that God has dramatically come into their lives through the baptism of the Holy Spirit. They believe that the Spirit can come to others in the same way, if they will open themselves. Consequently, they are eager to share their faith with others. They do this in organized ways, through the activities and structures of their churches. They witness individually to friends, business associates, even to customers. Members of the FGBMFI are encouraged to invite their friends to meetings to enjoy the fellowship and to hear inspiring speakers. Neo-Pentecostals are eager to share their faith and to pray that those to whom they witness will receive the baptism of the Spirit.

It is not clear whether Neo-Pentecostals make most of their converts from nonChristians or from nonCharismatic Christians. In either case, converts swell the ranks of conservative Christianity. It is virtually impossible to know how many converts are made by Neo-Pentecostals.

Most church membership statistics are reported by denominational agencies. Since Neo-Pentecostalism exists both within and outside traditional denominational structures, it is difficult to get a numerical profile on the size of the movement or its growth patterns. There was enough activity and growth in the movement in the late 1960s and early 1970s to warrant considerable media attention. But the media moved on to other things in the latter part of the 1970s and the spotlight was removed from Neo-Pentecostalism. Leaders in the movement say that it grows apace, in this country and in many other parts of the world, particularly in Latin America. As one tries to understand the growth of conservative religion in the 1970s, Neo-Pentecostalism must be given recognition as a major component of that phenomenon.

• *Suggestions for Further Reading*
for Context and Perspective

Anderson, Robert M. *Vision of the Disinherited: The Making of American Pentecostalism.* New York: Oxford University Press, 1979.

Hamilton, Michael P., ed. *The Charismatic Movement.* Grand Rapids MI: Wm. B. Eerdmans Publishing.

Harrell, David Edwin, Jr. *All Things are Possible: The Healing and Charismatic Revivals in Modern America.* Bloomington: Indiana University Press, 1975.

Nichol, John Thomas. *Pentecostalism.* New York: Harper and Row, 1966.

O'Connor, Edward D. *The Pentecostal Movement in the Catholic Church.* Notre Dame IN: Ave Maria Press, 1971.

Quebedeaux, Richard. *The New Charismatics: The Origin, Development and Significance of Neo-Pentecostalism.* Garden City NY: Doubleday & Co., 1976.

Ranaghan, Kevin and Dorothy. *Catholic Pentecostals.* New York: Paulist Press Deus Books, 1969.

Sherrill, John L. *They Speak With Other Tongues.* Old Tappan NJ: Fleming H. Revell Co., 1964.

Synan, Vinson, ed. *Aspects of Pentecostal-Charismatic Origins.* Plainfield NJ: Logos International, 1975.

Synan, Vinson. *The Holiness-Pentecostal Movement in the United States.* Grand Rapids MI: Wm. B. Eerdmans Publishing Co., 1975.

CHAPTER FOUR

On Being "Moonstruck": A Look at the "Cult" Movement

One of the more dramatic developments of the late 1960s and the 1970s was the rise of a number of religious groups that were greatly out of the ordinary, what some people called "weird" or "crazy." Some observers designated these groups as "alternative religions" or "new religions." But the title that caught the public imagination and which was perpetuated by the media was the term "cults." This term communicated the idea that these groups were not just denominations that one joined and participated in while still going about as a respectable, if unobtrusive, member of middle-class society. Membership in a cult required one to abandon the ways of mainstream society and adopt a distinctive lifestyle. Usually included in that life-style was leaving home and/or school and going to live with other cult members, totally immersing oneself in the activities and thought patterns of the group. One often was required to give all his or her possessions to the cult, both to help support the group and to signify the member's total commitment to it.

Because the vast majority of the converts to these cults were people in their late teens and early twenties and because they exhibited such total involvement in the cults, the sudden increase in the number and visibility of these groups caused alarm in the minds of many people. This single-minded behavior that rejected traditional middle-class values and conduct caused many people, particularly parents whose children had joined a cult, to believe that the youth could not have joined voluntarily.

They could not, so this reasoning went, have willingly turned their backs on home and family; they must have been coerced or tricked into joining the cult. Accusations of kidnapping, instant hypnosis, brainwashing, mind control, and virtual imprisonment of young people were made against the cults. Many people, and a large portion of the media, became convinced that youth were being manipulated by cult leaders who were, in reality, money-hungry exploiters.

But that was not all. At least two examples of the "cults" displayed even more ominous dimensions. In 1971 the Charles Manson "family" was convicted of the murder of actress Sharon Tate and some of her companions. In the proceedings of the trial it became known that the "family" had lived in a commune in the desert, seemed to worship Manson himself, used dangerous drugs freely, and engaged in promiscuous and unconventional sexual behavior. In November 1978 more than 900 members of the People's Temple, under the leadership of Rev. Jim Jones, died, either by their own hands or by those of the cult leadership. This mass suicide/murder horrified the nation and, even more than the Manson family case, brought to the attention of the public the evil potential of cults. These were the two most dramatic examples of cult membership gone wrong, but there was a widespread tendency to assume that all cults were dangerous. Cults generally were categorized as unwholesome, harmful to their members, and as holding great potential for evil for the society as a whole, not to mention the families which were disrupted by having young people leave home to give their allegiance to a cult.

The purpose of this chapter is to bring some clarity and understanding to the "cult phenomenon." Particular attention will be directed to a central question: What is a cult? Concepts and categories from the sociology of religion will be used to answer the question. Since the Protestant Reformation in the early sixteenth century, and certainly in the modern world, scholars and others have been trying to make sense of the great variety of religious groups which have come into being. In order to do that categories and conceptual tools are needed. Theologians and historians have worked at the task, but sociologists have been more helpful. Unfortunately, in trying to bring some order to the plethora of religious groups, not all sociologists agree. In trying to distinguish between mainstream groups and cults, sociologists have either emphasized theology or structure. That is, some have argued that mainstream groups are conventional in theology while cults are deviant, while others contend that organizational structure makes the difference: mainstream groups are rather tightly organized while cults are unstructured and virtually amorphous. Either principle, used singly, is simplistic. Professors Rodney Stark and William Bainbridge of the University of Washington have proposed a theory that combines these two approaches in a very creative way.[1] Their scheme pulls diverse phenomena and theories together into a coherent whole. Because I think they are not only helpful but right, this chapter owes many of its ideas to Stark and Bainbridge, although most of the categories are common to the sociology of religion.

To clarify the nature of cults, however, it is necessary to provide some background. In order to be understood, cults need to be compared with other types of religious groups. The bulk of this chapter is a typology of religious groups with examples from the late 1960s and the 1970s. The basic feature of this typology is the issue of the relation of a religious group to its environment.

• *Churches*

The analysis begins with the *church type* of religious group. A primary characteristic of a religious group that falls into this category is that it accepts the social environment in which it exists. That is, a church type group feels at home or comfortable with the larger society within which it lives. That is not to say that the religious group sees nothing at all wrong in society. It may disagree with individual events or even some trends in the society, but the church type sees no fundamental disagreement between its values and prevailing cultural values. The church type is, as one scholar has written, a "religion of culture."[2] One reason that the church type sees no major discontinuity between itself and its social environment is because its members tend to be of the middle or upper socioeconomic classes. People who are at least rather comfortable in terms of wealth and who derive that wealth from partic-

---

[1]Rodney Stark and William Sims Bainbridge, "Of Churches, Sects, and Cults: Preliminary Concepts for a Theory of Religious Movements," *Journal for the Scientific Study of Religion* 18 (June 1979): 117-131.

[2]H. Richard Niebuhr, *Christ and Culture* (New York: Harper and Row, 1956) 83-115.

ipation in the economic system valued by the society are not likely to be hostile to the society. This compatibility with the "system" carries over into their religious group membership.

Theologically, the church type favors contact with the larger society and, indeed, tries to influence it. (That it tries to influence society is an indication that it is not *totally* satisfied with the quality of the society). The classic example of the church type is Roman Catholicism in medieval times. In the West, prior to the Reformation, Catholicism was virtually the only religion in existence. In addition, an establishment form of church-state relations made Catholicism the official religion of the state. In short, Catholicism had a monopoly. In the attempt to create a Christian society, the church sought to dominate the society and to influence it in every way possible. The church's impact on society was magnified by its easy access to political structures and regular participation in them. In the United States there is not a union of church and state, so the church type cannot work to Christianize the society by working through society's structures in a formal or official way. The church type group tries to Christianize American society by evangelizing as many people as it can and by trying to influence the society in other ways, often by making moral pronouncements on the issues of the day. Yet in spite of all its attempts to influence society, the church must be described as not hostile to society, but friendly toward it. The church type accepts and feels compatible with the social environment in which it exists.

Examples of the church type include virtually all of the mainstream denominations in America. The United Methodist Church, the Presbyterian Church in the U.S., the Christian Church (Disciples of Christ), the Episcopal Church, and many others illustrate this category very well. The members of these churches are middle to upper class in social status. They feel they are a part of mainstream society and they expect their churches to be socially acceptable. The denominations and individual congregations thereof try to influence society through actions and pronouncements, but everybody assumes that they accept and feel more comfortable than uncomfortable with the primary characteristics of American society.

• *Sects*

In contrast to the church type, the *sect type* religious group is characterized by rejection of the social environment in which it exists. The sect regards the society around it as evil. The sect does not accept prevailing cultural values, but rather sees them as wrong. There is a radical difference between the values of the sect, based on its distinctive theology, and those of the larger society. From the sect's viewpoint, the culture is not only corrupt, but also corrupting. The sect believes that the evil of society is so strong and pervasive that if the sect has very much contact with the society it will be infected and ultimately destroyed. To protect itself from the evil influences of society, the sect attempts to separate itself, either physically or intellectually. A sect that separates itself physically goes to some uninhabited place where it simply will be insulated from society's evils by distance. A sect that separates itself intellectually fosters a different value perspective and life-style from the mainstream society. Of course, that is true of a sect that separates itself physically, but the difference is that the group that separates itself intellectually continues to live within the society, in spite of its evil character. It attempts to ward off society's evil influence by maintaining a set of values and behavior patterns different from those characteristic of society (and members of church type religious groups). A sect is a "religion against culture."[3]

The sect is often very evangelistic, but for the opposite reason from the church type. It may be more zealous in its evangelism than the church type, as well. The sect tries to win converts, not to make the society more Christian, since it conceives that as impossible, but rather to snatch people out of the evil society. Evangelism is essentially a rescue mission. Sects struggle to convince people that the only hope they have to be saved when the end of time comes is to become a part of the saved community—namely, the sect doing the evangelizing.

Members of sectarian groups are usually at the lower end of the socioeconomic scale. They are not in the mainstream of the economy and

---

[3]Ibid., 45-82.

the privileges and opportunities it offers, and therefore they see themselves at odds with the society. There is a process that sociologists call "sect to church progression." If the majority of the members of a sect improve their socioeconomic standing, if they move up into the middle class category, then the characteristics of their religion will change. Their attitude toward the society will cease to be so negative and will become considerably more positive.

A sect is always schismatic, that is, it is a splinter from a previously existing religious group. A sect is created by people who *left* another group to seek a more nearly perfect community. The sect may be a schism from a church or from another sect. Theologically, the sect often claims to continue the theology of the parent group, but in a pure and undefiled form; it accuses the group from which it has split of somehow departing from its own traditional theology (usually by becoming more "worldly" or churchlike). Those who disagree with the profanation of the traditional faith split off to hold and live by that faith in a pure and pristine way. The sect, then, is characterized by the belief that it is the preserver of the true faith, intensely held even in spite of the allurements and/or the attacks of the evil society. Consequently, sect type groups are characterized by a "true believer" mentality: "we are right and all those who differ from us are wrong."

An important example of a sect-type religion is Classical Pentecostalism, discussed extensively in chapter three. The members of these various groups fell in the lower range of the socioeconomic scale and they rejected, or at least strongly suspected, their social environment. They split off from the Methodist tradition and went beyond that tradition to recover the gifts of the Holy Spirit that are mentioned in the New Testament. Thus they could argue that where the Methodists (and all other "worldly" churches) had abandoned a true and strict adherence to Christianity, they held the original faith with accuracy and intensity; the "full gospel." There was definitely a "true believer" dimension to Classical Pentecostalism (and still is). But the process of sect to church progression has occurred in certain of the Pentecostal denominations such as the Assemblies of God.

• *Cults*

A third major category of types of religious groups is the *cult type*. This is a more complex type than either of the other two and is somewhat more difficult to describe. Cults also live in tension with their social environment, although sometimes not as overtly as sects. Cults tend to regard the society and its dominant values as evil or at least incorrect. There are some cults that promise to help their adherents achieve what the world values, health, wealth, and happiness. But these cults believe that the values or perceptions of reality of the world are wrong, so that if one adheres to the commonly accepted ideas of society, the commonly desired goals will never be reached. The cult, then, proposes an alternative view of reality that, it says, is the true path to the desired goal. Because some cults do promote a success-oriented goal, it is not possible to generalize that all cults are made up of people at the lower end of the socioeconomic scale; some are not. Indeed, many of the newsworthy cults of the late 1960s and the 1970s were joined primarily by middle- and upper-class youth. But the cult still makes a distinction between itself and its social environment by perceiving the latter as wicked or at least mistaken. It is a fundamental characteristic of cults that they do not endorse the prevailing cultural values and/or views of the nature of reality.

Whereas sects are always schismatic, cults are not. Whereas sects claim to perpetuate the old truth in pure form, cults propagate new and original perceptions. This is a primary characteristic of cults, that they claim to have truths or insights that are unique to them. Of course a cult may share some theological ideas with mainstream religion, but it is made distinctive by adding new truth or, at the very least, a new interpretation of the old theological ideas. Cults are ordinarily begun by a charismatic leader—charismatic not necessarily in the Pentecostal sense, but in the sense of having inherent leadership qualities—who proclaims that he or she has new revelation from God and/or has discovered a new way of understanding traditional theology. A cult will often have a new Scripture that supplements or replaces the Bible. This new truth, of course, is at variance with society's (or mainstream religion's) way of looking at things. The cult perceives the society to be evil or at least ignorant of the true nature of reality as it has been revealed to the cult leader and is now in possession of the cult.

In distinguishing between types of cults, a contrast can be made between "innovation cults" and "importation cults." Innovation cults are developed within a particular society as a new thing—Mormonism was an innovation in the early nineteenth century American religious scene. An importation cult is brought into a host culture from outside—as is true of the Unification Church or Hare Krishna. This category is somewhat ambiguous, however. While a group may be a cult in the host society, it may not have any cult characteristics in the country where it was born. While Hare Krishna is widely regarded as a cult in the United States, it may not be considered a cult at all in India, the country of its birth. There it may even have church type qualities as a "denomination" of Hinduism.

One way to define a cult, as we have seen, is by recognizing its theological deviance, or, in a less pejorative-sounding phrase, recognizing that it represents an independent religious tradition in society. But cults have also been designated as groups with little organization. A problem with that concept is that some cults are highly structured. Stark and Bainbridge have proposed that not all cults can be lumped together in terms of their organization, but that there are rather at least three degrees of organization and structure (or lack thereof) that characterize cults.

Audience cults have almost no structure or organization. As social organizations, they are very diffuse. Membership (a term used here very loosely) is principally a consumer activity. Adherents of the viewpoint may gather together occasionally to hear a lecture or to worship, but usually do not. Members of audience cults receive the doctrines in which they believe primarily through books, magazines, or other publications. An example is astrology. Astrology teaches that the stars and planets have an influence over people's lives and that one can in fact predict the tendencies in one's life by knowing one's astrological sign or, with more precision, having one's horoscope calculated for the precise day of one's birth. It can hardly be said that astrology is *new* truth, since it is a concept that has existed since antiquity, but it is still one that is different from, if not contrary to, the way most Americans view history, reality, and the conduct of their lives. Those who believe in astrology may attend classes or the lectures of an astrological society, but they may not. One can believe in astrology and nurture that belief by only reading astrological columns in newspapers or by going to one's supermarket or bookstore to buy horoscope literature.

A *client cult* is somewhat more organized or structured than an audience cult. The organization is found mainly among those offering the service or the theology—at the point of origin more than at the point of reception. The relation of the cult to its members resembles the relationship between a therapist and patients or between a counselor and counselees. There may well be more opportunity for members of the cult to attend formal activities, lectures and the like, but there is no ongoing congregation. An example is spiritualism, the belief that the spirits of those who have died continue to live and are available for the living to contact. Again, this can hardly be called a *new* truth; it has existed since ancient times (one thinks of King Saul's going to the witch at Endor to summon the spirit of his deceased mentor, Samuel, in 1 Samuel 28:3-20). But it is an alternative view of death and life thereafter. Mediums claim to be able to facilitate contact with spirits of dead loved ones, friends, or associates. A spiritualist might attend a number of seances conducted by the same medium, but those attending the several seances might change each time. What is constant is the activity of the medium, not the shifting constituency of seance attenders. Each of those attending the seances is presumably a true believer in the validity of spiritualism; each is a client of the medium with only the most tenuous relationship with the others.

• *The Most Visible*
and Alarming of the Cults

Cult movements are the most organized of the several types of cults. Cult movements have definite, visible leadership and groups or congregations that meet regularly. Here the word "member" can be used in its usual sense, for in this type one attends meetings on a regular basis and participates in a congregation with ongoing group identity. Indeed, a cult movement often makes heavy demands on its members, expecting them to conform to the life-style of the cult. It is sometimes the case that a cult movement will have not only a continuous and recognizable group, but will also require its members to live in a commune or some other kind of constant community in which commitment and obedience is total and absolute. Of course, those who choose to be members of such a highly structured, intensely demanding group will be very loyal to it.

An example of a cult movement is the Children of God, mentioned in chapter three, a group organized in the late 1960s by David Berg, more commonly known as Moses David. Moses David began his organization as a Christian group designed to appeal to young people and especially to rescue them from the drug-oriented counterculture. From the beginning the group had a fundamentalist theology, but it soon began to take on unique characteristics. Moses David began to demand that his followers give up all that they had and come to live permanently with the group. He soon took them out of the city into the "wilderness," where they could supposedly live the pure Christian life away from the vile world of drugs and materialism. High-pressure evangelism sought to convince potential members that the world is completely evil, that it soon is to come to an end, and that they needed to be with the only group that would stand a chance of survival, the Children of God. Those who joined were expected to join the group in the wilderness and pledge their total loyalty to the group, since only it represented God's will, as interpreted by Moses David. Coming to live in the wilderness obviously meant that one would leave family, friends, and school, since education was simply the perpetuation of the evil system of the world. The only thing worth knowing was the Bible and the writings of Moses David.

Moses David was a prolific writer: he produced over the years a large number of pamphlets or booklets known as "Mo Letters." Although they addressed a variety of issues, particularly the evil nature of the world and especially the United States, the Mo Letters very often focused on sex. Indeed, Moses David seemed to be preoccupied with sex. It is clear that he was not dedicated to the Christian tradition of fidelity within marriage or to abstinence from sexual intercourse prior to marriage. Moses David encouraged women to dress and behave to emphasize their sexuality; it was a gift from God not only to be appreciated but to be flaunted. In the late 1970s it was reported that the Children of God had changed its name to The Love Family and that it encouraged its female members to use sex as a way of luring converts into the group, to be "hookers for Jesus." Mo's publications did not use photographs, but were very skillfully and realistically illustrated so that his publications on sexual themes could be described, strange as it seems, as religious pornography.

Because of extremely bad publicity accusing them of brainwashing, breaking up families, economically exploiting their members—not to mention their views and activities in regard to sex—and because Moses David was convinced that the United States is the most evil place on earth, the Children of God left this country in the mid-1970s. After that the group conducted its affairs, figuratively and literally, in other countries, notably those of Latin America.

The hostility the Children of God engendered calls to mind that there is a relationship between the structure and organization of a cult and the public's attitude toward it. An audience cult rarely stimulates opposition for the obvious reason that it is virtually invisible, since there are hardly any membership rites. The same is true for client cults. Although there is the possibility of somewhat more visibility for this kind of cult, because the activities are those of interested individuals rather than dynamic congregations, there is rarely any opposition raised against them. Most people involved in client cults are middle or upper class, "respectable" members of society. When cult movements stimulate opposition, this is because of a highly visible ongoing congregation. Of course, it is not simply the existence of a visible group that causes opposition; what creates the opposition is that the cult movement is often a high demand/high loyalty group for which people may drop everything to take up membership. As Stark and Bainbridge summarize it, "The rule seems to be, the more total the movement, the more total the opposition to it."[4] In addition, a cult movement is often quite willing to vocalize its view that society is evil and/or ignorant of the truth, which also raises the anger of the society.

One other distinction between cult movements that helps one to understand how and why these groups attract opposition is the difference between individual-transforming and world-transforming groups. Individual-transforming cults promote change in individuals; they try to help individuals integrate their personalities, solve personal problems, deal with the stresses of life, or adapt to the expectations of society. Normally, although not always, cults of this sort do not seem to attract as much opposition as those that aim at world transformation. These may try to help individuals in their everyday living, but their primary goal is to change the world. These cults promote sweeping, structural changes in the society with the ultimate goal of bringing in a new world order. Since they go much beyond working only with individuals, they are highly visible. Because what they have in mind for the new world is based upon the theology of the cult, the vision of its founder and leader, it is unlikely that many people in the mainstream of society approve of

---

[4]Stark and Bainbridge, "Of Churches, Sects, and Cults," 128.

the cult's plans for the world. For that reason, resistance to the cult often becomes intense.

Of the two most well-known and controversial cult movements that came to public view in the late 1960s, one can be described as individual-transforming, the other as world-transforming.

• *An Individual-Transforming Cult:*
Scientology

Scientology is the brainchild of LaFayette Ronald Hubbard. L. Ron Hubbard (his followers often refer to him as "Elron") was born in 1911, the son of an American naval officer. Like so many military dependents, Hubbard traveled rather extensively during his childhood and youth and was exposed to Oriental, as well as Western culture. That experience clearly influenced the ideas of Scientology, as we shall see. Hubbard claims to have a university and graduate-level education, but observers who have studied his life challenge that claim.

In addition to his activities as an explorer, aviator, and pulp fiction author, Hubbard thought deeply about the nature of human beings, especially their mental processes and the disorders thereof. In 1948 and 1949 he began to formulate a concept of the human psyche and therapeutic procedures to be used in instances of mental malfunction. He first made his ideas available to the public in 1950 in an article, "Dianetics: the Evolution of a Science," published in *Astounding Science Fiction* magazine. This article and several that followed it elicited a large number of positive responses from the magazine's audience. Hubbard elaborated his ideas in 1950 in *Dianetics: The Modern Science of Mental Health.* The book rapidly became a best seller. People around the country began to practice the procedures of Dianetics and it became clear that there needed to be a method of training people in its techniques and responding to inquiries. Also in 1950 Hubbard founded the Hubbard Research Foundation. Soon, formal branches of the Foundation were established around the country. These branches were essentially mental health therapy centers, dedicated to the use of Dianetics to alleviate the psychic problems of their clients.

After a flurry of growth, Dianetics centers began to decline all across the country. This was because the number of recruits/clients decreased significantly. There were four primary reasons for this decline. One was that the affairs of the Foundation were not well managed. The various centers, which were essentially franchises, did not receive the benefit of good central management or advertising. Second, some people got what they came for, a cure for their mental or emotional problems, and went on their way. They did not maintain an ongoing relationship with the local Dianetics center. Apparently whatever "satisfied customer" statements they might have made did not offset the negative publicity Dianetics was getting. That negative publicity gives us the third and fourth reasons for the decline. Many people, it turned out, did not get what they came for. Dianetics claimed to be a form of psychotherapy, but many were not helped to deal with their psychic problems. Dianetics was also roundly criticized by the medical/psychiatric profession. Many doctors called it simplistic or shallow, others went so far as to say that it was dangerous—potentially destructive to a person who already suffered from psychological problems. Furthermore, they claimed that Dianetics was dispensed by persons who were ill-trained to deal with the great complexities of the human mind.

The result of this decline caused a severe financial crisis for the Hubbard Research Foundation. A large number of Dianetics centers closed. Hubbard was abandoned by most of the inner circle of Foundation trustees who had encouraged and supported him in the early days. It appeared that Dianetics was close to its demise. In response, Hubbard announced that he had refined his theory and had realized new dimensions of it; he called his recast concept "Scientology." These new dimensions of the theory branched into the realm of the spiritual. Scientology was a religion! It was not long until there was a Founding Church of Scientology, with L. Ron Hubbard as its president. In the 1960s the church took on international proportions, having spread to Western Europe and other parts of the world. Wherever it gained any kind of following and visibility, it also created controversy. The medical community, religious leaders, and government officials all took notice of it and, usually, condemned it. In England, where Hubbard had moved his international headquarters, Scientology was banned. In Australia Scientology was subjected to governmental investigation as a dangerous element in society. In America, the Food and Drug Administration and, later, the FBI took particular note of Scientology as posing both health problems and possibly having been involved in evasion of taxes.

Why has Scientology attracted so many negative responses? Scientology is essentially a therapy system for psychological disorders. It not only claims to be able to solve a wide range of psychological problems, but also to help even the healthy to reach a higher level of performance; to allow one to actualize his or her potential. Scientology asserts the existence of two minds in a person, the analytical mind and the reactive mind. The analytical mind could be called pure intelligence and it functions with computerlike efficiency as long as it is not interfered with by the reactive mind. The reactive mind operates as a defense mechanism for the analytical mind. It is the function of the reactive mind to absorb all pain, psychological traumas, or the psychic effects of any threats to the individual's survival. The fact that the reactive mind replaces the analytical mind at the time of trauma is a good thing, for it protects the analytical mind from psychic injury. The problem is that the reactive mind is essentially a recording device. It does not merely deflect these traumatic experiences away from the more fragile analytical mind, it keeps them within itself. The memories of these mishaps are not on the surface ready for immediate recall the way one remembers a telephone number, but rather they are at the subconscious level. These subconsciously remembered unfortunate experiences are known as "engrams."

However, these engrams stored in the reactive mind have a direct affect on our conscious lives. If, at a later time in our lives, we have an experience similar to that which originally caused an engram, our reactive mind takes over from our clear-thinking analytical mind and causes us to behave in a fearful or irrational manner. If, as an infant, I was frightened and/or bitten by a dog, that experience would be stored in my reactive mind as an engram. Later, even in my adult life, I likely would have an inordinate fear of dogs, even gentle dogs, so that I might break into a cold sweat or irrationally feel the need to flee when encountering a dog. Even though I would have no conscious memory of the original experience, it would nonetheless affect my conduct in troublesome ways.

This concept/process has very broad dimensions. The analytical and reactive minds are the principal components of what Hubbard calls the "Thetan," which can best be described as one's soul. Consequently, when the reactive mind deflects an unpleasant experience from the analytical mind and stores that mishap within itself, one's very soul is encumbered with that engram. The problem is magnified by the fact that the Thetan does not live for one physical existence only, but rather can be reborn repeatedly, a concept of reincarnation. Thus the Thetan with which one is born may have been collecting engrams for many lifetimes and all of these may show up in the phobias and episodes of irrational behavior one experiences. So, to continue the example, my problem may not only be a fear of dogs, but it may include a multitude of expressions of what happened to my Thetan during previous lives and the time I was a fetus, as well as what may have happened to me during my infancy and youth.

Consequently, a person may be going through life as a "bundle of nerves," not living up to his or her intellectual potential, behaving in strange ways, full of fears. Naturally, Scientology is the method by which one may be relieved of those problems and become an integrated, confident, whole personality. The name Scientology has given to that ideal state is "clear," that is, clear of engrams.

The procedure for reaching the clear state is to identify the engrams, bring them to consciousness, that is, to the level of the analytical mind, and to confront them rationally. That is done by a process known as "auditing," best described as a therapeutic interview or conversation between an auditor and a client. It is the function of the auditor, through conversation, to help the client identify the engrams that are the causes of the problems that prompted the client to come to Scientology in the first place. The auditor is aided by the use of a machine called an "E-meter." An E-meter is a simple skin galvanometer that detects changes in the small electrical current in one's body. The client holds a small tin can in each hand. The cans are connected to the meter by wires. The auditor leads the client through a series of questions designed to get into the reactive mind and identify an engram. The auditor knows that he or she has come to a sensitive area when the needle on the E-meter moves. An engram has been identified. Now the auditor must ask ever more probing questions in that area to bring the engram to the surface for analysis; to help the client to see the irrationality of it, to expose it to light, to eliminate it.

The road to clear is not an easy one. It is entirely possible that an individual has many personal problems to be treated. Consequently, auditing (also known as "processing") is a lengthy enterprise, requiring many sessions. Scientology has developed a series of stages to be moved through in the process of becoming clear and it has developed different procedures of auditing appropriate to each stage. In addition, there are what might be described as self-help courses available to clients, the completion of which are essential in becoming clear. These courses involve developing communications skills, sharpening memory and perception, and better utilizing one's native intelligence. The Church of Scientology cannot offer these services free of charge. There are fees for each one of the auditing procedures at each level. The cumulative amount of these fees is great. People frequently pay as much as $5,000 for their work in Scientology, although there are stories of people having paid $10,000, $15,000 or even more.

But why would people not pay that kind of money for what Scientology has to offer? Not only does it offer a church, in which one can worship (although Scientology seems to have no God-concept), be married and buried, but one can also take advantage of the church's pastoral counseling services, as they have been described here. Scientology, particularly in its early days, claimed that if one reached the clear or Operating Thetan levels, one could lead a truly remarkable life. If one were clear, one would not only be free from psychological problems, but would be virtually, if not totally, free from physical ailments. One would be able to grow new teeth, levitate objects (and perhaps oneself), and learn, remember, and reason with almost superhuman powers. One would be able to communicate with striking clarity. (One assumes that this communication would be only with other clears, since preclears would not yet have the highly refined perceptual tools to be able to understand.)

Scientology, then, is a cult movement of the individual-transforming type. It is a cult because of its new truth, its new perception of the nature of reality as it refers to the human psyche, although it bears similarity to Freudian psychology and analysis and, in its concept of reincarnation, to certain Oriental religions. (I have heard Scientology called "pseudo-Freudianism with Hindu overtones.") But one could argue, in spite of some peculiarities of its original ideas, that it appears to be a benign cult that may actually help people. What has caused all the opposition?

Opposition has been directed toward Scientology for a number of reasons. The medical community has pointed out that Scientology, by its very nature, deals in a very important and highly technical area, the human psyche. The trouble is that those who do it, the auditors, are hardly trained for the task. Not all of them are clear, most of them have been trained only in Scientological theory and methods, they have no medical background, and thus they are dangerous. Furthermore, the E-meter is not an adequate diagnostic tool. It was for this reason that the Food and Drug Administration originally began to monitor Scientology and even seized some of its literature and devices. In short, most medical people who have given Scientology any attention feel that it is quackery.

Other critics have pointed to the amount of money that is taken in by Scientology. It is essentially a franchise church, with the bulk of the revenue earned from auditing going to L. Ron Hubbard. The criticism is that it is not really a church, it is a business that has been made a church for tax advantages. It is charged that Scientology makes huge profits from those who are vulnerable, who may be grasping at straws in the hope for a better life and who may not be able to pay. In addition, it is often charged (sometimes by persons who used to participate in Scientology) that great pressure is exerted on people to keep going, to buy the next course, to go still another direction within the maze of Scientology therapy to try to reach clear. In this way the individual is put under greater psychological stress or, if he or she continues, perhaps less psychological stress but more financial strain.

Critics of Scientology also charge that it does not deliver. It may help people in some ways, but the expectations built up about what one can become by reaching the clear level are false hopes because there is virtually no evidence that clears are able to do the things Scientology advertises. For people who already have psychological difficulties in some form or other, unfulfilled hopes may be harmful, especially coupled with the expenditure of large amounts of money.

Naturally Scientology denies these criticisms. It claims to be a bona fide church that specializes in the counseling/psychological ministry. But Scientology has gone beyond claiming that criticisms are untrue and countering them with its own story. It has been active in trying to prevent anything even mildly critical from being written about it. It has taken legal action against authors and publishing houses, often suing for libel after a work has been published and trying to prevent the publication of books and articles that have not yet been released. It has been aggressive in trying to prevent the media, both print and electronic, from reporting anything that would reflect negatively on the church. In the middle 1960s, the church even went to the extent, under Hubbard's orders, of declaring that "Suppressive Persons"—those either inside or outside the organization who have been critical of it—are not to be the subject of ethical treatment, but may be denied by action of Scientologists their rights, freedoms, even life itself. In the late 1970s the church moderated its extreme reaction to critics, but it still was very thin-skinned about opposition in any form. Even though Scientology is an individual-transforming cult movement, it is an authoritarian one with L. Ron Hubbard definitely in command, offering a service based on dubious theory and willing to combat critics vigorously.[5] It is for those reasons that some people have feared the expansion of Scientology.

• *A World-Transforming Cult:*
The Unification Church

An example of a world-transforming cult movement that caused a storm of controversy and criticism in the late 1960s and the 1970s is the Holy Spirit Association for the Unification of World Christianity, or Unification Church, founded and led by Rev. Sun Myung Moon. Rev. Moon was born in Korea in 1920. During his youth he apparently was a spiritually sensitive person who was subject to dramatic religious experiences. When he was sixteen he had a vision of Jesus in which he was told that he would be a messenger of God who would complete Jesus' unfinished mission. Understandably inspired by that experience, when he became an adult he began to preach the Christian gospel. During the Korean War he was imprisoned by the North Koreans. His imprisonment gave him a hatred for Communism and gave his later followers the opportunity for some accounts of his extraordinary activities, such as the story that when he was released from prison, he carried a wounded friend on his back for 400 miles to safety in the South.

After the war Moon went back to preaching and soon founded his own church. Either because of the nature of his theology or because of his aggressiveness, or both, he was not accepted by other Korean Chris-

---

[5]Beginning in 1983, it became questionable whether Hubbard was still in command. A fierce power struggle erupted in the church between some young "hard-liners" who were loyal to Hubbard and some disenchanted followers, including Hubbard's son, who claimed that Hubbard was either dead or mentally ill, since he had not been seen publicly since March 1980. However, in late 1983 a judge ruled, in the son's suit trying to gain the assets of the church, that because tape recordings of Hubbard's voice had been received by the court he was still alive and in effective control of the church.

tians. There is also the story that he got in trouble with the law—according to Moon, because of his anti-Communism (a strange occurrence in a very anti-Communist country) or, according to other Korean Christians, because of morals charges. Meanwhile his church grew apace and began to expand to other countries, including the United States. The beginnings in this country were small but promising. In the middle 1960s Moon came to America for a visit; in 1968 he came to stay. It was shortly after that that the church began to gain great visibility. That was by design, since Moon seems to crave attention, and he also thought the notoriety would help his church to grow. It did, but opposition to his church also grew. Of all the cult movements active in the 1970s, the Unification Church seemed to receive the most hostility. There are many reasons for this.

The theology of the Unification Church is unique. The church may be easily classified as a cult movement because its theology is definitely new truth, a twist on Christian tradition that has never come along before. The Unification Church has a book, the *Divine Principle*, that it accepts as inspired truth alongside the Bible. It is in this book, God's revelation to Rev. Moon, that one finds the theology unique to the church.

In order to understand Unification theology, one has to go back to Adam and Eve. God created the first couple to live in perfect innocence. Their task in life was to "be fruitful and multiply." Since they were perfect, their children would be perfect also. Consequently, the perfect first family would begin the process of filling the earth, generation after generation, with perfect offspring: a paradise on earth. However, the entire process went wrong with the fall of Adam and Eve. Satan, in the form of a snake, seduced Eve and had sexual intercourse with her, thus corrupting her and causing the spiritual fall of humankind. Eve, in turn, seduced and corrupted Adam, and his sin represented the physical fall of humankind. Since they now had sinned they could no longer be perfect parents and their sin was passed on to their children, thus infecting all humanity. If salvation were ever to come, it would have to be through reversing this process so that there would be perfect parents to have perfect children to eventually produce the perfect family of humanity.

The Unification Church teaches that, in addition to the necessity of reintroducing perfect procreation into the human system, in order for the sin of Adam and Eve to be removed humankind has to pay reparation for its sin—that is, humans have to pay the penalty for having sinned against God. From time to time certain worthy individuals came along to lead men and women in the process of making reparation to God for having sinned. People such as Abraham, Moses, David, and the Hebrew prophets lived righteous lives and even taught great theology in order to show humanity how to come back to God. But humankind did not follow and so the sin was not paid for. In addition there is no indication that any of these worthies even approached the perfect parenthood with their spouses that is finally necessary to recreate the intended paradise on earth.

In due time Jesus (the second Adam) came. Here was a man of God who could certainly set humanity back on the right track of perfection. However, the Unification Church teaches that Jesus was not completely successful in his mission of bringing salvation to humankind. Along with his teaching ministry, it was necessary for Jesus to marry the perfect wife and to have perfect children in order to begin the process of repopulating the earth with perfect inhabitants. Unfortunately, Jesus was prevented from this marriage by his untimely death. The church teaches that in his death and resurrection, Jesus accomplished humanity's spiritual salvation. But that was only a partial salvation, since humanity's fall was both spiritual and physical. Consequently, Jesus was a partial failure and humanity, since his time, has had only incomplete salvation available to it.

It would be left to the third Adam or Christ of the Second Advent to finish the salvation that Jesus had begun. The Unification Church teaches that in our own time the Christ of the Second Advent has come and the physical salvation of mankind has begun. Who is this savior-figure? The church says that he was born in Korea around 1920 and that in the early 1960s he married one who is presumed to be the perfect wife. Rev. Sun Myung Moon was born in Korea in 1920 and in 1960 he married Hak Jan Ha, who one assumes is the perfect wife. Throughout the 1970s the Unification Church was rather coy about making a definitive public statement that Rev. Moon is the Christ of the Second Advent, here to accomplish mankind's physical salvation and thus bring the process to a successful conclusion, but it is clear that members of the church think that is the case. This is attested when Rev. Moon and his wife preside, as perfect parents, at mass weddings of young members of the church. For these couples the ceremony means that they, too, can be perfect parents and have perfect children to begin to repopulate the earth with redeemed people in the hope of recreating the original utopia.

One of the principal doctrines of the Unification Church is that Communism is completely evil. The problem, of course, is that Communism is officially atheistic and hostile to religion. The result is that Communism rejects the ethical standards that are to be derived from a belief in a sovereign God. But if humankind rejects an absolute ethic of righteousness, then it is doomed. Consequently, the existence of atheistic Communism with its teachings contrary to Judaeo-Christian ethics is a menace to humankind. It must be stamped out.

The United States has a decisive role to play in the elimination of world Communism. America is God's chosen nation (even though Korea is the new Israel), chosen for the specific purpose of defeating Communism. America was founded on the basis of the Judaeo-Christian ethical system and it consequently has the moral resources to be the antithesis of Communism. However, America is in danger of losing its role of God's chosen nation and chief opponent of Communism. The reason for this is that America itself is weakening its moral fiber, primarily through a relativistic, "do your own thing," attitude. The people of America are not as strong in their moral values as they once were. Furthermore, the American government has gotten soft on Communism, as demonstrated by its recognition of the People's Republic of China.

The answer to this dilemma is for America to return to its former moral rigor and anti-Communist stance by adopting the true religion, the Unification Church, as the religion of the nation. Here the real meaning of "Unification" becomes clear. The goal of the church is to unify all religions within itself, since only it can provide the dynamism to rally the people to commitment to combat Communism and to establish a viable moral order in the world. Although the Unification Church gives lip service to American law and government, its ultimate purpose is to overcome the separation of church and state and religious pluralism in this country to make itself the official and only religion in America. Once America has been won to the truth, then it will be necessary to expand the horizons of the church to the rest of the world, although the church is already active in other lands trying to advance its program. Furthermore, there is evidence that the church is interested in imposing its ideas on all other institutions—scientific, industrial, political—within various societies. In this country the Unification Church has involved itself, usually under another name, with all kinds of scholarly conferences, both scientific and humanistic, and any number of commercial enterprises. The church seemingly wants to become, either overtly or covertly, the dominant—if not the only—religion in the world. Of course, the Unification Church would deny any deviousness and argue that it is actually for the benefit of mankind that its views and ethics should be pervasive.

A movement to change the world needs multitudes of committed followers who are dedicated to the task of carrying the message of Unification theology. Consequently, the Unification Church is very evangelistic. While a group like Scientology makes a service, albeit one couched in the guise of a church, available to those who come to take advantage of it, a world-transforming group like the Unification Church aggressively goes out to recruit members. For this recruitment the church has received some of its harshest criticism. The church has utilized methods that many consider dangerous to get swift conversions and intense commitments; commitments to the group and the world it envisions, not to the world as it is or even to the recruit's families. The church has drawn potential members in a variety of ways. One way has been direct evangelism, in which members of the church would go into the streets or on campuses and talk to people about coming to an interest group, or, more often, "come over for dinner with me and some of my friends tonight." At other times, posters or ads in campus newspapers have appealed to student's idealism: "Do you want to help to make the world a better place? Come to meet others who feel the same way you do at such-and-such a place at such-and-such a time." In these initial contacts, either in person or in print, the name of the church is usually not mentioned. The interested person goes to the meeting and often discovers that he or she is the only stranger in the group, or at the most, there are only a few more. He or she is surrounded by members of this group that has invited him or her to come. There is nearly always a meal and very friendly conversation directed at the potential recruit, who is made to feel immediately welcome and very important.

At the end of this first meeting, the recruit usually is invited to a week-end retreat, often in a place away from the campus or the person's home. Here the atmosphere is the same; friendliness and acceptance. There are lectures on the need in the world for people committed to goodness; on the need to blunt the force of international Communism.

In between lectures there are food and activities. Indeed, the literature abounds with stories of how recruits are kept busy all the time, late into the night, so that they are tired and, theoretically, more susceptible to being influenced by the lectures and by the "love bombing" they are receiving from church members. It is said that they are never allowed any privacy for rest or reflection.

At the end of the week-end retreat, the recruit often is invited for a longer retreat, perhaps four or five days in length. If he or she goes—and many do because, in spite of the pace of the meeting, people have been friendly to him or her—the routine is repeated. Critics of the Unification Church, and they are legion, claim that these meetings are examples of high pressure tactics that can only be called "brainwashing," "mind control," or "a kind of hypnotism" that lowers the recruit's resistance to the invitation to join the church. Furthermore, it is only late in the process, actually after the recruit is "in the clutches" of the group, that the names of the Unification Church or Rev. Moon are mentioned. By that time, critics charge, it is too late to back out.

Of course, the church denies any devious or unethical behavior in its recruitment process, but rather says that it is simply showing interest and concern for young people and they respond by becoming members of the group. There is evidence that a significant number of potential converts simply do not return after the first or second meeting, thus casting the brainwashing theory into some doubt. But a large amount of literature, both by outside critics and by former members, indicates that some people do respond to the church's intensive recruitment in a rather mindless or "programmed" way. This has been a major source of the opposition to the group, much more than the content of its theology.

The amount of revenue taken in by the Unification Church and the method of raising it has also been a sore point for opponents of the cult. A movement that has world transformation as its goal needs a huge amount of money. In normal circumstances, the problem for a cult is how to gain its necessary economic base without having its members corrupted by the larger society. In the case of the Unification Church, the method was to have its members solicit funds from the general population but then to return to "headquarters" to live in a controlled environment with other members. Members were expected to spend long hours on the streets, in shopping centers, or in any place where they would have access to large numbers of people. They sold nuts, flowers, candy, candles, and other items that would have an immediate appeal. The church placed heavy demands upon its members/solicitors, setting daily goals of how much money each person must raise. There are reports of young people working themselves to exhaustion trying to meet these goals. This is one more example of brainwashing, the church's critics contend, because people do not normally work so diligently when none of the proceeds come to them. Supporters of the church, however, point out that they are highly motivated because they are working for the redemption of the world. There have also been instances when the church peddlers have not been completely open about who they represented when they asked for a contribution or tried to sell an item. Rather than acknowledging that the money went to the Unification Church, the vendor often would say that the money was going to support of a drug rehabilitation program, or a camp for poor children, or an orphan's home, etc. The church has been charged with advocating "heavenly deception," that is, that it is justified in not telling the entire truth if the ultimate goal is to make a paradise on earth through the Unification Church plan. Church leaders acknowledge that, in their zeal, solicitors sometimes were not entirely truthful in their claims, but insist that deception is not a policy of the church.

The solicitation of funds has been very successful. The accusation has been made that the bulk of the money raised by the church is for the pleasure of Rev. Moon and other leaders, while the rank and file membership are poorly housed, clothed, and fed. There may be some truth to this charge, for the church has been able to buy or initiate businesses and to purchase some very valuable real estate. But the church is not of the opinion that wealth is bad, if it can be used for the ultimate goal of the redemption of the world. Indeed, it wants to show that following the program of the church will eliminate poverty and provide better lives for people. Yet many people believe that the church is really out to control as much of the economy of America (and other countries) as it can, for its own benefit.

From this brief survey it is possible to see that the Unification Church was a very controversial organization throughout the 1970s. It is a totalistic movement, which has the reforming of the nation and then the world as its goal. Because of these characteristics, which include what many contend is the control of converts, it has elicited a storm of criticism. But the fact that this group, Scientology, and a number of other cults have been the stimulus of fear and the recipients of accusations raises again the question with which this chapter began: Are cults, by their very nature, evil?

• *Cults and Value Judgments*

The answer to that question is, no. The terms "sect" and "cult" are sociological terms used to identify certain kinds of religious groups and to distinguish them from other kinds. The terms are neutral; there is nothing in the terms that implies that sects or cults are either good or bad. The terms are merely descriptive; they carry no value judgment. The media have done a great disservice in perpetuating the commonly held idea that cults are always and necessarily evil. That is just not true. A cult is inherently neither good nor evil, it is just different. It could be that some would interpret that very difference as bad. To the extent that cults teach new perceptions, and that is a fundamental characteristic, they are theologically deviant and thus may be regarded as bad by the mainstream. But to be consistent with that viewpoint is finally to reject religious pluralism, one of the great strengths of American society. To make this point is not to deny that some cults may have very unfortunate and even destructive characteristics; the examples of the Manson group and the People's Temple again come to mind. A good number of serious scholars and medical personnel have called attention to the harm that some cult practices may do to some individuals' psyches and/or to family unity. These situations are causes for genuine concern. But the 1960s and 1970s should have taught us that there is certainly diversity within the religious experience and even within categories. Just because some cults have unwholesome dimensions does not mean that they all do. The appeal here is for discernment and discrimination. Let us not paint all religious groups, including cults, with too broad a brush. Cults are not, by their nature, either good or bad; each one must be considered on its own merits.

• *Suggestions for Further Reading
for Context and Perspective*

Barker, Eileen, ed. *Of Gods and Men: New Religious Movements in the West*. Macon GA: Mercer University Press, 1984.

Bromley, David G. and Anson D. Shupe. *Strange Gods: The Great American Cult Scare*. Boston: Beacon Press, 1982.

Ellwood, Robert S., Jr. *Religious and Spiritual Groups in Modern America*. Englewood Cliffs NJ: Prentice-Hall, 1973.

Enroth, Ronald. *Youth, Brainwashing, and the Extremist Cults*. Grand Rapids MI: Zondervan Publishing House, 1977.

Evans, Christopher. *Cults of Unreason*. New York: A Dell Publishing Company Delta Book, 1973.

Glock, Charles Y. and Robert N. Bellah, eds. *The New Religious Consciousness*. Berkeley: The University of California Press, 1976.

Hubbard, L. Ron. *Scientology: The Fundamentals of Thought*. The Publication Organization World Wide, 1956.

Needleman, Jacob. *The New Religions*. Garden City NY: Doubleday, 1970.

Rudin, A. James and Marcia R. Rudin. *Prison or Paradise? The New Religious Cults*. Philadelphia: Fortress Press, 1980.

Shupe, Anson D. and David G. Bromley. *Moonies in America: Cult, Church, and Crusade*. Beverly Hills CA: Sage Publications, 1979.

Sontag, Frederick. *Sun Myung Moon and the Unification Church*. Nashville: Abingdon Press, 1977.

What is Scientology? Based on the works of L. Ron Hubbard. Los Angeles: Publications Organization of the Church of Scientology of California, 1978.

White, Mel. *Deceived: The Jonestown Tragedy*. Old Tappan NJ: Fleming H. Revell Co., 1979.

Wilson, Bryan. *Religious Sects*. New York: McGraw-Hill Book Co., 1970.

CHAPTER FIVE

On Living
in Strange Times:
The Causes of It All

In previous chapters I have described the trends of the 1960s and 1970s, concentrating on the events of the late 1960s and later, when American religion moved away from the social activism of the mid-1960s into a more conservative mood. A prominent manifestation of that shift has been the increasing popularity of conservative theology and conservative churches, including Neo-Pentecostalism and high-intensity cult movements. Why has all of this happened?

• *The Need for Meaning in Life*

Many church leaders, particularly those in the declining liberal denominations, asked that question frequently during the late 1960s and 1970s. For them, it was a matter of life or death. They needed to find out why they were declining and why their more conservative counterparts were thriving—if for no other reason, so they could borrow some strategies from conservatives. In 1972, *Why Conservative Churches are Growing*—written by Dean Kelley, a Methodist and a liberal—suggested some answers. Kelley asserted that churches decline in strength and numbers of members if they are lenient in their social controls and reflect the culture around them. Conversely, churches grow if they are strict in their demands on their members and if they provide those members with meaning for their lives. Kelley did not focus on conservative theology per se as the reason that some churches grow. In fact, he wrote that it is conceivable that churches with liberal theology could grow if they did the right things. The "right things" would be to demand a high level of commitment from their members and to give them, in response, an explanation of life in ultimate terms, that is, meaning. In fact, Kelley believed that a better title for his book would have been "Why Strict Churches are Strong," rather than the one the publishers chose. It just turns out that the bulk of the churches that are strict and that are adept at providing meaning are conservative churches, whose style of theology does lend itself to absolutism, or a least to high demands for commitment from adherents.

Kelley argued that for the church to be true to its own mission it must supply people with meaning for life. He meant that one of the primary functions of religion is to help people make sense out of life, to explain life and death in ultimate terms. Humans, for all their wit and cleverness, are frail beings. One of the things that distinguishes them from the rest of the animals is that they know that they are frail; they are very aware of their finitude and they want ways of dealing with it. To grasp the full impact of Kelley's argument, one must ponder the human condition.

In his seminal attempt to define religion and to describe the religious impulse, William C. Tremmel has expressed the essence of our frailty with power and eloquence. "Religious behavior," Tremmel writes, "is a complex response to those aspects of human existence which are horrendous and nonmanipulable." These phenomena "threaten to destroy basic human values, and even life itself." They create in human beings not simply fear but terror and dread. They are, also, "beyond direct human control." They are inevitable and, without religion, unmitigated. Death is perhaps the most readily apparent instance of such a "religious problem." But "living," Tremmel reminds us,

> can also be horrendous. Indeed, for many people death is not the most terrible thing a person ever has to face. . . . For those who live past tender years, the basic tragedy of living may not be in death, but in disillusionment: in the discovery that life must be lived in picayune ways far beneath the expectations of youthful dreams and ambitions. For many sensitive people, the trauma of life, the horrendousness, comes in the lost beauty of life, the lost ecstacy of living, in the dulling of expectancy by the hard facts of mundane existence, in the gen-

eral loss of youthful ideals before the calculating motion of the years. The real frustration is not that life must end, but that it must be lived in little ways.[1]

Because these horrendous phenomena are built-in to the human condition, Tremmel adds, they are not subject to human manipulation. Human beings can delay death, but they cannot dismiss it. Such phenomena deny to every person "those conditions that are essential to genuine human life—such things as life itself, a sense of personal worth, an awareness of moral integrity."[2]

Another way the human condition can be described is to notice that only human beings can ask—indeed, must ask—themselves "existential questions" about the "nature of existence." Who am I? What does it mean to be me, different from you and all others? What does it mean to be a person of this sex, race, and nationality, at this particular place and time in history? From where did I come, and why? Is there any purpose to my living? What are my talents and abilities and how will I use them? Will my living make any difference in the world? Does anybody care? What is the nature and the meaning of death? What does it mean to cease to exist? Or, given a belief in life after death, what does it mean to cease to exist in the form that has been my total experience?

These kinds of questions must be answered or, at the very least, seriously engaged. As both Kelley and Tremmel clearly point out, the one institution or activity that can provide satisfactory answers is religion. No such answers are to be found in social clubs, business and commerce, education, science and technology, entertainment and recreation, as important as all those things may be. Only religion can provide us humans with ultimate meaning in our lives. Kelley writes that providing meaning for life is "the indispensable function" of religion.[3] It is the function of religion to explain to people the purpose of existence, the nature of reality, the character of the beings or forces that determine destiny. Re-

---

[1]William C. Tremmel, *Religion: What Is It?* (New York: Holt Rinehart and Winston, 1976) 35-37.

[2]Ibid., 39.

[3]Dean M. Kelley, *Why Conservative Churches are Growing,* rev. ed. (New York: Harper and Row, 1977), Chapter IV.

ligion attempts to explain the absurd and to make sense out of the pain and what often seems to be the craziness of life.[4]

Kelley argues that meaning is communicated, in those churches that are doing the best job in their peculiarly religious function, in such a way that something is demanded from those who receive the message. That message is: God has done something that gives meaning to your life, but you must respond with commitment. In Kelley's phrase "meaning = concept + demand."[5] He characterizes people who are struggling to live their lives in the world as saying: "Words are cheap; we want explanations that are validated by the commitment of other persons. . . . What costs nothing, accomplishes nothing. If it costs nothing to belong to such a community, it can't be worth much."[6] The thesis of Kelley's book is that some of the churches in America have been trying to function as churches without purveying that which is most characteristic of religion—meaning. They have been lenient in their demands upon people and the gospel that they have preached has been couched in terms of "this is one way of looking at it." The churches that took this approach in the 1970s declined in membership or only held their own. On the other hand, those churches that preached the gospel with the confidence that they were the possessors of the true faith and that expected people to respond with commitment and activity on behalf of the church grew in the late 1960s and throughout the 1970s. Although Kelley's book produced heated discussion about the validity of his thesis, I have been persuaded by his arguments and believe that he was much more right than wrong. Consequently, this chapter builds and expands on his general thesis.

The decline in membership of mainstream denominations was serious enough that leaders of many of those groups wanted to find out what was going on. For that reason, from 1976 through 1978 a group of scholars and denominational leaders held a series of workshops in which church membership and demographic data were examined. The result of

---

[4]Ibid., 38.

[5]Ibid., 52.

[6]Ibid., 52-53.

this study was *Understanding Church Growth and Decline 1950-1978*[7] and a companion volume, *Where Have All Our People Gone?*[8] After examining a mass of data, which was not completely consistent, the study concluded that the largest shift in mainstream church membership population occurred among those people less than 39 years of age, with an especially precipitous drop in church participation among those between the ages of 21 and 29. Liberal churches did not lose people of other age categories; the drop in their statistics was due to the defection of young people from their ranks. Conservative churches grew not so much because people from liberal churches transferred their membership into conservative churches; instead, the latter did a better job of retaining the loyalty of their young adults—they just did not lose as many. That argument seems a little unlikely, since many conservative denominations showed a numerical gain in the 1970s. But even if they are true such trends do not in any way disprove or even discount Kelley's concept of strict-church growth.

In fact, several authors of the study acknowledged that they found nothing with which to disagree in Kelley's thesis. The greatest problem was that it was too narrow, they believed. In trying to account for church growth and decline, they correctly made a distinction between internal factors, such as theological modifications, and contextual factors, such as population migration. They accused the Kelley thesis of ignoring contextual factors and of concentrating on internal factors only, namely, the articulation of strict, demanding theology, which focuses on trying to answer existential questions. The accusation is essentially true, but it is certainly possible to see the connection between Kelley's argument and cultural trends and historical events that made the desire of people to find meaning in their lives all the more intense. The internal factors that Kelley spells out are directly related to many trends in the world since World War II, particularly during the 1960s and 1970s.

Furthermore, the authors of the study on church growth and decline asserted that the growth of conservative churches and the decline of the

---

[7]Dean R. Hoge and David A. Roozen, eds., *Understanding Church Growth and Decline 1950-1978* (New York: The Pilgrim Press, 1979).

[8]Carl S. Dudley, *Where Have All Our People Gone?* (New York: The Pilgrim Press, 1979).

liberal churches in the 1970s had to be the result of short-term factors. They emphasized factors of the immediate past, since prior to the 1970s all American religious groups, liberal and conservative alike, had grown. Indeed, the decline or stagnation of many of the liberal denominations in the 1970s had been the reversal of two hundred years of church growth. The most immediate response to this is that the remarkable 1960s and 1970s are short-term events, as viewed from the perspective of church history. But one can also speak of a cumulative effect of the events since World War II; cultural tendencies and historical events, the effects of which came to a head in the 1970s. It is an oversimplification to say that only recent events could have provided the context for the church membership/activity tendencies of the 1970s.

Dean Kelley has argued that the churches that effectively supply meaning for people's lives are those churches that seem to have the most vitality. But an objection must be raised! Has that not always been the case? Have not frailty, mortality, and the inability to completely accomplish one's dreams always been part of the human condition? Why is it that now, in recent times, those qualities of finitude seem to respond so much more positively to the ministrations of religion that tries to give meaningful, definite answers to questions of existence? Is there something about our time that makes such theology, with an accompanying demand for response, more relevant than in past times?

A plausible argument can be made that the dramatic events of the past two decades account for the gyrations in religious activity and church membership in this country. We have lived through and continue to live in the midst of a series of cultural traumas. It sometimes is argued that people of every generation have faced crises and cultural novelties that made their lives uncertain. That is undoubtedly true. But the 1960s and 1970s have presented Americans (and all others on this globe as well) with spectacularly new problems, and the solutions seem more and more elusive. There has been a kind of cumulative effect to these cultural traumas. Throughout most of the 1960s, as the first of the truly startling changes/advances began to penetrate into our lives and as we continued the kind of naive optimism about human abilities we had inherited from previous generations, things seemed to go pretty well. It was in those days that "secular religion" flourished and church attendance went down in most denominations. But, as we moved into the 1970s and the events and cultural changes of that decade continued to flood in upon us, we began to be overwhelmed with the enormity of it all and we began to lose our confidence that we could manage on our own. Frailty, unfulfilled lives, fear of death have always been part of the human experience. But the strange times of the 1960s and 1970s caused us to see these horrendous phenomena as we had not seen them before. Many (not all) people began to turn to more meaning-oriented religion, and they seemed to find that meaning in more conservative denominations. The religious trends of the 1970s were part (along with increasing political conservatism and a nostalgia for the "good old days"—the 1950s) of a reaction against the 1960s and the increasing complexity of our lives as we moved into the 1980s.

• *The Traumatic 1960s and 1970s*

A quick review of the major developments of the 1960s and 1970s may help us recall the profound impact these happenings made on our lives. In the area of technological developments, consider these items, not listed in any order of importance:

Space exploration and travel. In these decades we were presented the spectacle of space ships, all the way from unmanned Sputniks, weather satellites, and deep-space probes of other planets, to manned craft orbiting the earth and, wonder of wonders, landing on the moon—all of this for the first time in human history.

Medical technology. Medicine made dramatic progress in these two decades in the areas of research for diagnostic and pharmacological purposes, in the development of sophisticated machinery and equipment, and in procedures. Perhaps the most dramatic example of all this was the development of heart-transplant operations. While perhaps not having the widespread applicability and benefit of other procedures, such as the related heart artery bypass operation, transplants effectively illustrated the profoundly spectacular innovations of medicine available to us.

The computer. The computer burst upon our consciousness and suddenly became a pervasive part of our culture. Computers invaded business, education, entertainment (oh, those "electronic games"), and manufacturing. The machines simultaneously relieved the tedium of many menial jobs and snafued our records so that we sometimes did not know from month to month what we owed on one or more of our many charge accounts. In the latter part of the 1970s, as computers became increasingly miniaturized, home or personal computers became available and forecasters predicted that they would cause a cultural revolution at least equal to the industrial revolution of the nineteenth and early twentieth centuries.

As people witnessed these scientific accomplishments, they could not help but be impressed with human abilities. Was there anything that we could not do, if we were determined enough? Was not *homo sapiens* truly self-sufficient? Surely the human potential for technical achievements was virtually limitless. Was it not the case that we could, within the foreseeable future, create the long-awaited utopia? Some people thought so; it was in those days that many individuals spoke of humanity come of age, a time when religion was becoming obsolete, of the death of God. But those ideas were naive even then. Contending against that optimism was the historical record that humans had not been able to move perceptively closer to a utopia or ideal society with the technology already available. There was not much reason to suspect that enhancing the sophistication of gadgets and procedures, as marvelous as they were, would make us the captains of our destiny into an idyllic future. There were also signs that our advanced technology was itself a mixed blessing; as it solved some problems it created others.

Technology threatened the environment. Almost overnight, as the 1970s began, the public became conscious that our environment was in serious trouble. For the first time more than just a few conservationists became aware that Americans were, and had been for some time, poisoning and destroying our air, water, and landscape. Although all of us participate in this despoilation of our natural habitat through the discarding of an enormous amount of waste, for example, it became clear that the largest contribution to pollution came from industrial and technological activities. The air was polluted by our excessive use of automobiles and by industrial emissions. Rivers, lakes, and even the seas were being contaminated by chemical wastes, many of which were quite toxic. Perhaps the most dramatic symbol of this problem was a river that caught on fire! Some people were fearful that the planet would not continue to be habitable unless there were dramatic changes in the way we treated our environment, certainly a prospect unknown to our forebears.

Nuclear proliferation. The major powers of the world produced ever more powerful nuclear weapons and increasingly sophisticated delivery systems for those weapons. Such weapons had been known since 1945, but in recent times many people began to despair that the weapons and delivery systems, given the instability of world politics, meant that the future of the human race was very much in doubt.

The energy crisis. Because of an insatiable need for energy for both industrial and home use, resources of fossil fuels appeared to be shrinking rapidly. The realization that these nonrenewable resources were being exhausted presented the prospect that society, as we moderns know it, might be doomed.

In the 1960s and 1970s technological developments presented the American population with prospects of prosperity, but also with gigantic problems. But these were not all. A wide range of social/political trends and events made those decades virtually unlike any other. In addition to the civil rights movement, violence in the streets, political assassinations, and the Vietnam war, there were other crucial challenges:

International crises. In the Cuban missile crisis of 1962 Americans came within minutes of war with the Soviet Union. In the almost endless bargaining to release American hostages in Iran in 1979-1980, Americans experienced the frustration of being powerless to do anything short of war to release their compatriots from an unjust captivity. In both cases the complexity of international politics demonstrated the limitations of American power.

Nuclear stalemate. Some progress was made in limiting the proliferation of nuclear weapons, but prolonged negotiations did not succeed in removing from the public consciousness the threat of nuclear annihilation.

Burgeoning population and shrinking resources. In those decades we became painfully aware that the beneficial advances of medicine have lowered the mortality rate sufficiently to cause world population to increase dramatically. This rapid increase in the number of people in the world put great pressure on the world's natural resources, particularly upon the capability to produce sufficient quantities of food. Thus in the late 1970s we became aware of the problem of massive world hunger. There have always been hungry people, but never in such gargantuan proportions as now. These great population pressures bode ill for political stability in the world, as nations of the Third World contend strenuously with each other and the rest of the world for food and other resources.

Automation and human labor. The development of computers and certain other industrial techniques presented serious problems, principally unemployment and/or the necessity for persons to retrain themselves to compete in the labor market. This development was most noticeable in the area of automation of mass production procedures. In the automobile industry and several others, robots are able to perform efficiently many tasks, thus taking jobs away from people. To be replaced or even challenged for one's job by a machine is a very disquieting occurrence.

Inflation and recession. Along with these problems, and compounding some of them, there was inflation accompanied by recession throughout most of the 1970s, becoming especially severe just as that decade ended. Bankruptcy, unemployment, frustration, fear, and complete despair became commonplace in American society. Certainly this was not the first time that economic problems had plagued the country, but it was the first time that inflation and recession arrived together. Combined with the other problems unique to the late 1960s and the 1970s, they made a psychically lethal mixture.

Bankrupt leadership. Just when all the rest of these problems converged in such a way that people needed to be able to rely on strong and competent national leadership to find solutions, the leadership itself was not equal to the task. Indeed, in certain glaring circumstances, it proved to be corrupt. In the early 1970s, the vice-president of the United States was forced to resign because of his income tax improprieties and later the president was forced to resign because of his own connivance and that of his staff in political espionage and coverup. Americans were shocked by these unprecedented events and, at the same time, had some of their worst suspicions about politicians confirmed. Throughout the rest of the decade there was a great deal of cynicism about politicians and the political process.

International Communism. In spite of the spirit of "detente" in U.S./ Soviet relations and more friendly relations with the Chinese Communists in the 1970s, there were still many Americans who were concerned about the continued threat of Communism to liberties in this country and abroad. The extreme right wing of American religion—those lumped together under the name Moral Majority—vocally and vehemently opposed Communism. The continuing international political turmoil did not seem to be solvable. The world was and continues to be a very complicated place in which to live.

Moral upheaval. Finally, in those years the country experienced a wide range of challenges to traditional social and moral values. One of these was the feminist movement. Although there had been those who had been campaigning for the rights of women since the mid-nineteenth century and even earlier, in the late 1960s and the 1970s this movement became more militant and more comprehensive in its goals. It did not have a single focus, such as gaining the vote, but demanded full equality for women in all aspects of society—in the boardroom, in the bedroom, in employment opportunities, in freedom from sexual stereotypes, in political participation. A guarantee of these rights through an amendment to the U.S. Constitution was sought with great agitation. This movement was supported with ardor by some, opposed with horror by others, but did not fail to be fascinating to almost everyone.

Somewhat related to the feminist movement and both consistent and inconsistent with it was a dramatic increase in sexual freedom. Sexual freedom was consistent with the feminist movement in that "liberated" women felt more free to use their bodies as they chose; it was inconsistent with it to the degree that the "Playboy philosophy," as it was known in the early days, tended to regard women as sex objects to be used and exploited by men. At any rate, the 1960s and 1970s were characterized by a dramatic increase in both sexual activity and in the freedom with which sex was discussed or flaunted through pornography in magazines, films, or soap operas. Many people saw feminism, greater sexual activity, and the pressures put on the family as related phenomena. The traditional family encountered enormous pressures of other kinds, too, ranging from increased leisure time for children to the difficulty of maintaining a particular standard of living. Whatever the reasons, the family unit was subject to great stress and divorce skyrocketed during those decades.

Another issue related to sexuality inflamed intense passions—abortion "on demand." Increasing numbers of women insisted that they had the right to do what they wanted in all matters related to their bodies, including the termination of an unwanted pregnancy by abortion. The Supreme Court agreed, at least if the abortion took place during the first trimester of pregnancy. Some people argued that abortion was simply a woman's legitimate free choice, a choice that had implications for the size of her family as well as her personal health, and that abortion could be a legitimate way of dealing with the population problem. Others considered it nothing short of murder and against the moral precepts of both

God and humanity. This issue inflamed intense passions on several sides of the debate.

Any one of these staggering issues is important and could easily demand the attention of an individual, if not a society. But taken together—they had to be taken together—they were virtually overpowering. It is no wonder that people felt threatened by the times in which they lived. It should not be surprising that a significant portion of the population felt the need to seek some sort of ultimate explanation of these events or at least some ultimate explanation of their fragile, temporal lives in the face of these forces. The impact of these cultural/historical trends was made all the more shattering by the pervasive influence of another aspect of our modern lives: the mass media, particularly television.

Although television had been available to many Americans before the 1960s and 1970s, it was in those decades that it became a pervasive influence in society. As such it became the disseminator of all the cultural changes and ideas that have been reviewed here. Americans were bombarded by television with information about breathtaking events throughout the world and were assaulted with new ideas, new life-styles, and challenges to traditional moral values. In creating this new climate television was supplemented by movies, print media, and various styles of rock music available through the radio, records, and tapes. It was not just in the news broadcasts that these fascinating and frustrating dimensions of society were thrust upon us, especially since not all the population watched the news, but also through the entertainment shows that new values became part of the American psyche. But conveying information about startling events and discoveries or depicting men and women in immoral sexual relationships were not the only dimensions of television's impact.

Evidence seems to indicate that television affects people at levels other than the cognitive or intellectual. Marshall McLuhan, a theorist of media, argued that television has been so pervasive in American life that one could mark differences in the generations by its advent. Those people who cannot remember the time when television was first brought into their homes are "TV children," in McLuhan's phraseology. The rest of us, those who can remember life before television, are nineteenth-century people. What makes us nineteenth-century people is that we still think in linear ways, in terms of subjects and predicates, logical arguments, the development of a train of thought. These patterns of thought were ingrained in us because we were reared on print media, a medium that particularly lends itself to such linear thinking.

But "TV children" do not think in such ways, argued McLuhan. They do not think in logical, progressive ways as much as they think in terms of images, impressions. A "TV child" is one who has been exposed to television throughout his or her life. Studies have shown that such people watch around twenty-two thousand hours of television between the ages of two and eighteen. One cannot look at anything for that long without receiving a definite impression. But television is a special case, said McLuhan, because it, in a sense, draws people into it. Because the viewer must fill in the image between the lines on the screen with imagination, he or she becomes a participant in what is happening on the screen. Television is not just a visual and auditory medium, it is also tactile or corporeal in the sense that it involves the whole person in what is being broadcast. There is an emotional involvement in television in the sense that there is a kind of participation in the program, not just in the hearing, seeing, and understanding, but also in becoming part of the action. But it is a *passive* kind of emotion. One participates by filling in between the lines on the picture tube and in that sense is involved in the action, but at the same time one is sitting in a chair with one's favorite beverage and food.

If McLuhan's theory is true, and it is arguably compelling, then TV children are part of a generation that has been inundated with the complex and changing world as it has been presented with startling immediacy. It has influenced TV children all the more because, given the nature of television itself, they have become vicarious participants in monumental events and value changes. For some, at least, it has been an overwhelming experience. Joined now and again by older people, they have sought some kind of integrating principle, some kind of concept to make sense of it all, something that would give ultimate meaning to life in these times. The living of life is difficult enough in any times, as Tremmel's poignant analysis reminds us. But in these times, in which the events and trends reviewed on these pages were thrust upon people both by experience and by the mass media—in "living color"—many felt the shock in such a way that they turned to what could give meaning to their lives. Dean Kelley has argued that this meaning has been found more often in strict religion promoting strongly held beliefs—conservative religion—and I believe he is right. This is the principal reason why conservative churches have grown.

I have reformulated Kelley's argument into three major points. Although this scheme is oversimplified, as most systematizations are, it may help to clarify why conservative religion grew so much faster than liberal religion in the late 1960s and throughout the 1970s. Conservative religion in our time is attractive to many people because it offers three things: authority, eschatology, and healing.

• *Conservative Religion*
Supplies Authority

Conservative religion is appealing to many because it offers certainty in an uncertain world. As one reflects on the times in which we live, one thing that seems obvious is the amount and rapidity of change we experience. There is a kind of craziness, if not chaos, in the world. Oh, for some certainty, something to hang on to, an anchor to provide mooring in this raging tempest! Conservative religion provides that certainty through its authoritative theology and life-style.

The churches that seem to have grown the most are those I have described as Fundamentalist or Establishment Evangelical. In general, they are dogmatic in their interpretation of the Bible and in their doctrinal assertions. Their view of biblical inerrancy leads them to believe that they know exactly what the biblical text means. It is the word of God, an infallible source of religious truth, and the truth is found in the plain sense of the words on the pages. Here is certainty; there is no equivocation as to the meaning of the Bible or its importance in living. For one who is insecure on the shifting sands of modern, relativistic, society, here is solid rock, a firm foundation upon which one can stand with confidence. To change the image, the Bible understood literally is the compass by which one can set a true course for life in a world that does not seem to know where it is going.

If the Bible provides assurance for conservatives in an unsure world, their doctrinal assertions do no less. Their theology rests upon the Bible; it is derived from the "plain truth" of the Bible. Given this view of the Bible, it is entirely possible for this style of religion to say in essence: "We know exactly what we believe and we know it is true." The slogan "God said it—I believe it—That settles it," may be a little simplistic even for some committed conservatives to affirm. But that is the gist of the doctrinal attitude of much of the religion that seemed to flourish in the 1970s. Again, the appeal is certainty. In a time when virtually any idea gets a hearing and when the spirit of relativism considers one ideology as valuable as any other, an adherence to precisely articulated classical Christian doctrine enables one to face these strange times with unassailable trust. There is great psychological security in being able to stand on such a firm foundation.

A society characterized by an anarchy of ideas often produces more than just intellectual confusion. In the absence of a clear ethical mandate people act on the ideas that they find most appealing. Consequently, our time is marked by a wide range of social evils, all the way from dishonesty in politics and industry to pornography and every sort of sexual perversion. In response to such hedonism or relativism conservative religion lays out a clear-cut Christian life style and expects its adherents to follow that code of ethics. On the basis of their reading of Scripture and the traditional moral doctrines of Christianity, conservatives generally adhere to an ethic which emphasizes monogamy, no pre- or extra-marital sexual relations, no abortion (occasionally with some very narrowly defined exceptions), and no pornography. It stresses the importance of the traditional idea of the family and tends to recommend the subservience of the wife and children to the husband/father. This ethic emphasizes that the body is the temple of God and thus demands abstinence from drugs, other than those legitimately prescribed, alcohol, and sometimes tobacco. It insists upon honesty in interpersonal relationships, in politics, and in the marketplace. These broad generalizations may work themselves out in various ways as different situations arise. But the point is that there are definite answers to the young people and adults who ask: "How should I live my life in these evil and confusing times?" The answer is not "Well, it depends on thus and so," or "Let's talk about it and see if we can figure out an answer." Rather the answer is that there are definite Christian moral rules and one must follow those. If that should seem rather restrictive, that possible liability is far overshadowed by the psychological certainty and security that may be derived from definitely knowing what the Christian life-style is to be.

"Eschatology" is part of the technical jargon used by theologians and other scholars of religion. It comes from a Greek word that means "last or final things" and thus, in its common usage, refers to the belief in the coming of the end of time. In specifically Christian theology it refers to the end of the world, to be accomplished by the second coming of Jesus Christ. In chapter three it was shown that a strong belief in the hasty coming of the end of time has traditionally been found mainly among the poor. But, particularly in the 1970s, a vivid eschatology began to surface among Neo-Pentecostals and other conservatives. Those people began to talk at length about how the end of time was to come soon, and the sooner the better. Now it is possible to consider why that is the case. I maintain that this emphasis on the end of time is one of the characteristics of conservative religion that makes it attractive to people in these unsettling times.

Actually, this interest in eschatology is a narrow focus on a much larger issue, namely, a view of history. Whether we realize it or not, we assume some things about the nature of history; that it had a beginning (Christian theology says it was through creation by God) and that it ought to have some kind of meaning. Couched in those terms, we hardly ever think about it and it is virtually never a topic of conversation at parties; yet a view of history remains part of our intellectual and emotional makeup. The problem is, history is all mixed up; for the past decade or two each year has seemed to be a little more strange than the one before. If we assume that history ought to have some kind of meaning, as we do, then we are frustrated because this chaotic history does not meet our expectations. Our anxiety can be summarized in the famous question: "Who's in charge here?"

Who *is* in charge here? The average person is likely to answer, "Nobody!" If that is true, then we are at the mercy of the cussedness of human nature or of fate. But conservative Christianity is able to give an entirely different answer. Based on the Biblical belief that God is going to bring the world to an end—that is, that when the end comes it will be because God will have caused it—it is easy to extrapolate from that to see God's hand in all of history. Of course, God's involvement in history has been a major ingredient in Judaeo-Christian theology from the beginning of the tradition and is held by the middle-of-the-roaders and liberals, too. But only conservative Christianity has been so vocal about God's guidance of history, partly because it has stressed eschatology so strongly. So, conservative Christianity is able to say with confidence that "God is in charge here."

In spite of the chaos and evil of the world, regardless of the disarray of history, God is in charge. That is a most reassuring concept, one that many people are ready to hear and accept. Not only does it provide confidence, but it also actually turns the disconcerting events of contemporary history into positive signs that God is indeed in charge. Eschatological thought in the Bible frequently points to tumultuous events as signs that the end is near at hand. One example from many that could be chosen is Mark 13, particularly verses seven and eight, which read: "And when you hear of wars and rumors of wars, do not be alarmed; this must take place, but the end is not yet. For nation will rise against nation, and kingdom against kingdom; there will be earthquakes in various places; there will be famines; this is but the beginning of the sufferings" (RSV). Consequently, literalistic Christianity can counsel its adherents (and potential converts) not to be dismayed by the wild events they are experiencing but rather to derive hope from them, for they are signs that God will indeed soon bring history to an end by the return of Jesus. They, as those who hold the true faith, will surely be among the victorious, the saints, when that happens.

The prospect of being among those who will receive God's blessing at the end of time is another reason that this concept of history is so appealing. That reward is a result of holding the true faith. To be among the blessed of God at the end of history is a motivation for living the ethical, righteous life demanded by Christianity. Living the good life will not only help to improve our society, but also will contribute to individual salvation at the end of time. That goal is very appealing to those who believe that this world is evil, corrupt, and going to hell. Finally, this prospect of the coming of the end of history is also a strong motivating factor in the evangelism promoted by conservative groups. One of the reasons that these groups are growing rapidly is that they work at it. That has frequently been true of conservative denominations, but in this cultural context their message is even more attractive, so they grow more rapidly than their liberal counterparts. Part of that message is a vivid eschatology. Here are people who understand history and believe the profoundly hopeful idea that God is in charge and that the ultimate illustration of that will be the soon-to-come climax. These people feel the ethical obligation to share that message with others, to rescue them from frustrating life now and damnation hereafter. Their view of history is a strong motivator for evangelism. And, because many people find meaning for their lives in this message, since it helps to give ultimate explanation for individual life and the course of history, they join and the movement grows.

• *Conservative Religion*
Supplies Healing

A third benefit that conservative religion offers to people is healing, broadly defined. First, and most basic, in the concept of healing is the idea of salvation from sin. The word "salvation" comes from a Latin root that means "health or healing." Christianity has always argued that it can provide healing from the sickness of sin, that it can restore any person's relationship with God, a relationship that was distorted and broken by sin. Obviously, that message is not the sole possession of conservative Protestants. But in this era it seems that conservative Protestants are most effective in persuading people of the truth of that concept. For those people who do not seem to be able to find meaning and purpose for life on their own, whose efforts to lift themselves up by the spiritual and emotional bootstraps and face these difficult times have been unsuccessful, the message of salvation through Jesus Christ is very attractive. For those who have attempted to find a meaningful or useful life through drugs, or alcohol, or promiscuity, or the commercial "rat race," or all of these—only to have the effort turn out to be one's own private hell—the message of spiritual wholeness and healing is very appealing. This is particularly so when membership in the saving community, the church, demands commitment and thus one can exhibit definite signs of having been saved. Again I quote with agreement Dean Kelley's word about the strictness of those groups that are growing: "What costs nothing, accomplishes nothing. If it costs nothing to belong to such a community, it can't be worth much."[9]

---

[9]Kelley, *Why Conservative Churches are Growing*, 53.

There is a considerably narrower dimension of healing which is also made available to people by some conservative churches—namely, physical healing. One of the gifts of the Holy Spirit that has been emphasized by Classical Pentecostalism is the gift of healing. This gift has been called upon in a variety of ways by Pentecostal groups, all the way from quiet and dignified prayers and the anointing of the sick individual with oil (see James 5:14-15) to the sensationalist and frenzied healing services of the tent revival or certain television evangelists. This same emphasis has been preserved in Neo-Pentecostalism, on the more dignified or controlled end of the spectrum, and thus is available to those people in the mainstream society who have chosen to participate in that style of conservative Christianity.

Another dimension of the healing offered by conservative Christianity is emotion. Surprising as it may seem, in this day of abundant entertainment possibilities and frenzied activity many analysts of American society see boredom as one of its greatest problems. They report that this is particularly true of young people, "TV children." Marshall McLuhan argued that regular viewing of television promotes emotionalism in people, albeit a kind of passive emotionalism. If this is true, then one can speculate that for TV children the level of emotionalism is so high that it takes ever more to excite them. Years of exposure to television and deafening rock music, along with the opportunities they have to go places and do things in a highly mobile society, have so conditioned young people that it takes ever more to stimulate them and give them emotional satisfaction.

The worship of liberal or middle-of-the-road churches seems not to have provided that kind of emotional gratification. Often liberal churches have a tradition of very formal worship; at least, even if they do not have such a liturgical tradition, they usually want to be dignified. But one of two things, if not both, seems to be going on in conservative churches. One of these is that in some of these churches the worship is less formal and actually stimulates emotional behavior. This is particularly true of Classical and Neo-Pentecostal churches. Although many of these have abandoned the older style of unbridled emotionalism and now conduct worship with a certain order, there is still an element of informality. It is still possible to find speaking in tongues and interpretation in the worship service. This may attract those who have a high threshold of stimulation. Recent research into church growth and decline has found that most of the people who have left liberal churches or remained in conservative churches are under 39 years old; the majority are between the ages of 21 and 29—"TV children" all. In the light of McLuhan's analysis of the kind of people that TV children may become because of their extensive exposure to electronic media, these results are not completely surprising.

Another dimension of emotionalism is the emphasis of conservatism on the personal nature of religious experience. Being "born again" means taking Jesus as one's personal Savior and experiencing a personal conversion of heart and life. Although the idea of accepting Jesus as personal Savior is not a recent theological concept and has been found in liberalism as well, in the liberal tradition it is principally an intellectual conception. But in conservatism it is more than an intellectual idea, it is a personal experience. Conservatives can often name the time and the place of their conversion because, unlike the usual liberal approach that sees becoming a Christian as a rather gradual process, conservatives very often think of conversion as a climactic, dramatic experience. It is an experience that, in itself, often involves emotion. Yet there is an ongoing emotional aspect to being born again in that it is an intensely personal thing to be able to say: "I have Jesus in *my* heart. *I* have been born again. Jesus is *my* Lord and Savior." Such a personal, individualized religious experience carries an emotional quality that is meaningful to many in our time. For those who are bored, and thus have real difficulty in finding "something to live for," and for those whose threshold of stimulation is high, the extremely personal and dramatic experience of being born again is very appealing; it is an experience of healing.

Another facet of healing, broadly defined, that conservatism provides is a sense of identity and individual worth. One of the most important of the "existential questions" is "Who am I?" In order to live creatively and with a sense of psychological well-being, one must have fairly clear conceptions of what it means to be a particular individual and of how one fits into society. The problem is that our society, with so many people and with its computerized, technocratic emphasis, tends to dehumanize people. It is so easy for a person to be just a face in the crowd. It is so common for a person not to be important to anybody else, or at least only to a few. It is endemic to our society for people to be thought of as numbers, or units of production, or consumers, but not so much as *persons* with personalities, aspirations, fears and worth. Students in schools and universities, workers in factories, nonworking women and men at home with only the soap operas for companionship, those imprisoned week in and week out in high-rise office buildings, military personnel, all these and more so often begin to feel that they personally do not matter to anybody, that they are just a cog in the machinery of whatever company or organization they are a part of, that nobody cares about *them* as persons.

This lack of individual identity and this loneliness cause many people to cry out for healing. Conservative religion responds well to such a plea. This is not to argue that liberal churches may not respond helpfully to such a call, for they often do, but conservative churches seem to be able to create more of a sense of community. Perhaps it is because there is more doctrinal uniformity in conservative churches—"You must believe like we do to become part of our church." Perhaps it is because they just work harder at it. But it is commonly said of conservative churches that they are warmer, friendlier, and more accepting than mainstream churches. For whatever reason, there is a strong sense of community in many fundamentalist or evangelical congregations. There is some danger that this may disappear as churches of this type are successful in gaining new members, for the larger the congregation, the easier it is to lose the personal touch and personal contact. But within a congregation with a strong sense of community, it is easy for a person to feel a sense of belonging and worth. One can answer the question of identity by saying: "I am a born-again Christian and have a feeling of unity with Christ and with those in this church that gives me a sense of security and that makes me whole." A sense of belonging, a sense of finding one's identity as part of the community, a sense of warmth within the faith: these things are quite commonly found within conservative churches that have a strong sense of theological identity. This is very helpful for one who feels cast adrift in the midst of an impersonal society.

Why did conservative churches grow in the 1970s? As a reaction to the events of the 1960s and the continuing difficult times. But this was not the first time that people had faced cultural crises and they certainly had faced the awareness of personal limitation, inadequacy, and the possibility of death before. Why did liberal and conservative churches respond differently in the 1970s than they had before? Because the cultural crises of the 1960s and 1970s were of such a profound nature and because there was a kind of cumulative effect to these events and trends which was simply overwhelming. Furthermore, the electronic media incessantly displayed political, scientific, and moral problems and, in the process, even changed the ways of thinking, perceiving, and reacting among the young and among the rest of us, as well. Many older folks are hooked on the tube, too. People simply have felt the need to be able to make some sense of it all and/or to ignore it. They have tried to put the craziness of our world behind them by putting something else in a predominant position in their lives. In Dean Kelley's terminology, people crave meaning in their lives. While moderate-to-liberal, mainstream, religion can and does provide this function for millions of Americans, in the 1970s many people turned to more conservative religious groups because they found there a strictly held doctrine with strong expectations of conformity. That discovery helped them both to make sense of or to find an ultimate explanation for the traumatic events of our times. It put something else at the center of their lives that would divert their attention from the turmoil. Conservative religion did this by providing authority, a view of history with a concentration on eschatology, and healing, broadly defined.

• *Objections to the Theory*

I suspect that a fundamentalist or evangelical Christian would respond to the analysis of this chapter with the observation that it is all very interesting and very wrong. I have argued that conservative churches have grown as a reaction to historical, sociological, and cultural events in the 1960s and 1970s. The conservative would say that this particular kind of church has been growing because God has been causing it to happen. This kind of theology and worship is most faithful to God and thus God, through the Holy Spirit, has been at work in the world giving success to the style of religion that is most faithful to God.

Leaving aside the question as to whether conservatism or liberalism is the style of faith most acceptable to God, a matter that must be left to personal choice, these two viewpoints are not incompatible. It is possible to believe that conservative churches are growing both because of historical, cultural trends *and* because God is causing it to happen. It has been an integral component of Judaeo-Christian theology from the beginning of the tradition that God works in history. Indeed, one of the most distinctive features of the Judaeo-Christian tradition, which is a major factor which makes it different from Oriental religions, is the idea that God is a participant in human affairs. As young people in the 1960s might have put it, "God is where the action is." God works through and is revealed in historical events. So it is not an either/or situation when one talks about contemporary trends in American religion to notice the pressures of society and the activity of God. Both may be true, as God may be working through even the most traumatic events of this era to accomplish the divine will in the world and draw men and women Godward.

Finally, if I have conveyed the impression that the late 1960s and the 1970s saw everybody in Protestantism join some conservative church, that is wrong. Millions stayed in mainstream, moderate-to-liberal churches, although those churches did decline in membership all through the 1970s. Furthermore, there was a significant portion of the population that did not go to any church or synagogue. Research in the late 1970s showed that there were some 63 million people who claimed to be religious, who held at least a moderately strong belief in God, but who did not go to any church.

One of the arguments against the Kelley thesis is that in the 1960s and 1970s young people tended to adopt life-styles that emphasized greater personal freedom with an attendant rejection of authoritarianism. They tended to seek greater self-expression, self-fulfillment, and individualism. They tended to turn their backs upon any structures or institutions that they perceived would thwart their free-swinging life-styles. The argument has been that since this rejection of authoritarianism seemed to be characteristic of a large part of the society, then Kelley was surely wrong in his argument that strictness and theological exclusivism were the characteristics that caused conservative churches to grow. It has been noted that the largest demographic shift in the 1970s was that persons under 39 years of age, particularly those between 21 and 29, left the liberal churches in large numbers. However, in conservative churches there was not a great loss of persons in that age category. It appears that what happened is that among those people who left the liberal churches there was the development of a rather freewheeling life-style. Some of them may have joined conservative churches, but it seems that the majority of them joined the ranks of the unchurched, those who continued to perceive of themselves as being religious but who were unwilling to participate in organized religion. Two important reasons cited were (1) they felt that churches were really interested only in perpetuating themselves and thus were more interested in raising the budget than in spiritual uplift and (2) they were rebelling against having been force-fed religion when they were children. However, most of these same young people expressed an interest in having their own children exposed to religious influences, so there is the possibility that many of these people, in the near future, may again become participants in some church. It will be interesting to see whether they return to some form of mainstream church that has a somewhat more relaxed style, or whether they will see the value of conservative religion in raising their children and, at the same time, find significant meaning there for coping with the strange times in which we live.

• *Suggestions for Further Reading
for Context and Perspective*

A Summary of Qualitative Research of the Unchurched. New York: Religion in American Life, Inc., n.d.

Dudley, Carl S. *Where Have All Our People Gone?* New York: The Pilgrim Press, 1979.

Hale, J. Russell. *The Unchurched: Who They Are and Why They Stay Away.* San Francisco: Harper and Row, 1980.

Hoge, Dean R. and David A. Roozen, eds. *Understanding Church Growth and Decline 1950-1978.* New York: The Pilgrim Press, 1979.

Kelley, Dean M. *Why Conservative Churches are Growing.* San Francisco: Harper and Row, rev. ed., 1977.

Marty, Martin E. *A Nation of Behavers.* Chicago: The University of Chicago Press, 1976. This book may be read as another author's perspective on the issues covered in the first five chapters of this book.

The Unchurched American. Princeton NJ: The Princeton Religion Research Center, 1978.

CHAPTER SIX

Mrs. O'Hair, Where Were You When We Needed You? Critical Issues in Church-State Relations

From the mid-1960s on few Americans had not heard the name of Madalyn Murray O'Hair. Mrs. O'Hair is an atheist, which does not make her all that unusual. But she is very outspoken about her disbelief in God and her suspicion of organized religion, and that does set her apart from others. Mrs. O'Hair's particular crusade is the strict enforcement of the concept of separation of church and state. She has been quite willing to initiate litigation and to speak out forcefully in order to see that separation is strictly maintained. Because of her willingness to "go public" on this issue so frequently, she is a controversial figure who has been treated shamefully by her detractors. To mention her is a proper introduction to this chapter both because she herself was a public figure during the period covered by this study and because she serves to point out that church-state issues were very much in the news. These issues were not just of intellectual interest, but rather had very practical implications for churches and other religious institutions in America, as they still do.

• *The Concept of Separation*

The founders of the United States were very much aware of the history of religious as well as political tyranny. Of course, the two were related, for in the history of the western world religion and government had typically been united. In that kind of union of church and state, heresy had been a political crime and the favored religion had received financial and political benefits from the state. To the framers of the Constitution that was an unacceptable situation, and they resolved that it should not exist in the new nation. Yet they apparently agreed that the matter of religious freedom was best left to the level of state authority, for in the original Constitution religion is mentioned in only one place. Article VI reads: "No religious Test shall ever be required as a Qualification to any Office or public Trust under the United States." This was a great advance toward religious freedom, since in most of the American colonies one was politically disenfranchised if he were not a member of the colony's established church. In the new nation political office was independent of one's religious belief or the lack of it.

However, many people were concerned that the Constitution was not specific enough about the rights due to the citizens and the individual states of the new nation and demanded that the lawmakers specify those rights. In 1791 a series of constitutional amendments, popularly known as the Bill of Rights, was ratified. The first two phrases of the First Amendment read: "Congress shall make no law respecting an establishment of religion, or prohibiting the free exercise thereof." These words provide for separation of church and state in the United States. Yet throughout most of our history it was assumed by most Americans that the religion clauses of the First Amendment applied only to the federal government. Indeed, in at least three states there was still an established church for some time after the ratification of the First Amendment. However, that assumption was changed by subsequent events in American history. In 1868, in the aftermath of the Civil War, the Fourteenth Amendment to the Constitution was ratified. One of the phrases of Section I of that amendment is: "Nor shall any State deprive any person of life, liberty, or property, without due process of law." In this century the courts have "incorporated" the First Amendment into the Fourteenth. That is, one of the liberties guaranteed to the citizens of states by the Fourteenth Amendment is the religious freedom articulated in the First Amendment. Consequently, it is now a settled point of law that the guarantees of the separation of church and state and religious freedom apply to local and state governments as well as to the federal government.

Although there is still some debate and disagreement as to the meaning of the First Amendment, as there is on all great philosophical principles, its meaning is commonly assumed. The establishment clause does not mean just that government may not show favoritism to only one religion but may aid all equally; rather it means that government must be neutral in matters of religion, neither aiding nor hindering religion or nonreligion. It means that a person may be religious in any way that he or she wants. One may hold any religious belief, or may ignore religion altogether, without government interference. The free exercise clause means that not only may a person believe as he or she chooses, but that one's beliefs may be put into action. Freedom of religion is not a matter of being able to believe whatever one wants, so long as he or she does nothing about it. One is guaranteed the right to allow religion to be the basis of one's behavior in public as well as in private. However, there is the limitation that governmental authorities may prohibit or curtail religious activity if that activity is harmful to others or to the moral fabric of society. The best way to illustrate these principles is to examine some decisions of the Supreme Court, which is the final arbiter, in "real life," of First Amendment questions.

• *Blue Laws and State-Required Theism*

In the 1960s and 1970s the Supreme Court faced important religious liberty questions. In fact, some principles were articulated by the Court during those years that are likely to influence church-state issues indefinitely. The first such issue to come before the Court in the 1960s was that of enforcement of Sunday closing laws. Those who challenged such laws argued that they have the effect of giving government support to observance of the Christian day of worship, consequently violating the establishment clause. In a case in which some merchants who had been arrested for selling prohibited items on Sunday made that argument,[1] the Court disagreed. Although the Court acknowledged that the Sunday laws had originally had a religious purpose—to protect the Christian day of worship from profanation—it held that they do not any longer. Now their purpose is to provide people an opportunity for a uniform day of

---

[1]*McGowan v. Maryland*, 366 U.S. 420 (1961). In reading legal citations, the letters in the middle refer to the bound volumes in which the case is reported. In the case of Supreme Court decisions, the "U.S." stands for *United States Reports*. The number to the left designates the volume in which the case is found, the number to the right is the first page of the case.

rest from their labors, a legitimate concern of the state in its public welfare policy. The laws are not unconstitutional and states or communities may have them for the welfare of their constituents.

In a separate case,[2] some Orthodox Jews claimed that the Sunday laws not only violated the establishment clause, but the free exercise clause as well. That is, not only did they give government sanction to the Christian day of worship, but they caused Sabbatarians (those who worship on Saturday rather than Sunday) economic disadvantage because of their religious beliefs. Sabbatarians were required by law to close their shops on Sunday; they were required by their religion to close their shops on Saturday. But their Christian or secular competitors could keep their shops open on Saturday, thus losing only one day of business instead of two. Consequently, the Sunday laws had the effect of putting the Sabbatarians at an economic disadvantage because of their religious practices, a violation of the free exercise clause. The Court responded by again saying that the Sunday laws were valid as a part of the government's public welfare concern. Furthermore, the laws did not prohibit Sabbatarians from practicing their religion, they just made it more expensive. Thus the laws were valid under the free exercise clause as well. Periodically, since these decisions, Sunday laws have been challenged in various courts around the country. But the challenges have generally been unsuccessful because the precedents established in these 1961 cases still stand.

In that same year the Court decided, in *Torcaso v. Watkins*[3] that government may not deny public office to atheists. The Maryland Constitution required that one declare a belief in God as a condition for public office in the state. The Supreme Court held that such a law was a violation of the establishment clause because it accorded believers a privilege denied to nonbelievers.

• *Public School Prayers*

One of the most volatile church-state issues of the 1960s and 1970s involved the question of state-mandated prayer and/or Bible reading in

---

[2]*Braunfeld v. Brown*, 366 U.S. 599 (1961).

[3]367 U.S. 488 (1961).

public schools. The controversy burst upon the public's awareness after two Supreme Court decisions of 1962 and 1963. In the 1962 case, *Engel v. Vitale*[4] the New York Board of Regents, which had regulatory authority over the state's public school system, had composed a prayer to be used in an effort to promote moral and spiritual training in the schools. The attempt had been made to write a prayer that would be nonsectarian enough not to offend anyone. The prayer was: "Almighty God, we acknowledge our dependence upon Thee, and we beg Thy blessings upon us, our parents, our teachers and our country." Local school districts had the option as to whether they would use the prayer, but if it were adopted, its recitation was to be required at the beginning of each school day. The Board of Education of New Hyde Park decided to use the prayer. The parents of several students filed suit, claiming that the prayer was a violation of the establishment clause.

The Supreme Court agreed with the plaintiffs. A state agency had written a prayer and a state law required that it should be recited in the public schools. The program was clearly a violation of the establishment clause, which prohibits government sponsorship of religion. The law did have a provision that any student who had objections to the saying of the prayer could be excused from the exercise. But this loophole was not enough to save the program because, according to the Court, the mere enactment of a law which puts governmental sponsorship or force behind a religious practice makes that law a violation of the establishment clause. To hammer home the point, the Court said that at the very least the establishment clause means that it is not the business of government to compose official prayers to be said by any of the American people.

So much for state-written prayers. But in 1963 the Court dealt with the question of religous observances in the public schools again, this time in a much more comprehensive case. In *Abington Township School District v. Schempp*[5] the Court dealt with laws that mandated the saying of the Lord's Prayer and/or the reading of ten verses from the Bible as a part of the daily opening exercises in the public school. As in the pre-

---

[4]370 U.S. 421 (1962).

[5]374 U.S. 203 (1963). This is the case in which Mrs. O'Hair was involved. She was known then as Madalyn Murray and her case was called *Murray v. Curlett*. It was combined with *Schempp* and heard at the same time.

vious case, the religious exercises were required, but an objecting student could be excused from participation. The Court found that the requirement of prayers and/or Bible reading was unconstitutional as a violation of the establishment clause.

In deciding this case, the Court articulated some new criteria or tests for adjudicating establishment clause cases. In order for a law to be declared constitutional under the establishment clause, it must have both a secular purpose and the primary effect of neither advancing nor hindering religion. That is, the first test of a law is that its intent must be secular. The second test is that even if the intent of a law is secular, its implementation or enforcement must neither advance nor hinder religion. Prayer and Bible reading in the public schools failed both the tests. The Court found that because both prayer and Bible reading were devotional exercises, the law requiring them in the public schools did not have a secular purpose. Rather, it had the purpose of promoting religious activity. In its implementation the law had the primary effect of advancing religion. This government promotion of religious activity was the very kind of thing the establishment clause was designed to prevent. Consequently, the requirement of prayer and Bible reading by law in the public schools was unacceptable public policy.

After the Court's decision in *Engel*, there had been a great cry of protest across the land. The principal charge had been that the Court had effectively shown hostility to religion and had, indeed, established a religion of secularism. Consequently, in *Schempp* the Court went to great lengths to try to show that its decision did not amount to judicial hostility to religion. Most specifically, the Court pointed out that the Constitution does not prohibit the teaching of religion in public school classrooms as a part of a school's regular academic offerings. The distinction was made between religion as devotional exercise and religion as instruction. The first was unconstitutional, but the second was acceptable. So long as religion was taught in such a way that it did not become a matter of worship or evangelism, but rather to show its place in history, art, or literature, such teaching would be understood to have a secular purpose and not to have the primary effect of advancing religion.

In spite of the Court's effort in *Schempp* to show that it was not antagonistic to religion, that message did not get through to a significant portion of the population. Echoing the anguish expressed after *Engel*, a new wave of protest swept across the nation. The attitude about what had been done is best summed up in the newspaper headline: "Court takes God out of the classroom"—that charge, of course, was completely false. Efforts immediately were begun to nullify or to circumvent the decision. Within two years after the *Schempp* decision 145 bills had been introduced in the U.S. House of Representatives and 40 in the Senate in order to amend the Constitution to permit voluntary prayers in public schools. When those initial efforts were unsuccessful the protest subsided for a while, only to be revived again late in 1971, when a constitutional amendment bill was narrowly defeated in the House. Since then there have been intermittent attempts to revive a prayer bill in Congress, although until the late 1970s these seem to have been rather halfhearted. But at that time, as religious conservatives became increasingly politicized, these efforts to overturn the Court's prayer decisions through an amendment to the Constitution were revived with a fervor reminiscent of the mid-1960s.[6] At that same time, since efforts to amend the Constitution had been unsuccessful, Senator Jesse Helms of North Carolina began an alternative approach to try to restore prayer to the public schools. In Article III, Section 2 the Constitution mentions several categories of cases appropriate to the federal judiciary. It then reads: "In all the other Cases before mentioned, the supreme Court shall have appellate Jurisdiction, both as to Law and Fact, *with such Exceptions, and under such Regulations as the Congress shall make*" (italics added). Senator Helms's idea was to employ the regulatory power of Congress mentioned in Article III to remove all cases involving prayer in the public schools from the jurisdiction of the federal courts so that such controversies could only be tried in state courts, closer to the will of the people. Some people supported such a plan enthusiastically, others opposed it as a serious threat to the Bill of Rights (which had never in American history been modified in such a way) and, Article III notwithstanding, as being an unconstitutional violation of the concept of the separation of powers. Most opponents of legally imposing prayer on the public schools (and there were many) were very concerned about these legislative efforts as the 1970s ended.

---

[6]On 18 May 1982 President Reagan sent a proposal to Congress initiating the process of trying to amend the Constitution to permit voluntary prayer in government buildings. This is the first time that a President in the 1960s or 1970s had even supported such an attempt, much less initiated the legislation.

• *Religion and Taxation*

Another church-state issue of major proportions was taxation of religious institutions. In 1970 the Supreme Court decided *Walz v. Tax Commission of the City of New York*,[7] a case challenging tax exemptions for property used for religious purposes. The Court found that such exemptions are constitutional because churches are not singled out for the exemptions that are also available to schools, hospitals, museums, and other charitable or cultural improvement institutions. Tax exemptions for religious property have existed for more than 200 years without having led to an establishment of religion. Most importantly, to levy a tax on religious property would compel governmental officials to become more involved with religion, but maintaining the exemption would avoid that excessive entanglement.

The *Schempp* and *Walz* cases have had an impact far beyond the specific issues with which they dealt. The secular purpose, primary effect, and excessive entanglement tests have formed the guidelines courts have used to decide all subsequent establishment clause cases. A law may be declared unconstitutional if it runs afoul of any one of the three tests; it must pass them all to meet establishment clause requirements.

The Supreme Court dealt with one other tax case in *Flast v. Cohen*.[8] Prior to that case the assumption had been that taxpayers did not have standing to file suit in federal courts. The concept of "standing" defines whether or not one has the status to be a legitimate litigant before a court. Since the judicial system is designed to solve controversies between parties, each of whom will be affected by the result of the case, in order to be a party to a suit one must show the court that the interest he or she presents is substantial and legally protected and that it has been injured or is in danger of injury. Taxpayer suits had not been allowed in federal courts because each individual taxpayer's contribution to the entire federal budget is so small that it was assumed that a single taxpayer could not show personal injury from the way that the government spent its money. But in *Flast v. Cohen* some taxpayers sued over the use of fed-

---

[7]397 U.S. 664 (1970).

[8]392 U.S. 83 (1968).

eral money in aid programs for church-related schools. The Supreme Court ruled that such taxpayers had standing to sue. If a plaintiff could show that tax money was actually used to finance a program that arguably was in violation of the establishment clause of the First Amendment, then that plaintiff would have standing to bring a taxpayer's suit. This was an important case, for it opened the doors to federal courts for many of the decisions regarding government aid to church-related schools in the 1970s.

Throughout the 1970s there were a number of other dimensions to the issue of the taxation of religious institutions, most of which had not been decided upon by the Supreme Court by the end of the decade. The Tax Reform Act of 1969 impinged on religious institutions in at least two ways. Prior to this legislation religious institutions not only did not have to pay income tax on the income derived directly from their religious activities, such as the contributions of members, they also did not have to pay income taxes on income derived from activities other than their religious mission, such as profit from a radio station or apartment house. This statute changed that. After 1 January 1976 churches were subject to taxation on their "unrelated income." However, because that was the case and because there were certain conditions that made even unrelated income exempt, the Internal Revenue Service required information forms to be filed, forms that described gross income and disbursements and whatever other information the IRS might require for the purpose of collecting taxes. However, "churches, their integrated auxiliaries, conventions or associations of churches" were exempt from filing the forms. This put the IRS in the position of defining "integrated auxiliaries, conventions or associations of churches," and the religious mission of churches in order to determine what agencies were subject to the information forms and possible taxation.

A number of denominations became alarmed at the potential for church-state violation that this provision presented. They claimed that a government agency is incompetent to define the religious mission of a church or to determine whether a particular agency has the function of a church. Churches insisted that for the state to define religious organizations would promote excessive entanglement between church and state and violate the establishment clause. In spite of church protests, government agencies persisted in defining religion and religious activity. Not only was the IRS involved, but also the National Labor Relations

Board, Office of Economic Opportunity, and other federal agencies. Consequently, as the 1970s came to an end, churches all across the land were becoming increasingly concerned about governmental intrusion into church affairs. Churches met in conferences to discuss how to deal with the situation and church bureaucracies gave increasing amounts of time to ways of coping with government interference into precincts that had formerly been protected by church-state separation.

One aspect of the government intervention controversy was resolved in 1979 in *National Labor Relations Board v. Catholic Bishop of Chicago*.[9] When unions sought to represent lay teachers in schools controlled by the Catholic church, the NLRB ordered representation elections. School authorities claimed that the NLRB lacked jurisdiction, for if it had jurisdiction this would have the effect of impermissibly entangling government with religion. When elections were held and the parochial schools refused to bargain with the unions chosen by the lay teachers, the NLRB found the schools guilty of unfair labor practices. When the schools challenged the NLRB's order to bargain, a federal court of appeals and the Supreme Court found in favor of the schools on the grounds that, in the National Labor Relations Act, Congress had not intended for church-operated schools to be covered by the statute. The schools' contention that the NLRB did not have jurisdiction over them was upheld. However, many other points of contention between religious agencies and government entities had not been settled by the end of the 1970s and that decade ended with churches sorely afraid of government intervention in their affairs.

One other illustration of government intervention in religious affairs was the case of Bob Jones University. A fundamentalist Christian school in the strictest sense of the word, the administration of the university held the position that interracial dating and marriage are forbidden by the Bible. In order to forestall such an event among its students, prior to 1971 Bob Jones admitted no black students at all. After that date, first married black students were admitted and, later, unmarried blacks. However, when unmarried blacks were added to the student body, rules were introduced that prohibited interracial dating and marriage, upon penalty of being expelled. Yet since the Civil Rights Act of 1964, public

---

[9]440 U.S. 490 (1979).

policy had been that racially segregated or discriminatory schools, including church-related colleges, should lose federal benefits and/or tax exemption. In line with that mandate, in the early 1970s the IRS revoked the tax-exempt status of Bob Jones University because its policy toward black students did not conform to public policy—that is, it first excluded black students and, later, did not treat them equally. The university sued to recover its tax-exempt status, arguing that its treatment of blacks was a matter of deeply and sincerely held religious beliefs and thus was protected from government meddling by the religion clauses of the First Amendment. Another way to articulate the college's contention is that government control over admissions policies of church schools deprives such institutions of the right to make decisions that very likely rest on theological or ecclesiastical bases. Such government policy negates the judgment of a church college regarding the best means to accomplish the religious goals the college has set for itself.

This sticky issue had not been settled one way or the other by the end of the 1970s, indeed, there had been conflicting court decisions on the case. Those aware of the conflict awaited a final resolution of the question with a sense of fascination, for they knew that however the issue was decided, it would have great implications for both public policy and religious institutions.[10]

Section 501(c)(3) of the Internal Revenue Code, a section that has to do with tax exemptions for charitable institutions, provides that an otherwise qualifying institution may not enjoy an exemption from income tax if it devotes a substantial part of its activities to "carrying on propaganda, or otherwise attempting, to influence legislation" or if it participates in or intervenes in "any political campaigns on behalf of any candidate for public office." In 1965 the IRS, invoking this part of Sec-

---

[10]The Supreme Court agreed to hear the Bob Jones University case early in 1983. On May 3 of that year the Court decided against the University, holding that an institution must be in conformity with public policy as defined by Congress to receive a tax exemption. The University's religious freedom argument was brushed aside by the Court, which said: "Denial of tax benefits will inevitably have a substantial impact on the operation of private religious schools, but will not prevent these schools from observing their religious tenets. . . . [G]overnmental interest substantially outweighs whatever burden denial of tax benefits places on petitioners' exercise of their religious beliefs." 103 S. Ct. 2017 (1983).

tion 501(c)(3), denied the income tax exemption of evangelist Billy James Hargis's Christian Echoes National Ministry. Hargis was a vehemently vocal fundamentalist preacher who opposed virtually every "liberal" cause and institution in the country. In 1964 he implored the listeners to his radio ministry to support the candidacy of Sen. Barry Goldwater for the presidency. He also recommended support of certain conservative candidates for Congress. Hargis's organization also contributed some of its own funds to the same candidates. When the IRS denied his tax exemption, Hargis sued the government in *Christian Echoes National Ministry v. United States*,[11] claiming that these political views were part of his religious beliefs. It is part of the Christian's duty, he argued, to combat "godless Communism." Hargis concluded that his advocacy of certain political policies was guaranteed to him by the religion clauses of the First Amendment. Furthermore, the case raised the issue of whether the government has the right to set limits on the activities and speech of religious institutions as they address public life, activities that they see as part of their ministry. A federal court of appeals held that the prohibitions of Section 501(c)(3) did not deny Hargis's right to practice his religion as he wished. It did not deal with the second question, which is the more important one. The Supreme Court refused to hear the case so, as the 1970s ended, religious groups all along the theological spectrum were uneasy as to how much they could exercise their ministries in the public arena and still be able to retain their tax exemptions. They were also frustrated by the increased role the government played in defining what a religious ministry is and what its scope may be—an unconstitutional activity of government, from the perspective of most churches and synagogues.

Another church-state conflict involving taxation emerged in the mid-1970s; the phenomenon known as "mail-order ministries." Since Section 501(c)(3) permits churches to be exempt from income taxes, some people got the idea that if an individual declared his or her home to be a church and became ordained so that he or she could be the minister of the church, then one could avoid paying personal income taxes. Not suprisingly, that idea rapidly gained popularity. The problem was:

---

[11]470 F.2d 849 (1972); 404 U.S. 561 (1972).

if I am an airline pilot or a plumber or a business executive, how can I also be ordained to be a minister? The answer came when some churches began to sell ordinations. The most visible of these were the Universal Life Church (this church did not sell the ordinations, but rather gave them away to whoever asked), the Basic Bible Church, and the Life Science Church. Whoever paid a fee (it could run as high as $1,500) could be ordained "for tax purposes" and thousands of people did. One variation on the theme was to declare a "vow of poverty," that is, not only to declare one's home a church but to give all worldly possessions to that church and then have the church pay one's living expenses. Whatever the technique, the point was to avoid paying income taxes. In the late 1970s the IRS came to realize that millions of dollars of tax money were being kept from the government in this way and the agency began to search out these "ministers" and to prosecute them for tax evasion. The bases of the prosecution are found in Section 501(c)(3), which requires tax exempt churches to be "organized and operated exclusively for religious purposes" and holds that churches may be exempt organizations only if "no part of the net earnings of which inures to the benefit of any private shareholder or individual." On the basis that these self-generated churches were not organized and operated for exclusively religious purposes and especially that the proceeds of the churches did benefit private individuals, the government was routinely winning mail-order ministry cases in the courts. However, the issue did raise the troublesome issue once more of the government's power to define the nature and role of a religious institution.

• *Religious Objection to Military Service*

Apart from the sensitive area of taxation of religious institutions, the Supreme Court confronted yet another church-state issue—this one raised by the war in Vietnam: the scope of permissible conscientious objection to military service. There had long been clear statements in the law that persons with religious objections to military service were to be exempt. In the 1960s the law said that such exemptions were to be based on "religious training and belief" stemming from "an individual's belief in a relation to a Supreme Being involving duties superior to those arising from any human relation. . . ." But, in response to the Vietnam war, there were some young men who claimed conscientious objector status but did not have a traditional belief in a personal God. In *United States v. Seeger*[12] the Court was willing to grant conscientious objector status even to those who did not have conventional religious beliefs. Arguing that Congress had used the words "Supreme Being" rather than "God" in the law in order to embrace all religions, the Court said that an unconventional religious belief would suffice to gain CO status if the belief "is sincere and meaningful [and] occupies a place in the life of its possessor parallel to that filled by the orthodox belief in God of one who clearly qualifies for the exemption." The effect of this case was to broaden the boundaries of legally recognized objections to war and, more than in any other case of the era, to come close to a judicial definition of religion.

The war in Vietnam was very unpopular with a large segment of the population, principally because it was waged without having been officially declared by Congress and because it was regarded by some people as an unjust intrusion into what was essentially a civil war in southeast Asia. Consequently, it is not surprising that some draft-age men tried to obtain conscientious objector status in order to not have to fight in that war, even though they would be willing, under different circumstances, to bear arms on behalf of the United States. However, the selective service law said that for a person to be eligible to receive conscientious objector status he had to have religious objections "to participation in war in any form." In *Gillette v. United States*[13] the Court upheld that provision of the law, deciding that one could not pick and choose his wars. Even though one of the plaintiffs was a Catholic, whose church historically had made a theological distinction between "just" and "unjust" wars, whereas other theological traditions had not made such a distinction, the Court claimed that its ruling was not preferring one church or religious tradition over another. The Court decreed that it was more evenhanded to treat all religions the same and it better served the nation's need for fighting personnel to uphold the law that a citizen must object to participation in all wars or be willing to fight in all wars.

• *Government Aid To Parochial Schools*

Another controversy the Court was forced to confront extensively in the 1960s and 1970s, stimulating passionate feelings in a large portion

---

[12]380 U.S. 163 (1965).

[13]401 U.S. 437 (1971).

of the population, was the issue of government aid to church-related schools. At both the elementary and secondary levels, there were many parochial schools around the country; most of them, then, were Roman Catholic. After the Civil Rights Act of 1964 and the school prayer decisions of the Supreme Court, an increasing number of Protestant church schools were founded. By the end of the 1970s it was claimed that three of these Christian schools were being created every week. Although many people believed that some of these schools were "segregation academies," the announced reason for the creation of these schools was that the public schools had declined in quality and that they reflected too much the moral relativism that permeated society. Then, too, Christian schools could freely conduct worship and teach their pupils theology.

In many cases the churches that sponsored these schools petitioned legislatures to pass laws that enabled parochial schools to receive some form of state and/or federal aid. The principal reasons for this were both practical and philosophical. The practical reason was simply the escalation of the costs of running a parochial school. This was particularly true for the Catholic church, since, after the Second Vatican Council, many nuns had renounced their vows or moved into activist roles other than teaching. Furthermore, there was a dramatic drop in the number of women entering religious orders. The pool of nuns available to teach in the church's parochial schools shrank drastically. The church was faced with hiring lay teachers to fill those slots once held by nuns, and lay teachers demanded much higher salaries than nuns, who typically had taken vows of poverty.

The philosophical reason was that parents who send their children to parochial schools are, in essence, taxed twice, once to support the public schools and once to pay the tuition of the school to which they have chosen to send their children. The argument was that the parochial school ought to get some form of government aid to meet some of its expenses so that it could lower part of this double burden endured by tuition-paying parents. Furthermore, advocates of state aid to parochial schools pointed out that those schools benefit society in much the same way as public schools do, namely, by helping to produce an educated citizenry.

Since that is a public benefit, the schools ought to receive some public money to underwrite their role in it.

From the mid-1960s on numerous pieces of legislation were approved granting some form of government aid to church-related schools, although very little of the aid was by direct monetary grant. Those who challenged these programs in the courts were, in nearly every case, taxpayers who sued under the expanded guidelines for taxpayers' suits allowed under *Flast v. Cohen*. In these cases, the Court considered several types of aid.

The Court approved lending of state-purchased textbooks to students in parochial schools. These books were not to be about religion, but rather about secular subjects usually studied in the public schools. The Court approved this type of aid under the "child benefit" theory, reasoning that the aid was going to the students, not to the school or to the church that sponsored the school, and that such programs have a secular purpose, given the content of the books.

The Court refused to approve a salary supplement program for teachers in parochial schools. The plan was that state money should be given to church schools to supplement the salaries of their teachers and to bring them up to higher standards. The supplements were to be given only to teachers of nonreligious subjects, who had to sign a statement that they would not inject religion into their classes in any way. The Court found the plan unconstitutional under the excessive entanglement test, because it would require continual surveillance of the teachers by state authorities to make sure that the teachers receiving the supplements in fact did not teach any religion.

A program designed to provide government funds for the maintenance and repair of parochial school buildings, except those explicitly used for religious teaching or worship, was struck down on the ground that it had the primary effect of advancing the religious mission of the schools. Such a program effectively subsidized the religious activities of the schools and thus was unconstitutional.

The primary effect test was also used to strike down a program of tuition reimbursements for lower income people. The idea was that poor people were effectively prevented from sending their children to parochial schools because of the high tuition such schools charge. If the state would provide money to make up the difference between what the poor were able to pay and the amount of tuition charged, then the poor would be able to exercise that option. The Court found that this had the impermissible primary effect of advancing religion through state funds; that is, the state was helping to provide an audience for religious schools.

The same program offered assistance to those of middle income to enable them to send their children to parochial schools—a tuition tax credit plan. Parents who were in the middle-income brackets could take a credit on their state income taxes that could be used to supplement their tuition payments. But the Court also declared this plan to be unconstitutional on the grounds that its primary effect was to advance religion, in that it encouraged parents to send their children to a church school by the indirect payment of state money.

Some states passed legislation providing for counseling and other psychological services for parochial school students, paid for with state funds. The Court declared such programs to be invalid under the excessive entanglement test. That is, even though the principal function of the professionals dealing with the students was to provide psychological therapy, the state would have to monitor them continually to make sure that no religious teaching would creep into their dealings with the students, which would have the effect of the state's paying for religious teaching. The surveillance necessary to prevent that from happening was itself an entanglement made impermissible by the establishment clause.

When a state wanted to purchase instructional materials, primarily audio-visual and laboratory equipment, for use in parochial schools, the Supreme Court invalidated the plan. The rationale was that even though the equipment obviously had no religious content, nonetheless religion so permeated the teaching in the church-related schools that the instructional equipment would have the primary effect of advancing the religious mission of the schools.

On the other hand, the Court was willing to approve a program of state financed testing for students in parochial schools, provided that the tests were state-prepared standardized tests concerning secular subjects and not teacher-prepared tests, into which some religious content might creep.

Since psychological therapy had earlier been struck down by the Court, a program was developed that would not provide therapy at all, but only diagnosis of speech, hearing, and psychological disabilities. The Supreme Court approved that program, with the provision that the physicians or other diagnosticians would not be employees of the parochial school. They would be strictly private professionals whose services would be provided to the parochial schools and whose fees would be paid by the state.

A different therapeutic services plan was tried, this time with the specific characteristic that the therapists helping parochial school students would be employees of the state or private therapists under contract and that they would do their therapy in locations away from the parochial school property. The Court approved this plan, finding that it had sufficient safeguards so that it would not amount to use of state funds to teach religion.

Finally, a program was developed whereby the state would provide funds for buses and other transportation to instructional sites away from the parochial school. But because the plan allowed the parochial school teacher not only to go along on the trips, but also to choose the sites that would be visited, the Court struck it down as a violation of both the primary effect and the excessive entanglement tests for interpreting the establishment clause. There was too much opportunity for the state to be subsidizing religious teaching in such an enterprise.

In summary, although there was a plethora of plans to provide government aid to parochial schools, the Supreme Court took a very restrictive view and approved only those proposals that could be demonstrated to be strictly secular in their impact. Textbooks in secular subjects, the administration of tests on secular subjects, and diagnostic and therapeutic services were allowed so long as those were done by nonparochial school personnel and, in the case of the therapy, away from the parochial campus. Although these decisions caused considerable consternation in the religious school community, they were consistent with the concept that the state should not subsidize or promote religion.

When one turns to the issue of government aid to church-related colleges and universities, however, the attitude of the Court was much different. In a case in which federal aid was to be provided to colleges for the construction of buildings that were not to be used for instruction in religion or for worship, the Court approved. In a much broader program in which funds were made available to church-related colleges not only for construction but for the support of virtually any program except instruction specifically in religion, the Court again applied its three-part test and found the plan to be constitutional.

The reason that the Court was much more lenient with church-related colleges than with their counterparts at the elementary and secondary level is that the justices perceived at least three significant differences between the levels. One is that usually colleges are not as permeated with religion as are lower-level schools. Even though a college is sponsored by a church, it is not as likely to advocate a particular theological viewpoint or to promote a religious mission. Second, most college faculties take very seriously the concept of academic freedom, not only for themselves but also for their students. That is, faculty members generally believe that at the college level, students need to have the freedom to be exposed to diverse views in the subjects they are studying. Third, the students themselves are more sophisticated and not as impressionable as students in lower schools. Consequently, they are not as subject to religious indoctrination as are younger students. For these reasons, the Court held that state programs that might be unconstitutional at the elementary or secondary level are acceptable at the university level.

While it was somewhat less vitriolic than the protest that arose over the Court's prayer decisions, there was also continuing controversy about the decisions concerning aid to parochial schools. This disagreement with the Court was most prominent in the attempt to get indirect financing of church schools through tuition tax credits. Although the Supreme Court had declared such tax credits unconstitutional in *Committee for Public Education and Religious Liberty v. Nyquist*,[14] Senators Daniel Patrick Moynihan of New York and Robert Packwood of Oregon repeatedly introduced a bill in Congress that would provide for such credits on the federal income tax for parents who sent their children to church-related schools, kindergarten through college. In spite of support for the bill by the Catholic church and other proprietors of parochial schools, by the end of 1983 it had not yet become law.[15]

• *The Free Exercise of Religion*

Virtually all the cases or issues reviewed so far were decided under the establishment clause of the First Amendment. But there were also

[14]413 U.S. 756 (1973).

[15]In 1982 President Reagan endorsed legislation for tuition tax credits.

some important developments in interpreting the free exercise clause. The chief of these was the case of *Sherbert v. Verner*.[16] Ms. Sherbert was a Seventh-day Adventist, a religion that prohibits work on Saturday. She was employed in the textile mills in South Carolina when her work week was changed to include Saturday. When she could not work out other work schedules to be off on Saturday, she quit her job. When she applied for state unemployment compensation, it was denied on the grounds that she had failed without good cause to accept work available to her. So, the question before the Court was whether a person could be denied unemployment compensation if he or she lost the job because of refusal to work on his or her day of worship. The Court responded in the negative. The free exercise of religion is a precious liberty in our tradition, said the Court, and one should not have to choose between economic survival and practicing one's religion.[17]

In deciding this case in favor of the Sabbatarian, the Court articulated a new test for deciding free exercise clause cases. The test is best expressed in a series of questions: (1) In the case before the court, has the government imposed a burden on the free exercise of the plaintiff's religion? Related to that question are two auxiliary questions: (a) Does the religion demand the kind of behavior in question and, (b) Is the plaintiff engaged in good faith in that religion? If the answer to this set of inquiries is negative, the case is over and the plaintiff has lost. If the answer is affirmative, the consideration must go on to the second major question. (2) Does a compelling state interest justify the burden placed on the exercise of religion? The state's interest must be of the greatest importance to take precedence over the free exercise of an individual's religion. If the answer to this question is negative, the plaintiff has won the case. If the answer is affirmative, the inquiry goes to the third question. (3) Does the state have an alternative way of achieving its goals

---

[16]374 U.S. 398 (1963).

[17]In a later case, *TWA v. Hardison*, 432 U.S. 63 (1977), the Court retreated from this ruling to a degree. Under the Civil Rights Act of 1964 an employer need not endure "undue hardship" to make "reasonable accommodations" to an employee's religion. The Court ruled that the airline was obligated neither to modify a Sabbatarian's work week nor to allow him to exchange work days with a nonSabbatarian employee, even if it meant that, absent these accomodations, the employee had to quit his job in order to continue to practice his religion.

rather than infringing on the free exercise of the individual's religion? If the answer is negative, the state has won its case. If the answer is affirmative, the state must adopt the alternative method and cease its assault on the plaintiff's religious exercise; the plaintiff has won the case.

This test of the free exercise clause was illustrated again in *Wisconsin v. Yoder*.[18] The Old Order Amish is a religious sect that believes that the "world," society, is completely evil. In fact, the Amish are a consistent example of the sect type that feels so threatened by the evil world around it that it tries to withdraw and maintain as much distinctiveness from the world as possible. As a part of trying to preserve a holy life-style from the cunning of the devil as he works in society, the Amish refuse to send their children to school for formal education beyond the eighth grade. They are afraid that if their children are exposed to the knowledge of the world beyond the level of education in the basics, the "three r's," they will be contaminated. But, in Wisconsin, the compulsory school attendance laws required children to go to school until they were 16 years old. The Amish objected to that because that would take their children beyond the eighth grade.

In deciding this case, the Supreme Court agreed that the state had placed a burden on the religious freedom of the Amish parents and children. Second, the Court recognized that Wisconsin had a strong interest in the education of children since an educated citizenry is so important to the welfare of society. But the Court ruled that that interest was not compelling enough to override the constitutionally guaranteed free exercise rights of the Amish. Consequently, the Amish were exempted from the compulsory school attendance law to the degree that they could end their children's formal education after the eighth grade.

A final case to be decided by the Supreme Court in the 1970s, also under the free exercise clause, was *McDaniel v. Paty*,[19] which dealt with Tennessee's law prohibiting ordained ministers from serving in the state legislature. Actually, the case came up over Rev. McDaniel's eligibility to serve in a state constitutional convention, but the eligibility requirements for serving in the convention were the same as for serving in the state legislature. The state Constitution, in the name of preserving the

---

[18]406 U.S. 205 (1972).

[19]435 U.S. 618 (1978).

separation of church and state, prohibited ordained ministers from serving in those political roles. The Court decided, however, that Tennessee's law was unconstitutional. In terms of the free exercise clause test, the law placed a burden on McDaniel's religious freedom in the sense that it required him to give up his rights as a citizen to serve as a legislator or to forego his role as a minister of the gospel. The Court determined that the state's interest was not sufficient to deny legitimately ordained ministers from serving in legislative roles. The rationale for the law was that it would preserve the separation of church and state. But the Court pointed out that in other states (Tennessee was the only state to have such a law) and at the federal level ministers had historically served in legislatures without having violated the prohibition against an establishment of religion. This argument from history showed that Tennessee's provision was an unnecessary burden on the religious liberty of ministers, that it was guarding against an abuse of ministerial roles that actually did not exist.

To summarize the activities of the Supreme Court in church-state cases during the 1960s and 1970s, it was a very important time. The Court handed down some decisions that had significant impact upon religious activities and that stimulated soul searching and controversy. Among these, of course, were the decisions on prayer and Bible reading as devotional activities in the public schools, followed by the long series of opinions ruling out most forms of government aid to parochial schools.

Of less visibility but of even greater significance were the definite tests formulated by the Court for interpreting both the establishment and the free exercise clauses. These are important because they are used by lower courts in determining the legitimacy or illegitimacy of any law being tried before them in a church-state case. It was in the declaration of these interpretive principles that the church-state decisions of the Court in the 1960s and 1970s are to have the most long-term significance.

• *Rescuing People From Cults*

Another church-state issue of some magnitude, although it was not brought before the Supreme Court, was that of "deprogramming" young people who had joined cult movements. There was an accusation, at least partly true in some cases, that cults "brainwashed" young people, capturing and holding them against their will through some kind of "mind control." While this was seen to be bad for the young people themselves, it had wider repercussions for parents, families, and friends of the cult members. The idea was that these young people could not have voluntarily joined such "offbeat" religious groups, that they surely would not have chosen to desert their families, friends, and careers; rather they must have been forced or tricked into cult membership. Since "nobody in his right mind" would do such a thing, they must not have been rational at the time; they must have been "brainwashed." Since these youth joined and remained in the cults because they were under some kind of spell or other overwhelming influence, extraordinary measures were required and justified in getting them out of the cults and restoring them to their families and a normal role in society. As one response, deprogramming was developed.

Deprogramming may be most simply described as "counter brainwashing." Its goal was to cleanse the cult member's mind of the theology of the cult, his or her loyalty to the cult leader, and any attachment to fellow cult members. Deprogramming was to break the almost mystical spell the cult leader and the group had over an individual, to restore to that person a loyalty to his or her family and its religion (if any), and to enable the cultist to return to life in the mainstream of society. Because the cult had so twisted the mind of its devotee, advocates of deprogramming asserted, their task was not easy and required extraordinary measures. It was not at all uncommon for the person being deprogrammed to be detained in a locked room for several days, sometimes with hands and feet tied. Often one would be denied adequate food and/or sleep until he or she would renounce the cult and give in to the demands and pleadings of parents and deprogrammers. During this time of physical restraint emotional and psychological stress would be built up by the deprogrammer's continuous discrediting, ridiculing, and profaning the cult leader and all he or she represented. The primary aim of the deprogrammer was to show the logical inconsistencies and the ridiculous nature of the cult's beliefs or practices. At the same time, the deprogrammer would try to convince the young person of the truth of his or her inherited religion and how much his or her parents loved him or her. The goal was to win the young person back to home and hearth. The deprogramming would continue until the deprogrammers were convinced that the cult member was "broken" and it was safe to release him or her to freely walk around in society again. The deprogramming procedure was often more extreme and demanding on the young person than the original conversion techniques of the cult that the parents and deprogrammers were attempting to discredit.

Of course, cult members did not often voluntarily subject themselves to that kind of treatment. Consequently, the first act in the deprogramming drama was often a kidnapping or some other kind of entrapment of the cult member. Usually the parents would hire professional deprogrammers, of whom Ted Patrick was the first and most famous. While the deprogrammers remained out of sight, the parents would lure their cult-member child to a prearranged site where he or she would be captured and taken away for the "cure." There are all sorts of accounts of this kind of adventure, from meeting a child at the airport or snatching him or her as he or she walked down a sidewalk to storming into the cult's commune, in each case to take the child away in a speeding car to the place of deprogramming. There were even some instances in which law enforcement personnel were utilized in apprehending the cult member for deprogramming purposes.

Such strong-arm tactics were not satisfactory for several reasons, not the least of which was that they were inefficient (sometimes the cult member did not show up). In addition, such methods often produced psychological trauma in parents who regretted kidnapping and forcibly restraining their own children. So the court proceeding of "conservatorship" became an alternative method of gaining possession of cultist children. Simply put, a conservatorship is an instrument by which a person may take over the assets and responsibilities of a person who becomes senile or in some other way becomes physically or mentally incapacitated so that one cannot administer one's own affairs. The conservator takes responsibility for the administration of those affairs and, often, for the care of the incapacitated individual.

Under the argument that the cult member was no longer mentally competent, because he or she had been brainwashed and was under the intellectual and emotional domination of the cult, the parents went to court and asked the judge to grant that they be the conservators, not so much of their child's assets, but of the child's person. When these requests were granted, the child was placed in the care of the parents for a specified length of time, usually 30 to 60 days. During that time the parents could do whatever they wanted to try to bring their child out of the cult, including the harrassment of deprogramming. It should be noted that the use of the word "child" here does not imply that all the subjects of conservatorship proceedings were minors. There were many instances in which the children were in their mid-twenties or even older.

The principal problem with such procedures is that they may well violate the First Amendment guarantees of religious freedom. They assume that any person who joined one of the cults did so through coercion, rather than voluntarily. There is some evidence that some of the cults did use some high pressure tactics to persuade some people to take up membership in the group. But that is a long way from the presumption that conversions were forced, which was usually the assumption behind the conservatorship proceeding. Furthermore, in such a proceeding the judge was willing to make a judgment about the moral quality of a religion based only on the testimony of anguished parents who were convinced that their children had been victimized. This was true because virtually all conservatorships were granted without the knowledge, much less the testimony, of the cult member in question. The point is that if there was a specific charge of wrongdoing on the part of the cult in reference to the child, that would be a legitimate cause for government intervention. But in these cases the judge simply assumed that since a cult was involved, it had done what the parents said it had done. In that sense the judge made a presumptuous judgment about the relative merit of that particular religious group. There is abundant legal precedent under the establishment clause that says that the government may not evaluate theology, that it may not determine the validity of a religious group. Many believed that the conservatorship procedure to get young people out of cults was a serious violation of our concept of the separation of church and state.

The broader practice of deprogramming also raised serious questions about religious liberty. Kidnapping or entrapment for the purpose of conversion is a violation of the religious liberty of an individual. In this case, the conversion was supposed to be (it did not always work) back to the cult member's former religion or to a religious viewpoint more acceptable to family or friends. The rationale was that the mind of the young person had been captured and that deprogramming was actually restoring freedom of thought and freedom of religion to the individual.

The extreme measure of kidnapping was justified on the basis that the brainwashed individual would not voluntarily come out of the cult. So, repressive measures were legitimate in the name of expanding the cult member's freedom. That is, at best, a dubious argument. It loses even more luster when one considers that the young person might have gone into the cult willingly and voluntarily. In short, the entire concept of deprogramming drew attention to the issue of religious liberty. This country is committed to the free exercise of religion. The concept of deprogramming, except in possibly the most extreme and narrowly defined cases, simply did not allow religious freedom to those who might even find membership in a cult movement meaningful and appealing.

This issue takes on even sharper focus when one realizes that sometimes people who were not even members of cults were subjected to deprogramming. A young man who had entered an Old Catholic monastery in Oklahoma City was lured away and deprogrammed. In another case, two women who had left the Greek Orthodox traditions of their families were deprogrammed, even though at the time they had no religious affiliation at all. It was just that their families wanted them back in the Greek Orthodox way of life. A woman in Canada who had converted to Roman Catholicism was caused to be deprogrammed by her Protestant parents, who wanted her to be a Protestant again. As the 1970s ended, deprogramming was quite frequently undertaken, especially since some professional deprogrammers promoted it in the interest of very high fees. However, many people believed that deprogramming not only had potential for real psychological harm for those subjected to it, but also that it was a violation of the principle of freedom of religion for all.

• *The Electronic Church
and Political Involvement*

In the mid-to-late 1970s another facet to American religion began to attract attention—the electronic church. There was a rapid increase in the number of radio or television ministries in the latter part of the decade. Generally, the thrust of this media ministry was fundamentalist. Of course, religious programs had been on radio and television for some time. In previous decades the majority of religious programs had been provided by mainstream, liberal or middle-of-the-road churches, with few exceptions. For some time the Federal Communications Commission had ruled that stations had to give away a certain amount of time for public service broadcasting and the bulk of religious programs had taken some of that public service time. But in the 1970s some fundamentalist media preachers became aggressive and forced the more liberal programs off the air or to less desirable times by buying the best times. Radio and television stations could hardly be blamed if they preferred to receive money for the time religious programs used rather than give it away; hence many of the conservative ministers became "prime time preachers." As they became so aggressive and dominated so much of the air time, they became part of the resurgence of conservatism that was the emerging characteristic of religion in the 1970s.

Not all of these programs were of the same type. Television ministries attracted most attention and were usually what people had in mind when they spoke of the electronic church. Some of the programs were simply telecasts of regular church services, like "The Old-Time Gospel Hour" of Rev. Jerry Falwell. This program was a broadcast of the 11 a.m. Sunday worship service from the Thomas Road Baptist Church in Lynchburg, Virginia. Another church service program was that of Ernest Angley, minister of Grace Cathedral in Akron, Ohio. Angley added to his program a videotape of a few minutes of a healing service from one of his many crusades around the country. This was perhaps the thing that distinguished Angley's program from the rest, since he was about the only one of the old-time healers left since Katherine Kuhlman died and Oral Roberts changed the direction of his television ministry. Another major church service program was Robert Schuller's "Hour of Power" broadcast, prior to September 1980, from the Garden Grove Community Church and, since that time, from his new Crystal Cathedral in Garden Grove, California. Schuller, the only nonfundamentalist of the major television preachers, preached "possibility thinking," a kind of theological and psychological assurance strongly reminiscent of Norman Vincent Peale's "power of positive thinking." To say that the programs of these ministers were only telecasts of regular worship services is not to imply that they were lacking in the kind of eye-catching, entertaining features that so well lend themselves to television. These services had their share of special music, quartets, toe-tapping gospel songs, and sometimes testimonials to heighten the interest of the home viewer. But the program was still a telecast of a regular worship service constructed to serve the needs of the congregation in the sanctuary; the main focus was on the sermon.

A second type of program was more clearly aimed at entertainment—a kind of religious variety show. The best example of this in the 1970s was "Oral Roberts and You." Broadcast from a handsome set and featuring handsome people, principally the World Action Singers from Oral Roberts University and Oral's son Richard, the program had a style and class that made it very good television. Of course, the centerpiece of the program was still a homily by Oral Roberts, but the sprightly and professionally done musical numbers were designed to create an attentive audience for Roberts's remarks. Another entertainment program was that broadcast by the Jimmy Swaggart Evangelistic Association. Jimmy Swaggart was both a preacher and entertainer, since he was a recording star in his own right. The program featured a Nashville-style band and Swaggart singing gospel songs, all of which led up to the message, delivered with camp-meeting enthusiasm by Swaggart. Viewers were also given plenty of opportunity to send in for recordings of Swaggart's songs. A third example of the entertainment program was that of Rex Humbard. Although the program was usually broadcast from Humbard's Cathedral of Tomorrow in Akron, Ohio (except when the program was a tape of a crusade), it did not have the traditional worship service format. Again, the audience was prepared for the message by a series of musical numbers provided by the Humbard family—both large and musically talented—headlined by Maud Aimee, Humbard's wife.

A third component of the electronic church was the teaching program. On "Day of Discovery," the teachers were Richard De Haan and Paul Van Gorder. Although the program usually had a musical number near the beginning, it mainly consisted of a lesson, a sermonic treatment of a Biblical passage or theme, delivered in a low-key, didactic manner without any of the histrionics found in some of the other kinds of programs

The fourth and final type of program was the talk show, patterned closely after the network talk shows. The conversations on these programs focused on evangelical religious topics. By far the two most famous were the "PTL Club" and the "700 Club." "PTL" meant both "People That Love" and "Praise the Lord" (some detractors suggested "Pass the Loot" as an alternative meaning) and was hosted by Jim Bakker and his wife Tammy Fay. The title "700 Club" referred to the original 700 people who responded to an appeal for financial assistance for the underwriting of the program, although the band of supporters had grown to many times that number by the end of the 1970s. The host of the "700 Club" was Pat Robertson, who was also the head of the Christian Broadcasting Network, of which the "700 Club" was the flagship program. Both programs appeared on stations all over the country and made a significant impact on religious broadcasting.

When the electronic church burst upon the consciousness of the media and the mainline churches, there was some dispute as to the scope and appeal of these programs. As various books and newspapers reported this phenomenon (and many did), the total audience of the various television ministries was reported to be as high as 130 million. It seemed that throngs of people were watching these programs, a perception that prompted grave concern that the electronic church was doing irreparable damage to the local church, that people were just sitting home in front of their television sets and not attending or contributing to their hometown churches. Many attributed the decline in mainline church attendance to this cause. However, research into the Arbitron and Nielsen viewer statistics for 1979 and 1980 indicated that the audiences of the various electronic church programs were considerably smaller than had previously been reported. In fact, those data indicated that the total audience was only about 10 or 11 percent of that 130 million. Furthermore, comparison of the figures between February and November, 1980, showed a significant loss in viewing audience for most of the ministries.

However, even though the original estimates on the size of the television congregation were grossly inflated, a large number of people watched. A combined audience of some 13 to 16 million is of some significance. Furthermore, many of those viewers sent in money to one or more of the electronic ministries, a fact which also did not go unnoticed by local pastors. The top four programs (Oral Roberts, Rex Humbard, Robert Schuller, Jimmy Swaggart) collectively received more than a quarter of a billion dollars in 1980. The next five most popular programs took in more than 100 million dollars. The television evangelists alternated between telling their audiences how successful their ministries were in saving souls and combating evil in society and how much they needed people to send in more money. There is no doubt that these programs consumed large sums, since they bought their television time and since they each had large computer-based direct mail operations.

As to whether the various television ministries actually were detrimental to local churches, by the end of the 1970s there was no conclusive evidence. Most observers discounted that fear. Because most of the electronic ministries were fundamentalist, they probably did not hurt the liberal churches significantly. People inclined to prefer a liberal church probably did not watch such programs anyway. On the other hand, liberal churches did decline in memberships at the same time that the electronic church seemed to be coming into its own, so it may be that at least some people in the mainline churches, perhaps those who were marginal members, made a theological shift under the influence of religious television and radio programs. Conversely, conservative congregations may have profited from these ministries. Many of the television ministers encouraged people to go to their local church and to contribute to it. It may be that some uncommitted people did that, while people who were practicing members of evangelical or fundamentalist churches were reinforced in their devotion to the local congregation by the television ministers. That most of the viewers of religious television were church members was attested when virtually none of the programs was broadcast at 11 A.M. on Sunday morning; that time just did not draw a large enough audience.

The reason the electronic church is an appropriate topic in a chapter on church-state relationships is the political dimension it took on beginning around the middle of the 1970s. For most of this century evangelicals and fundamentalists have tended to avoid political involvement. They argued that the only legitimate goal of Christian activism was to save souls. When this idea was coupled with the attitude that politics was, at best, a dirty and corrupt business, evangelicals and fundamentalists simply stayed out. That changed for a significant portion of the conservative community in the mid-1970s. Liberal evangelicals, the "young evangelicals," became active in Christian social activism. But many of those on the extreme right wing of conservatism turned aboutface and became political activists, too. They perceived that American society was rapidly being ruined, that it was characterized by corruption, and that the rottenness was rapidly spreading. They felt that if Christian people (by whom they meant the "born-again") did not get involved immediately, it would be too late, that America would be beyond repair.

Right wing Christian leaders were very specific about the cultural factors that caused their sudden political involvement. Their concerns included:

Widespread pornography, in print, in the movies, and on television.

The gay rights movement. It was bad enough that there were homosexuals, practicing what others considered to be a perverted style of sexual relations, but worse, they had "come out of the closet" to parade their sexuality and to become very visible in society.

Abortion. Many conservatives were appalled at the Supreme Court's decisions of 1973, *Roe v. Wade* and *Doe v. Bolton*, which allowed virtually unlimited freedom to abort a fetus in the first trimester of pregnancy. Along with many Catholics, they considered abortion to be murder and launched a comprehensive attack against it, with the hope of pushing through Congress and the states a Constitutional amendment to prohibit it.

The Equal Rights Amendment. Many conservatives considered the ERA to be potentially dangerous to the family and to the dignity of women.

School prayer. State sponsored prayers in the public schools had been prohibited by the Supreme Court.

Advancing Communism and liberalism. Not all conservatives considered these two to be synonymous, but many did. It was these "godless" attitudes that undergirded, supported, and promoted many of the more specific conservative targets. Late in the 1970s a new label was uncovered that became the code word for all philosophies the right wing did not like: "secular humanism." The secular humanists were the cause of the bulk of America's ills and it was up to born-again Christians to root out and destroy this corrupter of America's young people, this menace to the nation's future.

One other factor caused the religious right wing to get involved in politics: the secular right wing. For some time right wing political organizations had been trying to unseat the moderate-to-liberal Democratic majority in Congress. In the very late 1970s some of the leaders of that movement began to realize that there was a great, untapped pool of supporters for their cause in the ranks of born-again Christians. Overtures were made and the leaders of some of the television ministries were persuaded that things were so bad in the country that they had to help to turn this nation around to conservative political and moral principles.

Consequently, several religiously-oriented political action groups came into being. Among the more well-known were:

Christian Voice. Perhaps the most obviously political of the group, this organization was specifically a Christian lobby group. The activity that gave Christian Voice its most visibility just before the 1980 election was its "Congressional Report Card," in which it gave grades to members of Congress based on their votes on key moral issues. Although it was not explicitly stated, the implication of low grades on the report card was that the member of Congress casting the votes was neither moral nor Christian.

National Christian Action Coalition. Organized in 1977, this group had the specific task of monitoring and lobbying on legislation pertaining to Christian schools.

The Roundtable. Although it was organized in 1980 by Ed McAteer, formerly of the Christian Freedom Foundation, the most visible individual in this organization was James Robison, a television minister from Fort Worth, Texas. It sponsored the National Affairs Briefing in Dallas 21-22 August 1980. This meeting was made notable not only for gathering together the entire galaxy of right-wing religious/political stars, but also by the appearance of presidential candidate Ronald Reagan, who delighted the assembled audience with his conservative rhetoric.

Moral Majority. This was the most famous of all the New Christian Right political groups. In fact, in the public mind all right-wing Christian political activity was subsumed under this title. Jerry Falwell was the organizer and president of the Moral Majority, although it is clear that he decided to organize the group under the pressure and guidance of some conservative secular political operatives. Moral Majority was the largest, best organized, and probably most influential of all the Christian right wing groups.

The relation between such groups and the electronic church is that various prime time preachers were very much in favor of the goals and objectives of the political action groups. They sensitized their listeners and viewers to be more in touch with what was going on around them and to try to change what they did not think conformed to Christian standards by writing letters to those in power and, even more importantly, by voting their convictions. So there was a relationship between political activism and some of the radio and television preachers, especially Jerry Falwell, James Robison, and Pat Robertson.

Of course it is no coincidence that this political activity of the religious right evolved and developed in time for the 1980 presidential election. Evangelical and fundamentalist Christians were heavily involved in the electoral process. When the results were in, the Moral Majority and others were quite willing to take the lion's share of the credit for the election of Ronald Reagan and for the defeat of several moderate and liberal Senators. Election analysis agreed that they did play a role in these events, although not as large as the groups claimed for themselves.

During the campaign and even after the election there was a good deal of criticism of the religious right by the press, by some moderate and liberal clergy, by some politicians, and by nonconservatives in the general population, who said that the religious right was violating the concept of separation between church and state. Because the Christian right was so clearly identified with a theological position and so clearly had a moral and theological agenda for its political activity, its involvement in the electoral process was a breaching of the high wall of separation between church and state. Not only was the religious right raising important specific questions about morality and public policy, its participation per se raised an important issue for the general public to think about. In the long run, the public debate about what separation means in the context of political participation by religious groups was beneficial.

But that the debate had to take place at all is disturbing, since the arguments against the political activity of the religious right were so clearly mistaken. To argue that the concept of separation of church and state bans religious groups from participating in electoral politics is just to misunderstand the concept. Liberals (and everybody else) should have known better. The free exercise clause guarantees individuals and groups the right to put their religious beliefs into practice. They may act on those religious beliefs through worship, meditation, fellowship groups, and political action. Supreme Court Justice William Brennan made this very clear in his concurring opinion in *McDaniel v. Paty*.

> That public debate of religious ideas, like any other, may arouse emotion, may incite, may foment religious divisiveness and strife does not rob it of constitutional protection. The mere fact that a purpose of the Establishment Clause is to reduce or eliminate religious divisiveness or strife, does not place religious discussion, association, or political participation in a status less preferred than rights of discussion, association and political participation gener-

172 • *Religion in Strange Times*

ally. "Adherents of particular faiths and individual churches frequently take strong positions on public issues including. . . vigorous advocacy of legal or constitutional positions. Of course, churches as much as secular bodies and private citizens have that right." *Walz v. Tax Commission.* . . .

In short, government may not as a goal promote "safe-thinking" with respect to religion and fence out from political participation those, such as ministers, whom it regards as overinvolved in religion. Religionists no less than members of any other group enjoy the full measure of protection afforded speech, association and political activity generally. The Establishment Clause, properly understood, is a shield against any attempt by government to inhibit religion as it has done here. It may not be used as a sword to justify repression of religion or its adherents from any aspect of public life.

Our decisions under the Establishment Clause prevent government from supporting or involving itself in religion or from becoming drawn into ecclesiastical disputes. These prohibitions naturally tend, as they were designed to, to avoid channeling political activity along religious lines and to reduce any tendency toward religious divisiveness in society. Beyond enforcing these prohibitions, however, government may not go. The antidote that the Constitution provides against zealots who would inject sectarianism into the political process is to subject their ideas to refutation in the marketplace of ideas and their platforms to rejection at the polls. With these safeguards, it is unlikely that they will succeed in inducing government to act along religiously divisive lines, and, with judicial enforcement of the Establishment Clause, any measure of success they achieve must be short-lived, at best.[20]

Just as liberal church people were active in the political arena in the 1960s, so conservatives had every right to be active in the arena in the late 1970s. However, after the ruling in the *Christian Echoes* case, that one's tax exemption may be taken away for political activity even though the activity is performed as a matter of religious principle, all groups need to be wary of doing themselves damage by their involvement in political activities.

However, the attitudes of the leadership of the Christian right did raise a church-state question. With its moral report cards and "hit lists" of politicians who did not meet its theological or moral expectations, the religious right infringed upon the spirit of Article VI of the Constitution. That provision declares that a person may not be given or denied a public office because of religious beliefs or lack thereof. There shall be no religious test for public office in the United States. When persons are

---

[20]435 U.S. 618 at 640-642 (1978).

seen to be fit or unfit for elective office *only* because they conform or do not conform to a particular theological standard—and that was the only basis the religious right used in evaluating candidates—then the spirit if not the letter of Article VI has been violated. The difficulty here, of course, is the question of enforceability. Suppose, for example, the Christian right was in violation of the "no religious test" principle; what corrective measures could be taken to solve that violation? This is a much more difficult issue than that in the *Torcaso* case. There the Maryland state Constitution declared that one had to affirm a belief in God in order to have an office in that state. A potential officeholder who could not conscientiously make such an affirmation brought suit and the Supreme Court declared the Maryland Constitution to be in violation of the federal Constitution. It was a matter relatively easily resolved. But when the violation is not written into any law, but rather is in the attitude, the political approach, of millions of people and the several groups into which they have organized themselves, then the issue of enforceability of the Article VI principle, of rectifying the problem of a kind of religious political imperialism, is virtually insolvable. Perhaps the only cure for this problem is education, alerting people that the "no religious test for public office" doctrine exists and that it must continue to be observed for our principle of the separation of church and state to mean anything and for elective office to be truly representative of all the people.

One other dimension of the religious right raised troublesome church-state questions. During the 1980 election and after, as the Moral Majority and the other groups savored their success and looked to the future, there was a good deal of talk about creating a "Christian America." America was slipping into the cesspool of immorality and degradation, but by becoming involved in the political process and electing only born-again Christians or those in sympathy with their goals (the Moral Majority claimed Catholic, Jewish, and Mormon members) to public office, this nation could be transformed into a Christian nation. Of course, the definition of "Christian" was a fundamentalist or extreme evangelical definition. America could be Christian only if it conformed to the born-again, rigid morality standards of the Moral Majority and those of a like mind. Such an attitude violates both the spirit and the letter of the religion clauses of the First Amendment. The framers of the Constitution were all too aware of historical examples of countries in which one particular religious viewpoint was given official approval and legal sanction to the exclusion of all others. It was because they knew of the abuse of the rights and the bodies of dissenters in those countries, a situation they wanted to avoid in their new nation, that they wrote the First Amendment. America has been, from its inception, a religiously pluralistic country. That pluralism has not only been permitted but also nurtured by the concepts of separation of church and state and religious freedom. To speak of a Christian America in which one viewpoint alone is the basis on which persons are elected and laws are passed is to destroy a religious heritage that has helped make our nation the beacon of freedom that it still is, in spite of our problems of racism and discrimination.

Many people intellectually or instinctively felt the objections raised here. Perhaps the spectacle of a theocratic society created by the Islamic revolution in Iran, led by the Ayatollah Khomeini, in which religious dissenters of all kinds were brutalized, sensitized some Americans. Indeed, some of their detractors used the term "Ayatollah" in referring to Jerry Falwell and James Robison, which was unfair but still made the point that many were exceedingly uncomfortable with the idea of a "Christian (fundamentalist) America." Jerry Falwell began to retreat from that image and to insist that he was aware of America's tradition of pluralism and religious freedom, a tradition he claimed to endorse. But at the same time he continued to insist that America had to be purified and that there was really only one way to do that, to instill fundamental Christian moral principles as dominant. Consequently, as the 1970s ended, the jury was still out on the church-state implications of the new Christian right, supported and urged on by the electronic church.

• *Suggestions for Further Reading
for Context and Perspective*

Bromley, David G., and Anson Shupe, eds. *New Christian Politics*. Macon GA: Mercer University Press, 1984.

Fackre, Gabriel. *The Religious Right and Christian Faith*. Grand Rapids MI: Wm. B. Eerdmans Publishing Co., 1982.

Falwell, Jerry. *Listen, America!* New York: Doubleday & Co., 1980.

Hadden, Jeffrey K. and Charles E. Swann. *Prime Time Preachers: The Rising Power of Televangelism*. Reading MA: Addison-Wesley Publishing Co., 1981.

Jorstad, Erling. *The Politics of Moralism: The New Christian Right in American Life*. Minneapolis: Augsburg Publishing House, 1981.

Kelley, Dean M., ed. *Government Intervention in Religious Affairs*. New York: The Pilgrim Press, 1982.

————————, ed. *The Uneasy Boundary: Church and State*. Philadelphia: The American Academy of Political and Social Science, the November 1979 edition of *The Annals of the American Academy of Political and Social Science*.

Maguire, Daniel C. *The New Subversives: Anti-Americanism of the Religious Right*. New York: Continuum Publishing Co., 1982.

Miller, Robert T. and Ronald B. Flowers. *Toward Benevolent Neutrality: Church, State, and the Supreme Court*. Waco TX: Baylor University Press, 1977, 1982.

Pfeffer, Leo. *God, Caesar, and the Constitution*. Boston: Beacon Press, 1975.

————————. *Religious Freedom*. Skokie IL: National Textbook Co., 1977.

Shriver, Peggy L. *The Bible Vote: Religion and the New Right*. New York: The Pilgrim Press, 1981.

CHAPTER SEVEN

Is God Color-Conscious
Or Color-Blind?
Black Theology
in the Church

Two of the most dramatic events of the 1960s and 1970s had to do with rights and freedom. Although World War II had been fought to preserve the liberties of America and the entire "free world," the 1960s began with many people in America still denied basic human rights and/or the opportunity for equal participation in the economic sphere of society. The two groups most active in their protests about their status, or lack of it, were blacks and women. The purpose of this chapter is to examine the religious dimensions of the black civil rights movement. The following chapter will explore religious feminism. Neither of these movements was born in the 1960s; each had a long heritage. But in the 1960s and 1970s they found unprecedented qualities of intensity and effectiveness. They each made a profound impact on society, so much so that we shall never be the same again.

• *Background of the Civil Rights Movement*

The civil rights movement, in which black people tried finally to throw off the shackles of a racist society, had antecedents in the late eighteenth, the nineteenth, and the early twentieth centuries, but it was renewed in earnest in the mid-1950s. Black people could not help but be offended by their experiences in the aftermath of World War II. The nation had gone to war to defeat a racist regime. One of the most demonic dimensions of the war, the Holocaust against the Jews, was based on racial hatred. In the war effort against the Nazis many blacks and other minorities had fought and even given their lives to protect the world against such malevolent bigotry. Yet when they came home as victorious soldiers they found their families still subjected to the same prejudices that American blacks had always had to endure and they themselves were subjected to the same old abuse. This was particularly true in the South, but no part of the country was free from racism. Great resentment built up among blacks who simply could not reconcile having fought against racial persecution abroad and finding themselves still second-class citizens when they returned home.

Black dissatisfaction with life in the United States was given greater specificity in the mid-1950s. In 1954 the Supreme Court handed down *Brown v. Board of Education of Topeka, Kansas*, declaring that racial segregation in public schools was unconstitutional. In 1896 the Court had decided *Plessy v. Ferguson*, holding that racial segregation was permissible as long as facilities were equal. From that time on segregation was practiced in most American social institutions under the concept of "separate but equal," although nearly always much more emphasis was put on "separate" than upon "equal." So it was in the public schools, with education provided to blacks characterized by incompetent instruction and inadequate facilities. The *Brown* decision was supposed to correct those wrongs, and blacks were momentarily jubilant about the decision. But when the Court took nearly a year to recommend implementation of its decision and then counseled "all deliberate speed," blacks knew they had rejoiced too soon. Indeed, noncompliance was the rule rather than the exception. Particularly in the South massive resistance greeted the order to desegregate public schools. A decade after *Brown* not a single school in Mississippi had been desegregated and only .004 percent of the black students in South Carolina were attending school with white children. The statistics for the rest of the Southern states were hardly better: Texas had the highest percentage of black students attending integrated schools ten years after *Brown*—5.5 percent. The most visible act of defiance to the Court's order took place in Little Rock, Arkansas in December 1957. In that instance school officials in Little Rock and the governor of the state, Orval Faubus, so completely resisted the integration of the schools that President Dwight Eisenhower, usually lukewarm in his support of desegregation, sent armed federal troops to compel compliance with the law. The adamant disobedience of both the spirit and the letter of the court orders for desegregation demonstrated to blacks in the 1950s that the privileged, powerful, and prejudiced would not voluntarily give up their views and practices; that blacks would have to wrest equality from them.

• *The Montgomery Bus Boycott*

Actually, the inaugural event of the civil rights movement took place in Montgomery, Alabama, a year before the Little Rock debacle. It happened in a most unlikely way. The law in Montgomery, as in many other cities in the country, was that black people riding buses should ride in the back. On 1 December 1955 a black woman got on the bus and, because she had had a day of hard work, sat down in a seat in the front of the bus, right behind the driver. When some white passengers got on and demanded her seat, the driver instructed her to move to the back of the bus. She refused. By this act Mrs. Rosa Parks ignited the modern civil rights movement. This particular act of defiance of the racial mores was not premeditated; it was rather a spontaneous result of her weariness that day. But Mrs. Parks had for many years believed strongly in racial equality and had worked for the National Association for the Advancement of Colored People in Montgomery. In fact, she had several times previously refused to ride in the back of the bus. Always before she had been evicted from the bus: this time she was arrested and taken to jail.

Leaders of the black community, of whom more than half were ministers, met and planned a boycott of the buses to protest Mrs. Park's arrest. The announcement of the boycott was made principally through leaflets and statements from the pulpits of the city's black churches. The next day, Monday, 5 December 1955, the boycott of the buses was virtually 100 percent successful, as black people went to work by foot or by car pools organized by black taxi drivers and other citizens. Churches served as pickup points and, as the boycott dragged on—it lasted a year, since there was stiff opposition from whites—churches organized alternative transportation systems for blacks.

The Montgomery bus boycott was significant not only as the beginning of the civil rights movement, but also for the emergence of Martin Luther King, Jr., as its leader. King was a young Baptist minister from a relatively prosperous background. He had come to Montgomery less than a year before, having just completed a doctorate in theology at Boston University, to be the minister at the Dexter Avenue Baptist Church. Although he had not been in the forefront of any black liberation activities in Montgomery or elsewhere, now, by vote of his fellow pastors, he was thrust into the leadership of the bus boycott. Once he had agreed to take the leadership, he did well, providing encouragement and ideology for the protesters. For example, on the evening of 5 December at an "encouragement rally" in one of the black churches King addressed an overflow crowd in these words:

> If you will protest courageously, and yet with dignity and Christian love, when the history books are written in future generations, the historians will have to pause and say, "There lived a great people—a black people—who injected new meaning and dignity into the veins of civilization." This is our challenge and our overwhelming responsibility.[1]

In addition to giving encouragement and motivation to the protesters, King also provided the method for the protest. Blacks were not to protest and boycott in a spirit of hatred and revenge, but rather in a spirit of love and hope for a better time in America. The method was nonviolent, passive resistance. King had become convinced of the rightness of this approach by reading Jesus and Mohandas Gandhi and by realizing that violence could do nothing but elicit violence from white opponents. Nonviolent resistance was to become the trademark of the early civil rights movement.

The Montgomery bus boycott was not begun in the black churches, and it was not precipitated by church leaders. But once the event had begun, almost accidentally, black ministers assumed leadership, putting their reputations, careers, and perhaps even their lives in jeopardy. The black church became the rallying point and source of inspiration for the protesters. Under the leadership of the religious community, the bus boycott demonstrated to blacks in Montgomery and beyond that they could effectively triumph over one aspect of white racism. It also demonstrated the feasibility and effectiveness of nonviolent, passive resistance. Above and beyond all that, it also resulted in the creation of the

---

[1]Quoted in Charles S. McCoy, "The Churches and Protest Movements for Racial Justice," in Robert Lee and Martin Marty, eds., *Religion and Social Conflict* (New York: Oxford University Press, 1964) 44-45.

Southern Christian Leadership Conference, founded in January 1957, with Martin Luther King, Jr. as its leader. SCLC became one of the most effective of the organizations fighting for black liberation throughout the 1960s and the early 1970s.

• *Sitting for Freedom*

The next major development in the civil rights struggle was the emergence of the "sit-in" strategy. On 1 February 1960, four black college students entered a segregated eating place in Greensboro, North Carolina, sat down at the lunch counter, and asked to be served. They were not. They remained at their places until the establishment closed. Although there was no preexisting network of blacks waiting for some signal to begin this method of protest against segregation, within days after the first sit-in blacks, primarily students, all across the South were engaged in this activity. Within two months, the practice had spread to 65 cities. Sit-ins were at first confined to restaurants and lunch counters where blacks would take up space until the place closed or they were removed by the police, which happened frequently. Soon sit-ins were organized in parks, swimming pools, theaters, museums, libraries, art galleries, and laundromats.

A variation on the sit-in was begun in May 1961. Federal rules forbade racial segregation in interstate travel facilities and some black students decided to call attention to the fact that those rules were routinely violated. Thus the "freedom ride" was born. In the face of severe ridicule and considerable violence, students rode interstate buses and entered areas reserved for whites in bus stations, including restrooms and lunch counters. These events caught the attention of the media and were broadcast across the country, stimulating considerable sympathy for the freedom riders.

In neither case was the strategy conceptualized or initiated by any church. The original freedom ride was sponsored by the Congress of Racial Equality. But once the activities were begun the black churches (and a precious few white ones) lent their support and facilities to the cause. Not only did the churches provide moral support, but they often served as training centers for freedom riders and those engaged in sit-ins, instructing them in nonviolent perseverance. Churches often served as organizing points for sit-in efforts and places where those who had been engaged in sit-ins or freedom rides could rest and have their bruises and wounds cared for, as was often necessary.

• *Protest in Birmingham*

In 1963 the Southern Christian Leadership Conference mobilized the blacks of Birmingham, Alabama, to launch a full-scale attack against what they felt was one of the most segregated, racist cities in America. Because Martin Luther King, Jr. was the leader and organizer of the protest, it was to be a nonviolent effort. Blacks intended to eliminate segregation from the city, particularly in stores and eating places, and to demand equality in job hiring and promotion. Their way of calling attention to these issues was by massive but peaceful marches through the city and by a boycott of all segregated businesses in the city—virtually all of them.

The political and business leaders of Birmingham resisted. The city government, in the person of its most visible symbol, Public Safety Commissioner Eugene "Bull" Connor, took extreme measures to destroy the demonstrations and to send the blacks back to stay "in their place" (a favorite Southern expression). Although the blacks were neither perpetrating violence nor destroying property, they were dealt with most harshly. The Birmingham marches were well covered by the media, so Americans and much of the world saw dramatic pictures of police beating blacks, including old women and children, with their night sticks, police dogs attacking marchers, and streams from high-pressure fire hoses knocking people off their feet. Part of the significance of Birmingham was that the treatment of blacks there began to evoke the sympathy of people across the nation and support for blacks began to grow.

Another significant feature of Birmingham was King's famous "Letter From Birmingham Jail." It was a most lucid, sane, and moving explanation of the civil rights movement and nonviolent demonstrations, and deserves to be considered a classic of modern American literature. King, like scores of his followers, was arrested and jailed in Birmingham. While in jail he received a letter from eight Alabama clergy who criticized him for creating confrontation in Birmingham, a city of which he was not a citizen, and of trying to go too far too quickly. From his jail cell, King responded to them.

Of the many topics King touched in the "Letter," two most worthy of note were the interrelated ideas of nonviolent direct action and civil disobedience. King pointed out that there were four steps in planning to protest racial segregation: analysis to determine whether injustice existed, negotiation, self-purification, and direct action. In Birmingham analysis did not take very long, since it was clearly a segregated city. Negotiations had been initiated by blacks, as they tried to work out plans for greater freedom of opportunity and participation in the government in Birmingham. They had been rebuffed, as the business and political leaders of the city absolutely refused to talk. With that crucial step denied them, blacks had prepared for demonstrations in the streets. The self-purification of which King spoke consisted of a series of workshops in nonviolence in which blacks were asked to examine their motives, to root out any feeling of revenge against whites, to ask themselves whether they were willing to accept derision and even physical abuse without retaliating, and to risk going to jail for their cause. Only after that did they go into the streets. King said that the purpose of the demonstrations, always nonviolent in nature, was to create such a tension-filled atmosphere that the oppressors would be willing to negotiate the demands of the oppressed after all. In this King let it be seen by all that the blacks were both a disciplined and a determined people.

In the process of demonstrating in the streets and sitting in at lunch counters, blacks broke many laws. They did so intentionally. King felt called upon to explain why they were so willing to practice civil disobedience. King pointed out that he and his followers believed that, in principle, the law should be obeyed. But there were just laws and unjust laws. A just law is consistent with the moral law or the law of God; it enhances and uplifts human personality. A law is unjust when it does not square with principles of morality, when it degrades the human personality, and when it is applied to some, specifically a minority, differently than it is applied to others. Segregation laws, he said, were obviously unjust laws. They did not square with the idea that all people are made in the image of God and are thus equally objects of God's care. They did not enhance the human personality in that they gave a false sense of inferiority to the oppressed minority and a false sense of superiority to the oppressing majority. They formalized difference rather than equality. Consequently, they could legitimately be broken. However, unjust laws could not be broken by protesters in a casual way and it was not the intention of blacks to do so. They were willing to pay the penalty for having broken the law, to be arrested and go to jail to further dramatize the rightness of their cause and their respect for the law. As King summarized it,

> One who breaks an unjust law must do so openly, lovingly, and with a willingness to accept the penalty. I submit that an individual who breaks a law that conscience tells him is unjust, and who willingly accepts the penalty of imprisonment in order to arouse the conscience of the community over its injustice, is in reality expressing the highest respect for the law.[2]

The "Letter From Birmingham Jail" was widely circulated and did much to explicate the nonviolent protest movement among whites and to prolong its usefulness among blacks.

• Black Power

But even as King wrote this fine document, the character of the civil rights movement was changing. Some people were becoming disenchanted with King's nonviolence. Blacks met such resistance and were treated so violently that some simply felt the need to retaliate. An organization called the Student Nonviolent Coordinating Committee (SNCC—pronounced "snick") was founded in the early 1960s and came into prominence around 1966. By that time it had outgrown its name and symbolized the changes occurring in the civil rights movement. Its membership was, by then, not adverse to the use of violence to try to force the whites of the nation to give in to black needs and desires. It represented a much harder line in blacks' attitudes about themselves and about white people. Under the leadership of Stokely Carmichael and, later, H. Rap Brown, SNCC advocated a new slogan: "Black Power." The term "Negro" was no longer acceptable; blacks had reclaimed an open pride in their color. They repudiated the notion that whites had imposed on them for so long, that black was a color of inferiority. SNCC was involved in a number of projects, but its primary function seemed to be to keep the issue of racism before the American people, never to let them

---

[2]Martin Luther King, Jr., *Why We Can't Wait* (New York: New American Library Signet Book, 1964) 83-84. The "Letter from Birmingham Jail" is included in this book.

forget the injustices done to blacks, to insist on the need for immediate reforms.

White support for civil rights had never been as extensive as King or the other black leaders had hoped it would be. In spite of the rather widespread sympathy for blacks generated by the excesses of the police of Birmingham and other Southern cities, by the middle of the decade white indifference had turned to resistance. By this time, many blacks, particularly those not under the direct influence of one of the nonviolent leaders, had resorted to violence. There had even been riots; one of the most destructive of these outbreaks of anger and frustration occurred in the Watts section of Los Angeles in 1965. Many whites were alarmed and offended by these excesses, while blacks were angered by lack of support from whites. Consequently, by the middle of the decade, blacks and sympathetic whites were retreating from each other because of mutual disenchantment. Because even liberal whites were no longer as supportive as they had been, blacks decided to proceed alone in gaining their rights. In fact, many began to feel that they were not eager for integration, just for desegregation: freedom and equal opportunity. All these feelings came to a focus in the phrase "Black Power." Many blacks began to turn away from the leadership of Martin Luther King, Jr. because they were not convinced of the ultimate effectiveness of nonviolence and because he was too willing to negotiate and sometimes even to compromise with white people. Thus, in the last half of the 1960s, the civil rights movement became more self-consciously black and militant.

Although King and his methods were losing popularity among blacks in the late 1960s, he was still the most prominent living symbol of the movement. When he was assassinated in 1968, anger and violence erupted among blacks all over the nation. King's death demonstrated, once and for all, that whites were not going to *give* freedom and equality to blacks, blacks were going to have to *take* it. The movement became even more militant.

The black church was not always in the vanguard of the civil rights movement, but it was a strong supporter of it. The churches provided invaluable leadership—especially in the person of King, but through others, also. Yet in the late 1960s the church seemed to be losing favor with blacks. Church attendance declined significantly. Young black people in particular seemed to be less interested in, if not hostile to, the church. As it became more militant, the civil rights movement seemed to move away from the church. All this is symbolized by the character of SNCC and the black power strategy.

However, it would be wrong to say that the black church became completely disengaged from the civil rights struggle. Church leaders were too dedicated to the cause to allow the church to become totally ineffective. In November 1967 the National Committee of Black Churchmen was formed as an organization to try to improve the economic condition of blacks. The most dramatic event to occur under the auspices of this organization was a conference on black economic development, held in Detroit in 1969. At that meeting James Foreman read a "Black Manifesto" that proposed a radical solution to the problems of black people. The document deplored the way whites had treated blacks over the years and demanded reparations payments from white churches and synagogues. The $50,000,000 demanded would be used for the economic benefit of the black community in projects such as a land bank for evicted black farmers, publishing and printing industries, a television network, and a black university. The manifesto was a very militant approach to the problem, delivered out of a black semichurch organization and aimed at the white religious establishment, which blacks felt was guilty of complicity in the racist character of American society and that, with a few exceptions, had been mostly unhelpful in the recent civil rights struggle. The document demonstrates how far the civil rights movement had come since the Montgomery bus boycott.

Even though the role of the black church in the civil rights movement was slightly ambiguous, the point is often made that its participation in the cause changed the church itself. C. Eric Lincoln, a black sociologist of religion, has gone so far as to say that the Negro church died in the civil rights movement. Lincoln distinguishes between the Negro church and the black church. The Negro church is the church that existed during slavery times and in the Jim Crow era since slavery. The generalization is usually made that the Negro church was an institution that helped Negro people cope with and defend themselves against slavery and the subsequent racism in America. The best way of coping was to think of the future when the troubles of this world would be over, so the Negro church had its eye on the next world: things may be terrible now, but there will be peace and security in heaven. It taught its people to trust in Jesus with the confidence that things would be better bye and bye. The generalization that the theology of the Negro church was completely otherworldly and consoling in nature is oversimplified, but it is essentially true.

Late in the 1960s, when black people finally realized that the structures of segregation were not going to go away without a struggle, the Negro church enthusiastically joined in and even gave leadership to the effort. With their new consciousness and determination, Negro people became black people and the Negro church became the black church. Lincoln describes the process:

> The "Negro Church". . . no longer exists. It died an agonized death in the harsh turmoil that tried the faith so rigorously in the decade of the "Savage Sixties," for there it had to confront under the most trying circumstances the possibility that "Negro" and "Christian" were irreconcilable categories. The call to full manhood, to *personhood*, and the call to Christian responsibility left no room for the implications of being a "Negro" in contemporary America. With sadness and reluctance, trepidation and confidence, the Negro Church accepted death in order to be reborn. Out of the ashes of the funeral pyre there sprang the bold, strident, self-conscious phoenix that is the contemporary Black Church.[3]

In spite of the fact that blacks were moving away from the leadership of Martin Luther King, Jr. at the time of his death, most historians credit him as the person who led the transition from the Negro church to the black church.

• *Black Theology*

In spite of its transformation into a more aggressive institution in the mid-1960s, the black church seemed to retreat from its previous activism as the decade closed. In a somewhat oversimplified way, it may be generalized that the initiative in the fight for freedom moved from the churches to the academy at the end of the decade. The black power emphasis began to be articulated as black theology, formulated by black university and seminary professors rather than by black pastors and laity.

---

[3]E. Franklin Frazier and C. Eric Lincoln, *The Negro Church in America* and *The Black Church Since Frazier* (two books bound as one) (New York: Schocken Books, 1974) 105-106.

The idea of black theology at first kindled the curiosity of many people: how could it be that there was a black theology, indeed, how could theology come in colors? The advocates of black theology responded that theology in America has always come in colors. They insisted that American theology had always been white theology ignoring the experiences and needs of black people. American theology had historically been influenced by western European thinkers in such a way that it was highly rational and logical rather than experiential. Certainly it was neither cognizant of nor sympathetic with the experiences of black people. During the period of slavery theological arguments had been used to justify and defend the practice of enslaving blacks. Biblical passages that reflected the practice of slavery in ancient times were used in the South to attempt to prove that the enslavement of blacks was the will of God. After emancipation, the white churches of the South and in other parts of the country were guilty of complicity in keeping blacks in second-class citizenship. White theology supported a kind of white supremacy that, at best, ignored the problems of black people. One of the clearest manifestations of this supremacist mentality was a theological manifest destiny ideology that America was God's chosen nation and thus Americanism needed to be spread throughout the world. This ideology was used to justify colonial rule over people of color throughout the world.

Even in the recent times of the civil rights movement, a white theology that idealized tranquility more than human rights told blacks to go slowly in their activities, not to "make waves." The practical effect of that idea, of course, was simply to delay justice. With few exceptions, at no time in American history did the white church or its major thinkers call into question the oppression of blacks, Indians, or any other minority. Black theologians, with some indignation, pointed out that there has always been a white theology and, since it had supported the oppressors, it needed to be replaced with black theology. White theology was of no value at all for black people. Again C. Eric Lincoln summarized it well.

> If Black people cannot trust white people and their systems of truth, it is obvious that the white man (who is already preoccupied with the consequences of his whiteness), cannot create an acceptable theology for Black people. The white man's perspective is distorted by his values, and his values are centered around the color of his skin and the salience of his economics. That is a fact that was never lost on Blackamericans, even when they were in physical bond-

age. . . . The central problem is that white theology has excluded Black people from its universe of discourse and from its area of meaningful concern. In so doing, white theology has encouraged the notion that Black people are somehow beings of lesser consequence in the eyes of God, that they are not capable of proper Christian witness and that, being so limited, God does not require or expect very much of them.[4]

The sources of black theology have not been the great philosophers and thinkers of the past so much as the Bible and the experiences of black people. In formulating black theology its spokespersons have not been nearly as concerned with what Plato, Augustine, Luther, Barth, or Tillich had to say as with the experience of slaves, of blacks living under Jim Crow laws and the constant threat of lynching, or of blacks in their pews under the Spirit-filled preaching of their unlearned but often saintly preachers. This is not to say that black theology has been or is irrational or illogical, but simply that it is based in experience, applying Biblical insights to the wounds of the tyrannized.

Black theologians insist that black theology is not just a phenomenon of the late 1960s and 1970s, but that it always has been a part of the experience of black Americans. They argue against the claim that the Negro church of slavery times or during Reconstruction was only a palliative for suffering blacks. It is true that the church did offer its participants a large amount of "pie in the sky bye and bye," the hope of the triumph of the next life as a way of coping with a miserable existence. But in subtle ways it also spoke of freedom and even defiance of slave owners or the racist society. Principally in sermon and song the church spoke, in veiled language, of freedom, of the underground railroad, and sometimes even of slave rebellions. After slavery ended, the black church contributed to a sense of black consciousness and dignity. The church was usually the only institution where a black person could have authority, be addressed by a title such as Mr. or Mrs., express emotion without being subject to ridicule, and exercise leadership and/or self-direction.

The theme of black theology is liberation. In its earlier, nascent, form and in its more recent overt expression, black theology speaks of liberation; freedom from the bonds of racism, hatred, and bigotry. It

---

[4]Ibid., 142, 144.

proclaims that being black is something in which to take pride. It announces that oppression and second-class citizenship are not acceptable and that blacks must be afforded their rightful place in society. It affirms the personhood of blacks and encourages them to claim their God-given human dignity. It also condemns the structures of society and the racist attitudes that have traditionally relegated blacks to inferior status and inflicted inhumane treatment upon them.

Black theology points to the great biblical themes of the Judaeo-Christian tradition as sources for its insights. God is a God of liberation: always on the side of the oppressed. How dramatically that has been demonstrated! In the Exodus of the Hebrew people from Egypt God saw the affliction of the people and led them from bondage. God put down the oppressor and lifted up the oppressed. The Exodus, then, is a dominant event or theme for black theology. God knows of the sufferings of the oppressed, disapproves of the oppression, and is caring enough and powerful enough to do something about their plight.

Black theology draws insights from the Hebrew prophets, that band of courageous individuals who spoke for God in ancient times of oppression and persecution. Although they articulated theology in many different ways because they spoke to a variety of situations, the principal message of the prophets was that God does not tolerate exploitation of the poor and powerless. Their theme is most succinctly stated in Amos 5:24: "Let justice roll down like waters and righteousness like an ever-flowing stream." God's standards are high for political and social life; they demand justice. The community or nation that does not have social justice cannot remain alive.

Of course, from the Christian perspective, God acted most dramatically in human history by sending Jesus. Here again, black theologians point out, God is demonstrated as the supreme liberator. Jesus came to rescue humankind from sin and all its manifestations. Jesus was Savior, history's most decisive act of liberation. Here God teaches, even more than in the Exodus or through the prophets, that anything that holds humans in bondage is wrong. God is on the side of blacks and other oppressed people; working against oppressors. Black theologians have argued that God is so much with the blacks that it must be said that God and Christ are black. To make such an affirmation is not as radical as it may seem; historically Christians have tended to depict Jesus as being like them, since they perceived that he gave his life for them. Just so, black theologians tended to think in terms of God and Jesus as black in order that blacks may more easily understand that God is not solely in the possession of white people. God and Christian theology are not the exclusive property of white western Europeans and Americans.

• *Varieties of Black Theology*

Black theologians, then, were unanimous in their view that there was a need for a theology aimed at the particular needs of black people, and that the thrust of it had to be the message of liberation. They argued that God endorses freedom and equality for all people and, indeed, is moving in history to achieve those goals. But not all black theologians saw their task in the same way. For some, black theology adopted such a militancy that *it* took on a racist flavor. While all black theologians deplored the fact that traditional theology has served the needs of white people over against everybody else, the more militant black theologians were so vehement in discrediting white theology that they seemed to assert black supremacy. This approach essentially advocated that blacks become independent in the theological/religious arena and that if whites were to participate at all, they must become black in their thinking. James H. Cone of Union Theological Seminary in New York, who was a pioneer in black theology and was one of its most articulate advocates, seemed to represent this view. On the other hand, there were some black theologians who advocated reconciliation between blacks and whites. To be sure, they insisted on liberation from all vestiges of racism and oppression, but they did so in such a way as to try to keep channels of communication and relationship open between blacks and whites. These people pointed out that oppression of a people is virtually as destructive to the oppressors as it is to the oppressed, since it gives them an unrealistic sense of superiority, and thus liberation is as beneficial to whites as it is to blacks. By making this point to whites they hoped that there would be a mutual recognition of rights by both whites and blacks and reconciliation would occur, to the benefit of the entire society. Of course, the most famous advocate of freedom and reconciliation was Martin Luther King, Jr. Among black theologians after King a representative of this view was Major J. Jones of the Interdenominational Theological Center in Atlanta.

A conundrum faced by black theologians has been the issue of the use of violence. Black theology came to the fore alongside black power; indeed, some have said that it was the religious manifestation of the black power emphasis. Many of the theologians saw that those who have privilege will not willingly give it up, that some power and violence are necessary for the oppressed to get equality. The pressing question for the theologians was whether violence was compatible with the Judaeo-Christian themes they were using. Of course, Martin Luther King, Jr. had made nonviolence the centerpiece of the early civil rights movement. But King was not able to win as many victories as some blacks thought he should and their mood began to turn toward a more confrontational style of protest. Then, too, whites seemed to pay more attention to spontaneous violence than to organized nonviolent protests. Some black theologians began to speak of the use of violence as a tool of last resort in gaining the liberty so long denied their people.

Although there were some disagreements among black theologians from the time they first spoke out, the various positions did not remain static. Throughout the 1970s there was some evolution of thought. One of the most radical and interesting of those developments was the adoption of Marxist categories by some black theologians, principally James Cone. This was primarily because of the influence of South American liberation theology. Latin America is generally characterized by rigid social stratification, with spectacular riches held by a few and abject poverty endured by the majority. Churchmen and churchwomen in Latin America, including nuns, priests and even bishops of the Catholic church, increasingly became concerned with the plight of the poor and, consequently, a liberation theology came into being during the 1960s and 1970s. The purpose of this theology was to try to deal with grinding poverty and oppressive power structures in the various countries of the region. In trying to come to grips with these momentous problems, theologians drew upon not only the Biblical themes of God's liberation of the oppressed but also the Marxist concept of the overthrow of the rich by the poor. The two could be combined to provide not only principle but also methodology as to how the poor should be lifted up.

James Cone and those blacks influenced by him used these Marxist ideas to articulate black theology. Cone pointed out that Martin Luther King taught blacks the necessity of the scientific analysis of a problem of racism. King clearly explained this in his "Letter from Birmingham

Jail." Although King never advocated or adopted a Marxist analysis, Cone came to believe that Marxism, with its concept of the elevation of the proletariat and the goal of the classless society, could provide the analytical tools and the methods to make a significant contribution to black liberation. It is probable that it is from this source that Cone and those of a like mind were willing to entertain the use of violence, since Marx advocated the rebellion of the poor against the rich. Of course, even for these black theologians the principal component of their thought was the good news of God's concern for the poor, God's love. It must be understood that they were not Communists. But they did believe that Marxist categories were useful tools for analyzing the social and economic problems of a society: they might instruct sincere Christians in how to try to apply God's love to society's problems. It is in that sense that they did not believe that the gospel and Marxism were incompatible. Other black theologians rejected the inclusion of Marxist insights into black theology; they believed that the gospel alone provided sufficient ideology and motivation for challenging white racism.

Black theology had to broaden its horizons beyond its original vision. It had to take notice of liberation theology, both its Latin American and African forms, and it had to acknowledge feminist theology. The reason that it had to take these other theological emphases seriously is because they had common interests and goals—namely, the breaking of the position of some power group and the elevation of the oppressed or disadvantaged. In order to facilitate the broadening of the awareness of black theologians regarding other liberation theologies, the Society for the Study of Black Religion was formed in 1970. In addition to the purpose of expanding knowledge, the society was to give black theology greater credibility as an academic discipline.

In December 1974 the Ghana Consultation on Black/African Theology met. Although most of the participants were academics and church people from various places in Africa, several black Americans attended. The discussion concerned what the American theologians could learn from the experiences of contemporary Africans and how they could draw upon their own heritage of African culture, distorted as it had been by slavery and subsequent oppression in America.

Of paramount importance for black theology was the conference on Theology in the Americas held in Detroit in 1975. At that meeting two hundred Latin American and North American Christians met for the presentation of academic papers and dialogue. The purpose of the conference was to carefully analyze Latin American liberation theology and its possible relevance to North America. But, because of the variety of participants, the conference also dealt with various theologies designed to speak to Native American, Chicano, Puerto Rican, Asian American, and white working-class churches in the United States. The conference focused on the socioeconomic exploitation of minorities, human rights violations, and class struggle in North and South America and what role theology and the church might play to alleviate these injustices. Papers from that conference were published and Theology in the Americas was made an ongoing project, with an office and staff. In the late 1970s other conferences were held in this country as a result of the Detroit meeting. One of these was the Black Theology Project that met in Atlanta in 1977 and considered the relationship of black theology to the black church. Another major conference, the Pan-African Conference of Third World Theologians, was held in Ghana in December 1977. Of more than 100 participants, 15 were black Americans. As at other such conferences, the participants sought cross-fertilization of ideas and the building of bridges of awareness and commonality.

Black theology was a phenomenon of the academy; this was particularly true after the most overt and aggressive civil rights activity died down around 1970 and the churches became more quiescent. But it is not true to say that black theology did not try to speak to the churches or that the churches were oblivious to the social difficulties facing black people throughout the 1970s. The black churches were confronted with the problem of trying to keep increasingly urbanized and secularized young people involved. At the same time they had to cope with at least some blacks who had moved into the middle class and received college education. They had to deal with both unemployment and sophistication among black youth. They had to continue to proclaim a message of human dignity and liberation—their mandate from black theologians—and at the same time help blacks deal with whatever successes the civil rights movements might have wrought for them.

There is some evidence that the black churches did at least a moderately good job of doing these things during the 1970s. One imperative for black churches is an educated clergy. From 1970 to 1980 the number of students in theological seminaries in the United States and Canada increased 59.7 percent, but the rate of increase among black students was

172.9 percent. However, even with such an increase, in 1980 black students made up only 4.4 percent of total seminary enrollment. So black churches were increasing the quality of their leadership, but much more remained to be done. Black churches, with a tradition of independence and rather strong congregational autonomy, saw the need to come together to pool their resources and intensify their effectiveness. In 1978 representatives from six black denominations met to form an organization, the Congress of National Black Churches. At the initial meeting and in subsequent ones, the CNBC identified four problem areas that it would address: theological education, evangelism, communications among black churches, and unemployment. In addition, the National Committee of Black Churchmen, founded in 1966, subsequently changed its name to the National Conference of Black Churchmen. It met annually throughout the 1970s and continued to try to address the wide range of social issues of greatest importance to blacks which had called it into being originally.

It is clear, then, that although the black churches were not as "up front" in the 1970s as they were in the 1960s, under the inspiration of black theology, the residue of prejudice that blacks face, and the dramatic economic burdens that many blacks continued to endure in the 1970s, they remained significant agents for consolation and change in the black community.

* *Suggestions for Further Reading
for Context and Perspective*

Appiah-Kubi, Kofi and Sergio Torres, eds. *African Theology En Route*. New York: Orbis Books, 1979.

Bass, Jack and Jack Nelson. *The Orangeburg Massacre*. Macon GA: Mercer University Press, 1984.

Cone, James H. *A Black Theology of Liberation*. Philadelphia: J. B. Lippincott Co., 1970.

──────────. *Black Theology and Black Power*. New York: Seabury Press, 1969.

Frazier, E. Franklin and C. Eric Lincoln. *The Negro Church in America* and *The Black Church Since Frazier* (two books bound in one volume). New York: Schocken Books, 1974.

Jones, Major J. *Black Awareness: A Theology of Hope*. Nashville: Abingdon Press, 1971.

King, Martin Luther, Jr. *Why We Can't Wait*. New York: Signet Books, 1964.

──────────. "Letter from Birmingham Jail," *Christian Century* 80 (12 June 1963): 767-773.

Lincoln, C. Eric, ed. *The Black Experience in Religion*. Garden City NY: Doubleday, 1974.

Torres, Sergio and John Eagleson, eds. *Theology in the Americas*. New York: Orbis Books, 1976.

Wilmore, Gayraud S. and James H. Cone, eds. *Black Theology; A Documentary History 1966-1979*. Maryknoll NY: Orbis Books, 1979.

CHAPTER EIGHT

All About Eve
and the Goddess:
A Layperson's Guide
to Feminist Theology

Of course, blacks were not the only people trying to gain liberation, recognition of rights, and equal opportunity during the 1960s and 1970s. There were many other minority groups struggling against some form of oppression. Although they are not a numerical minority, women as a group had developed a sense of having experienced discrimination and inferior status. Consequently, women set about trying to break the ideology and patterns of behavior that denied to them fulfilling personhood.

The problem, as feminists saw it, was that historically and universally women have been subordinate to men. In virtually all historical periods and virtually every culture men have been dominant and women subordinate. Men have defined the proper roles for themselves and for women and have not allowed women either to redefine the roles or to break out of their confinement. Feminists have employed the word "patriarchal" as the proper label for this kind of male oppression. Patriarchal society has historically stereotyped women as "the weaker sex." Because they were assumed to be the weaker sex, they were assigned definite sexual and family roles; women were things of beauty to be enjoyed, were to be the source of male sexual gratification, and were to stay at home minding the children. Who has not heard that "woman's place is in the home?" There are other cultural stereotypes. Men have been perceived as being aggressive, analytical, powerful and thus were obliged to take the dominant and more highly valued roles in society; decision maker, breadwinner, leader. Women, on the other hand, have been categorized as passive, emotional, nonanalytical and thus were relegated to what were considered secondary roles; mother, homemaker, always sheltered from the hustle of the competitive world. If women did work outside the home, as they have done increasingly in this century, the values of patriarchal society made women feel guilty about being away from home and hearth and the greater value accorded to men prevented women from being given the same compensation as men for equivalent work.

Turning specifically to religion, feminists insisted that the subordination of women has been given much support, indeed a rationale, by the Judaeo-Christian tradition. Although many other religious traditions, in their own way, also foster an unequal society, feminists believe that the Judaeo-Christian tradition is, undoubtedly, patriarchal. From the creation story, which has been interpreted to mean that men were to be dominant over women (the woman's proper role is to be the "helpmate" for the man), to the maleness ascribed to God, the tradition has been responsible for the subordination and sometimes the persecution of women. God is Father and thus male, God's son Jesus is obviously male and consequently it has been natural to assume that the male sex is superior. God made men and women in his own image, but the male was created first and the female second, from the body of the male ("Adam's rib"), so, again, women are to be subordinate. These images of the maleness of God, Jesus and the Holy Spirit have become the keystone of a symbol system that has pervaded western society. Feminist thinkers pointed out that humans live by symbols, that symbols have power in that they help structure our ways of thinking. Consequently, the symbol of God as male has done very much to form our thinking about the structures of reality, about how men (and women) have perceived themselves and their relationships. The result of this has been the societal value that women are to be married and to find their identity and their proper roles in life in relation to their husbands. This is well summarized by Judy Grahn's poem:

> you are what is female
> you shall be called Eve
> and what is masculine shall be called God.

and from your name Eve we shall take
the word Evil
and from God's the word Good.
now you understand patriarchal morality.[1]

Not only has the Judaeo-Christian tradition provided the cultural mentality that has contributed greatly to the subordination of women in the western world, but within its various specific groups women historically have been denied leadership positions or even full participation in religious activities. Although there are examples of women playing enormously creative and important roles in one or another religious group, generally these roles had been defined by men and normally were subservient to those played by men. In these contexts, women felt shunted aside, discriminated against, unfairly treated. The editors of a recent collection of feminist essays on religion have clearly articulated this perception.

> It is precisely this sense of injustice that lies at the heart of the first feminist criticism of religion. Most of these criticisms originated in an often inarticulate sense of exclusion from traditional religious practice or theology. Women who felt called to be rabbis, priests, and ministers frequently found themselves barred from these vocations. Orthodox Jewish women who wanted to participate fully in worship were excluded from the praying community and seated behind a screen. Catholic and Protestant women who wanted to serve communion were asked, instead, to serve church suppers. Women in every congregation heard phrases such as "God of our Fathers," "men of God," and the "Brotherhood of man" preached from the pulpit. Everywhere they turned, women found signs reading "For Men Only."[2]

Just as black theologians had perceived that theology comes in colors, so women contended that it has come in genders. Just as "white" theology functioned to subordinate and serve as the justification for the oppression of people of color, so also has "male" theology operated against females. Just as black theologians tried to articulate a theology that would neutralize the effects of white theology and serve to liberate

---

[1]Judy Grahn, *The Work of a Common Woman* (New York: St. Martin's Press, 1978) 137.

[2]Carol P. Christ and Judith Plaskow, *Womanspirit Rising: A Feminist Reader in Religion* (San Francisco: Harper and Row, 1979) 3.

black people, so have many women tried to counteract cultural and ecclesiastical patriarchy and formulate a feminist theology.

• *Historical Background*

Of course the feminism of the late 1960s and 1970s was not the first effort by American women to improve their cultural/economic/political status. The "first wave" of feminism swept across the nation in the nineteenth century. This feminist impulse grew, in part, out of the abolitionist movement. Among the several women who were active, even leaders, in the movement to free the slaves, Sarah and Angelina Grimké are perhaps the most famous. The abolition movement was an impetus to feminism both in terms of its theme of freedom for the oppressed and because it gave some women opportunities to assert themselves in ways that did not conform to the traditional stereotype. But there was also a stimulus for feminism that was not derived from an external source—namely, women's impatience with and anger against the injustice of inequality imposed on them by patriarchal society.

In the realm of religion, many women asserted themselves in ways that were not necessarily in conformity with the prevailing attitudes about women's roles. Women broke out of the stereotype and, in the process, made an enormous contribution to religion in the nineteenth century by organizing and administering missionary societies affiliated with various denominations, raising about $6 million and sending out 694 single women missionaries. By 1900 the societies were supporting 389 missionary wives, 856 single women missionaries, and 96 physicians of both sexes in foreign missions alone. Comparable work was being done in home missions, although the scope of such work is not quite so clear because figures are harder to find. These societies were responsible for numerous orphanages, hospitals, and schools around the world.[3] They primarily employed single women who were eager to perform the same tasks as male missionaries. Consequently, they tapped a

---

[3]Virginia Lieson Brereton and Christa Ressmeyer Klein, "American Women in Ministry: A History of Protestant Beginning Points," in Rosemary Ruether and Eleanor McLaughlin, eds., *Women of Spirit: Leadership in the Jewish and Christian Traditions* (New York: Simon and Schuster, 1979) 306.

great resource for the churches and at the same time gave women exciting new vocational opportunities. To prepare these women for missionary work the societies developed mission schools (not seminaries, which did not admit women in those days) that concentrated on instruction in Bible and mission techniques. Most of the faculty at these schools were women, another unusual characteristic for the time.

Their experiences in mission work led many women to desire other roles in the church, especially as ordained ministers or priests. But in most denominations ordination was not available to women. The ordination of Antoinette Brown in 1852 to the ministry of the Congregational Church, the first woman to be ordained in this country, has been viewed as a signal event—the exception rather than the rule.

In the early twentieth century, most of the missionary societies that had been administered by women were absorbed by other denominational agencies, often without consulting the women, much less securing their approval. Occasionally women were able to retain positions of leadership in these newly organized missionary groups, but in many cases the reorganization was a power grab by male denominational leaders. In most denominations the missionary schools were closed and the female teachers dismissed. Some women accepted all this in the name of greater efficiency and nonduplication within denominational structures. But other women were greatly angered by it and saw in these denominational maneuvers one more illustration of patriarchy at work in the church.

Activity in missionary societies was not the only manifestation of religious feminism in the nineteenth century. One of the famous crusades of the time attempted to abolish beverage alcohol; it was spearheaded by the interdenominational Women's Christian Temperance Union, founded in 1874. The WCTU, understanding its primary role to be education, played a significant role in arousing the country to the evils of alcohol. Its most effective leader was Frances Willard, but it rallied the interest and utilized the talents of women all across the country. The leadership of the WCTU also contributed to the organization in 1895 of the Anti-Saloon League, an organization of both women and men applying political pressure to stop the sale of beverage alcohol. It was principally because of the influence of the League and the WCTU that the Eighteenth Amendment became law in 1920. Again, religiously motivated women were able to influence national life in ways that did not fit stereotypical roles.

Some women believed the Bible was the heart of the problem of patriarchal religion and society. They saw the connection between the oppressive nature of their society and the churches of which they were members, and the male dominance themes that pervaded Biblical literature, at least as the Bible had traditionally been translated and interpreted. Some feminist leaders, such as Sarah Grimké, called for women to learn biblical languages and study the Bible for themselves to find the message of liberation that had been masked by male-dominated interpretation.

Women took up the challenge. Some prepared themselves as biblical scholars and even participated in the Society of Biblical Literature, the professional society for biblical scholars, in the late nineteenth and early twentieth centuries. The most famous result of trying to break the male bias in Bible interpretation was *The Woman's Bible*, published in 1898. This was a new translation and commentary done by a number of women led by Elizabeth Cady Stanton. These interpreters argued that the biblical literature was greatly influenced by the patriarchal culture of the ancient world. Rather than rejecting the Bible as being worthless for women, however, they affirmed that there were messages in the Bible that did not reflect those anti-feminist times and that those passages were much more supportive of the importance of women in family and social structures than anybody had previously acknowledged. They believed that the Bible could be studied from a woman's point of view and found to affirm the equality of women with men.

In the late nineteenth and early twentieth centuries religious feminism was very much in evidence. Feminist historians have uncovered the names of a multitude of women in the Jewish, Catholic, and Protestant traditions who were active in the cause of women's rights in society at large and also within their own religious traditions. But with the absorption of the women's missionary societies into denominational structures and the ratification of the Eighteenth and Nineteenth (female suffrage) Amendments, feminism lost most of its momentum. The first wave was over.

The second wave of feminism, including feminist theology, began in the late 1960s and lasted throughout the 1970s. Several factors reignited the movement. Many observers believe the principal agent was the publication of Betty Friedan's *The Feminine Mystique* in 1963. In that book Friedan pointed out that American society tended to stereotype women as homemakers and mothers, contending that those roles were the proper ones for women and that if women wanted more of a public than a private life they were somehow maladjusted. That constricting model of the proper role of women in society was reinforced and even propagated by the media. Friedan argued that women should break out of that mold and be their own people, as much involved in the "real" world as men. In 1966, the National Organization for Women (NOW) was formed with Friedan as cofounder and first president. NOW was created to dramatize women's causes in American society, particularly the proposal and ratification of the Equal Rights Amendment to the Constitution. Still another cause for the resurgence of feminism was that during the political activism by young people in the mid-1960s many women activists had been relegated to secondary roles by their male counterparts. They reacted against making the signs and running the ditto machines while men took to the streets and "ran the revolution." The increase in single parent families and the worsening economic conditions in the country both drew more women into the market place and into encounters with male prejudice.

In the area of religion, one of the first contributions to modern feminism was an article published in 1960 by Valerie Saiving Goldstein.[4] Little noticed for more than a decade, this article began to attract considerable attention in the mid-1970s. Goldstein argued that traditional theology contained a masculine bias. Historically the Bible has been interpreted and theology has been formulated principally by men; their work has demonstrated a masculine bias, even at the most fundamental points of faith such as the doctrines of sin and grace. Goldstein called for a theology more sensitive to the situation of women.

In 1968 Mary Daly, a Catholic theologian and teacher at Boston College, published *The Church and the Second Sex*, which became an important document for the feminist movement in religion. In her book Daly analyzed the Catholic Church's attitude toward and its treatment of women and found a distinctly bad record. She argued that the church had regarded women as inherently inferior and that it had been a primary

---

[4]Valerie Saiving Goldstein, "The Human Situation: A Feminine View," *The Journal of Religion* 40 (April 1960): 100-112, reprinted under the name Valerie Saiving in Christ and Plaskow, eds., *Womanspirit Rising*, 24-42.

agent of oppression. But she still had hope then that the church could be made more sensitive to the inherent equality of women with men in society and, indeed, in the church. Not much was written on religious feminism in the 1960s, and there was little activism. But following publication of Daly's book there was an explosion of literature and activism that gained momentum throughout the 1970s.

As with black theology, the principal starting point for feminist theology was experience. Women could draw on a long tradition of having been alternately ignored and oppressed in society and the church. Their experience of having been dominated by men and male-centered institutions was one of dehumanization. Any theology appropriate for women would have to account for the subservient roles they had traditionally played and to provide a way for women to combat that centuries-long indignity. But women had another experience that influenced their feminism, what many called "the experience of their bodies." While most feminists rejected what they considered an artificial dichotomy between men and women—namely, that men are inherently aggressive, analytical, and powerful whereas women are inherently passive, nonanalytical, and emotional—yet women are obviously physically different from men. Women, then, have a different body experience: menstruation, pregnancy, giving birth, and lactation. A feminist theology had to draw on those body experiences as well.

In the attempt to develop a theology that took seriously both the experience of oppression and the experience of female physicality, there were basically two modes of response, the revolutionary and the reformist. Advocates of the former tended to think that the Judaeo-Christian tradition is hopelessly and irreformably sexist. Because they saw no future for women within either Judaism or Christianity, they chose to turn their backs on them and look for other religious traditions that might have more to offer to women as a way of dealing with being a woman in the modern world. The reformists agreed with their revolutionary sisters that the Judaeo-Christian tradition is quite sexist in theory and practice, but they did not believe that it was irreformably so. Consequently, their attempt to formulate a theology appropriate for women was to go back to the tradition to celebrate female dignity and the value of women. They searched in the Bible and in the history of the synagogue and the church for real-life examples of women who played creative, important roles in the religious institutions of their respective eras, in the face of patriarchal prejudice imposed upon them. These reformists believed that patriarchalism is not endemic to the Judaeo-Christian tradition. In their feminism they were calling the tradition back to a core truth that, for Christianity, was expressed by Paul when he wrote: "...there is no male and female; for you are all one in Christ Jesus" (Galatians 3:28).

• *Recovery of the Goddess*

Revolutionary feminists recovered ancient religions with female deities as an alternative to the rejected patriarchal Judaeo-Christian tradition. These religions with female deities are much more appropriate for women, they felt, because they have the potential of being more meaningful to women's experiences. The patriarchal religions of Judaism, Christianity, and Islam are relative newcomers onto the stage of history and, although they have become very powerful religions, do not represent the more ancient and original religious impulse of humanity. Revolutionary feminists pointed out that history shows that prior to the development of the major religions of the modern world, earliest humanity had religions that normally focused on the forces of nature. In these nature religions, virtually without exception the deities were female. These traditions stemmed from many cultures: the ancient Mediterranean, pre-Christian European, Native American, Central American, African and others. There are many deities associated with these various traditions, among whom are Artemis, Kore, Tana, Diana, Hecate, and Kali. So, for this revolutionary feminism, there was a multitude of deities to which they were willing to give recognition and honor. By whatever name these goddesses were called, they each were thought of as a personification of nature. Nature goddesses were thought to speak most powerfully to women, since each woman's body experience is a microcosm of the cycles of nature, of the seasons of the year, of birth, growth, and death.

Among revolutionary feminists the moon was a popular symbol of the forces of nature personified by the Goddess. That is, there was perceived to be a symbolic connection between the 28 day cycle of the moon and the 28 day cycle of menstruation. Also, unlike American culture, which idealizes youthful, beautiful people, the Goddess religion can stimulate respect for women at every stage of life. Again, this is symbolized by the cycles of the moon: the new moon suggests youth, the

Maiden; the full moon suggests mature women, the Mother, giver of life; the waning moon suggests the old, wise woman, the Crone.

What did Goddess religion offer to women? Carol Christ, one of the principal advocates of this style of feminism, wrote of several benefits. Goddess religion acknowledged female power as independent and legitimate. "Power" means that the divine principle is within women. That it is independent and legitimate means that women who recognize the divine within them no longer have to rely on men for self-definition, as was the case under patriarchalism. Goddess religion is an affirmation of the female body and the life cycle expressed in it. This theology is an affirmation of the goodness of the body, rather than the implicit "anti-*body*" prejudice that has historically lurked just below the surface in western religious traditions. With the Goddess, women need no longer be regarded as descendants of the sexual temptress, the carnal Eve. Awareness of the Goddess stimulates Goddess-centered ritual, focusing the energy that flows between beings in the natural and human world. Finally, Goddess religion breaks old religious stereotypes and provides a basis for a reevaluation (and rejection) of the bondages and heritage with which women have had to contend.[5]

The Goddess religion to which revolutionary feminists turned was not just an intellectual idea, a belief. It worked itself out in practical forms in the rituals of witchcraft, often known as "wicca." The word "wicca," from which witchcraft comes, seems to have been derived from the Indo-European roots "wic" or "weik," which mean to bend or turn. Thus a witch is a person skilled in the craft of shaping, bending, or changing reality. This was right in line with feminist goals of reinterpreting and reforming patriarchal society into one that respected both sexes as equal. Consequently, there were some covens (groups for worship) for women and men, although usually women were in the leadership roles, but there were some covens for women only. These practiced rituals that glorified the Goddess, the human body, and the environment. Because the Goddess is a personification of nature, witches were often very sensitive to environmental concerns: Mother Earth had been

---

[5]Carol P. Christ, "Why Women Need the Goddess: Phenomenological, Psychological, and Political Reflections," in Christ and Plaskow, eds., *Womanspirit Rising*, 277, 279, 282, 285.

damaged as much by patriarchal society as women had. The rituals of the wicca covens drew power from Mother Earth and from the consciousness of the assembled participants. There were also rituals of self-blessing to be used even when one was not in the sisterhood of a coven, by which a woman could honor her own divinity, her own identity with the Goddess. This was a private but powerful self-affirmation.

Devotion to the Goddess was not found among the majority of religious feminists, but this revolutionary position was well articulated by others, in addition to Carol Christ. Some of the other spokeswomen for this viewpoint were Sheila Collins, Starhawk, Naomi Goldenberg, Zsuzsanna Budapest, and Merlin Stone. Charlene Spretnak summed up the thinking of this faction very well.

> The revival of the Goddess has resonated with so many people because She symbolizes *the way things really are*: All forms of being are One, continually renewed in cyclic rhythms of birth, maturation, death. That is the meaning of her triple aspect—the waxing, full and waning moon; the maiden, mother, and wise crone. The Goddess honors *union and process*, the cosmic dance, the eternally vibrating flux of matter/energy: She expresses the dynamic rather than static, model of the universe. She is *immanent* in our lives and our world. She contains both female and male in Her womb, as a male deity cannot; all beings are *part of Her*, not distant creations. She also symbolizes the power of the female body/mind. There is no "party line" of Goddess worship; rather, each person's process of perceiving and living Her truth is a movement in the larger dance—hence the phrase "The Goddess Is All."[6]

• A Different Kind of Revolutionary

A revolutionary feminist who took a different route in her protest against patriarchal religion was Mary Daly. Her approach was not to reject Christianity by going into nature religion. Rather, she rejected Christianity by completely redefining its core symbolism to make it into something new. As noted above, in *The Church and the Second Sex* Daly castigated the Catholic Church for its oppression of women, but still held out some hope that the church, after the reforms of the Second Vat-

---

[6]Charlene Spretnak, "Introduction," in Spretnak, ed., *The Politics of Women's Spirituality: Essays on the Rise of Spiritual Power Within the Feminist Movement* (Garden City NY: Doubleday, 1982) xvii; italics in original.

ican Council, was moving to rectify its past. This, she then believed, increased the possibility for equality for women within the church.

However, in her second book, *Beyond God the Father: Toward a Philosophy of Women's Liberation*, Daly wrote a "post-Christian" philosophy of women's liberation. Here she asserted that God functions as an idol that legitimates patriarchy, "his" male nature justifying the dominance of males over females. That idol obviously had to be eliminated. But it was not enough simply to change the pronouns, to speak of God as "She" or "Mother." Though Daly spoke of "castrating" sexist theological language and concepts, simply changing the gender of God would not be sufficient. The problem is that it is not just the gender of the word "God" which is patriarchal, but God's very nature and attributes. God has been perceived as transcendent, "high and lifted up," to use the phrase from Isaiah 6:1. God has been understood to be the pinnacle in the hierarchy of being. Since God is transcendent, the Supreme Being, *and* male, women have been perceived as the "subordinate other," not only of God but of his fellows-in-gender. Daly said that to liberate women truly God must never more be thought of as male or as endorsing hierarchical relationships. For women to cease to be the "subordinate other," God must not be conceived as the male "superordinate other."

For Daly the God "beyond the Father" is beyond both gender and hierarchicalism. She simply described God as be-ing, using the hyphenated term in order to imply dynamism. Because God is dynamic, moving in everything which has be-ing, the word "God" should not be a noun, but a verb. God is the Verb of Verbs and is in constant activity, thus negating static hierarchical relationships. Furthermore, one cannot speak of the gender of a verb. The result of all this is that the hierarchies of divine and human, male and female, human and natural that grow out of the biblical record are negated. Daly felt that the result of this process would be an androgynous society—in her definition, a society in which female and male would be absolutely equal.

In 1978 Daly published *Gyn/Ecology: The Metaethics of Radical Feminism*, in which she departed from traditional Christianity even further. She now spoke of the divine be-ing as "Goddess," although it does not seem that she meant the same thing by that term as the wicca-following feminists. She now argued that men are inferior to women and that the ideal society would not be androgynous, but one in which the traditional social order would be inverted.

Radical black theologians have asserted that God is black. That may be somewhat shocking to those who have never had a stereotypical concept of God challenged. But the style of feminist theology represented by Mary Daly was much more radical because it called into question and redefined the very nature of God. The "God of the Exodus" theme of liberation appealed to blacks and other minority races. But discrimination based on gender obviously cuts across all racial lines and is independent of minority/majority status. In that context the liberation theme is not just to challenge the authority figures, it is rather to destroy all aspects of the hierarchical advantage of males. Since that advantage is based largely on the pervasive symbolism of the maleness of God, Daly's extreme feminist theology redefined the nature of God and so became the most radical of theologies.

• *Feminism for Reform*

As noted earlier, there was another style of feminism which saw as clearly as the revolutionaries the patriarchal nature of the Judaeo-Christian tradition, but yet did not want to leave it. The goal of these feminists was to reform the tradition, to call it back to its true nature of regarding women and men as equals. A primary example of this was Rosemary Ruether, a Roman Catholic and serious churchwoman, a theologian and church historian. For Ruether, the principal reason for the oppression of women is that the ideology from Greek culture influenced early Christianity and caused some modifications in its original views on reality. The result of this was the creation of a dualism that views reality in terms of opposites. Some of the dualisms that have persisted in Christian history are the distinctions between sacred and secular, individual and community, soul and body, material and spiritual, this world and the next, and male and female. Males tended to be the culture-creating agents and thus associated the negative side of these dualisms, body, material, this world, with women. Ruether said that these dualistic views must be replaced with new views and cultural symbols if women are to be relieved of the oppression they have endured. Women can and must take the initiative in this transformation of cultural views and values.

The key to cultural transformation is the distinctly Judaeo-Christian message of God's power to liberate the oppressed, as it was articulated by the Hebrew prophets and by Jesus, both in his teaching and in his actions. Ruether emphasized the same kinds of themes that black theology lifted up: God's love for the oppressed and God's power to break through hardened social structures. Ruether did admit that the themes of liberation and equality have been obscured and perverted in history; even the church has betrayed them. But she insisted that these cultural accretions and interpretive perversions can be stripped away to return to the essential vision. She was a reformist, wanting to purify the tradition of its abuses and to reaffirm the original possibility of the equality of the sexes before God.

Of course, the central question here is how one knows what the essential and original ideas of the tradition are. Ruether's answer is that they are to be sought through biblical and historical scholarship. A large part of the explosion of reformist feminist literature in the 1970s focused on biblical and historical studies. Feminism had a sizable cadre of highly qualified scholars—Ruether was one—who were seeking to show that the Judaeo-Christian tradition does contain themes of liberation and that, given these insights, the tradition could purify itself of sexism.

• *The Bible in Reformist Feminism*

Both reformers and radicals have noted that the Bible is full of patriarchal symbols and language. It reflects a male-dominant perspective, one in which women, children, and slaves are subservient and, in a real sense, invisible. That is what caused many feminists to give up on biblical religion altogether, to see it as not only irrelevant to them but as part of the problem.

Feminist biblical scholars insist, however, that it is possible to find in the Bible not only oppressive language but also language and concepts that both transcend and negate the patriarchal material. Ultimately the Bible speaks of the redemption of humanity and social structures by the power of God. Prophetic literature in both testaments shows that any cultural-conditionedness that leads to the oppression of anybody on the basis of sex (or race or class) is wrong. The core of the theology of the Bible shows that even those passages that reflect male dominance may be transcended by the concept of God's concern for the liberation of all oppressive structures. The task, then, of feminist interpretation is to penetrate the sexist language of the Bible in order to lift up the liberating themes. The task is not only to emphasize the passages that obviously reflect the equality of all persons before God and so condemn the illegitimacy of all oppressive social orders, but also to examine the patriarchal passages to show that, in reality, they are much more reflective of the equality of the sexes than they appear to be on the surface. A pioneer work of this sort was an article by Phyllis Trible, "Depatriarchalizing in Biblical Interpretation," in which she demonstrated that certain Old Testament passages that seem to assert the idea of male dominance do not do so at all. Without distorting the texts she showed the passages to be quite compatible with the idea of the importance of women in Hebrew society and certainly in God's scheme of things. An example of this approach is this summary of a section of the article:

> Although the Old Testament often pictures Yahweh as a man, it also uses gynomorphic language for the Deity. At the same time, Israel repudiated the idea of sexuality in God. Unlike fertility gods, Yahweh is neither male nor female; neither he nor she. Consequently, modern assertions that God is masculine, even when they are qualified, are misleading and detrimental, if not altogether inaccurate. Cultural and grammatical limitations (the use of masculine pronouns for God) need not limit theological understanding. As Creator and Lord, Yahweh embraces and transcends both sexes. To translate for our immediate concern: the nature of the God of Israel defies sexism.[7]

• *Historical Studies*

The scholarship of reformist feminists was extended to postbiblical periods, both in Judaism and Christianity. This research was designed to show the patriarchal oppression in the history of western religious institutions. This catalogue of negatives was told for the same reason that modern Jews tell of the Holocaust; that people should not forget it, in order that it might never happen again. To tell the stories of the oppression of women was to raise the consciousness of society so that such

---

[7]Phyllis Trible, "Depatriarchalizing in Biblical Interpretation," *Journal of the American Academy of Religion* 41 (March 1973): 34. Footnotes omitted. Other good examples of a wealth of literature that could be cited are two articles that appeared in the *Journal for the Study of the Old Testament* 6 (February 1982): Elisabeth Schüssler Fiorenza, "Feminist Theology and New Testament Interpretation," 32-46, and Rosemary Radford Ruether, "Feminism and Patriarchal Religion: Principles of Ideological Critique of the Bible," 54-66.

abuses might disappear. But there was also a positive dimension to this scholarship. That was to tell the stories of women who made significant contributions to the spirituality and/or to the well-being of religious institutions in their times. In an essay in which she traces the stories of two Medieval English women who made significant contributions to the church, Eleanor McLaughlin writes:

> The general outlines of the thesis, that Christian faith and institutions have been in certain times and under certain conditions radically supportive of women and informed by women's experience, will be illustrated primarily from the history of the spirituality of the high and late Middle Ages. . . .[8]

This is a succinct statement of the methodology of the historical work by feminist scholars, although many of them worked on periods other than the Middle Ages, of course. Others who were prominent in the biblical and historical scholarship of feminism were Letty Russell, Barbara Brown Zickmund, Krister Stendahl, and Elisabeth Schüssler Fiorenza.

There were also conservative scholars who counted themselves as feminists. Some of these were "Establishment Evangelicals," but most were of the left-wing "Young Evangelical" viewpoint. In order to reinterpret the obviously patriarchal character of the Bible, some of these scholars argued that the biblical authors did not mean what it seems that they meant, that there is a meaning below the surface meaning of the words and that deeper meaning is what the authors intended. Others simply argued that the biblical texts were culturally conditioned by their patriarchal historical context and that these passages can be either discounted or radically reinterpreted to make them conform to humanitarian/feminist standards. Prominent among those evangelical feminist scholars were Letha Scanzoni, Nancy Hardesty, Paul Jewett, Virginia Ramey Mollenkott, Lucille Sider Dayton, and Donald Dayton. In 1975 an Evangelical Women's Caucus was formed and, in the same year, *Daughters of Sarah*, an evangelical feminist monthly magazine, began publication.

At the same time that feminist scholars were making significant advances in revisionist biblical and historical scholarship they tried to crack

---

[8]Eleanor L. McLaughlin, "The Christian Past: Does it hold a Future for Women?" *Anglican Theological Review* 57 (January 1975): 39.

the male dominance of the leadership of the Society of Biblical Literature, the American Academy of Religion, and the American Society of Church History, the major professional societies in the field. Their goal was to gain more participation in leadership structures in order to secure greater recognition of feminist concerns and themes by the organizations. By the end of 1980 they had not been able to make much progress in those efforts. In order to present their concerns and to gain some visibility they did form a Women's Caucus in the American Academy of Religion.

• *The Need for a New Language*

Feminists tried to make scholarly communities aware of their concerns, but they also had much broader objectives. One of these was to sensitize people to the need for "inclusive language," both within the framework of the church or synagogue and in the society generally. Language communicates ideas, viewpoints, attitudes, cultural and individual mindsets. Language that communicates male dominance reflects and often encourages the tendency of society, including its religious institutions, to relegate women to a secondary, subordinate state. With the resurgence of feminism, its advocates encouraged the use of inclusive language that treats both sexes equally and no longer reflects a dominant-subordinate relationship between men and women. This attempt to substitute inclusive language for traditional sexist language was part of the consciousness-raising dimension of the women's movement. A document written for the faculty and students of Vanderbilt Divinity School helpfully summarized this issue into four areas.[9]

1) *Human references*: The references we often make about people, in conversation and within historical narrative, frequently reflect male dominance. But feminists insisted that alternative methods of expression should be found. For example, "mankind" more properly may be referred to as "humankind" or "humanity." One frequently speaks of "man" when referring to the human race. But the words "all of us," "everyone," or "human beings" might just as easily and more appropri-

---

[9]Nadia Lahutsky et al., *Toward a More Inclusive Language for VDS/GDR* (Nashville: Vanderbilt Divinity School, 1979).

ately be used. Feminists said that in referring to nonclergy in a church or denomination, it is better to use "lay persons," "lay people," or simply "laity" rather than "laymen," unless one is referring only to the males in this group.

2) *References to God*: As we have seen, many feminists were convinced that thinking of God in male terms has led to the male dominance that has been such a distressing part of human history. This identification of God has been used as a justification for a patriarchal style of family and of society. Furthermore, who is to say that God has only male qualities? Is not God creator of both sexes? Must not those qualities found in females also be part of the Creator's character? Since God is comprehensive, it is appropriate sometimes to use language which reflects the feminine side of God, terms such as "She" or "Mother." But feminists also pointed out that there are gender-neutral terms that can be used for God, terms such as "Most High," "Creator," "Redeemer," and "Friend."

3) *Liturgy*: Creeds, confessions, prayers, litanies, sermons and hymns often use gender-oriented language, not only to refer to the Divine but also to refer to the recipients of salvation. Here again feminists argued that language could be made inclusive without altering the meaning of what was being said. They called on clergy to use sermon illustrations that were inclusive and to recognize that women have roles other than wife and mother; they need salvation from the complexities of modern life just as much as men. Confessions of faith can recognize that salvation is for all; that in referring to Christ's role it is better to say "Who for humanity's sake, and for our salvation. . ." rather than the traditional "Who for us men, and for our salvation. . . ." Hymns present problems for inclusive language, since there are considerations of rhythm and cadence, but feminists felt that it is not unreasonable to expect that "Good Christian Men, Rejoice" could become "Good Christian Friends, Rejoice" or that "Faith of our Fathers" could be "Faith of our Parents."

4) *Bible translation*: Because of the cultural context of its authors, the Bible uses patriarchal language at many points. Obviously many passages refer to men specifically and that language ought to be retained as it is, said feminists. But when "man" is used in the generic sense, even the words of Scripture should be modified to make it more inclusive. For example, Psalm One begins with the statement "Blessed is the man who walks not in the council of the wicked. . ." and carries the male motif throughout. Feminists argued that the Psalm should be "Blessed are

those who walk not in the council of the wicked. . ." with appropriate plural verbs throughout. The meaning of the passage is not lost, indeed, it is intensified, since it refers to all the righteous. Feminists insisted that it is possible to modify passages throughout the Bible to make them more obviously express what the authors intended, namely, that God's activity and saving love is not exclusive; that it encompasses all the human race, not just half of it.

This feminist desire to rephrase the English Bible moved from the theoretical to the practical in 1980 when the National Council of Churches, the holder of the copyright for the Revised Standard Version of the Bible, decided to publish an inclusive-language lectionary based on the RSV. The decision to publish a lectionary was a compromise between those who wanted an inclusive-language edition of the Bible itself and those who wanted no such thing, since they felt that the text of the Bible, seen as God's word, is inviolable. The decision was to publish the lectionary with inclusive language for use in worship in order to see how such language was accepted in churches and as a "trial balloon" for a possible inclusive-language edition of the Bible in the future.[10]

• *Ordination to the Ministry*

Religious feminists of the reformist variety were committed to the church or synagogue. Consequently, they not only wanted to make those institutions more sensitive to feminist concerns, they wanted to serve them. One practical way that reformists wanted to serve their respective institutions was through the ministry. But even here the way was not easy, for the various religious bodies had, at the very best, equivocal attitudes toward women in the ministry.

World War II had tended to cause people to reexamine the role of women in the workplace, since many women had worked in war-related

---

[10]The lectionary was published on 17 October 1983. It precipitated a storm of reaction, much of which was negative. The principal criticisms were that it was a concession to a social fad, that it rewrote history to the extent that the Bible is a historical document, and, most importantly, it tampered with the form of God's revelation. The negative judgments notwithstanding, by 27 November 1983, the lectionary was in its third printing and the National Council scholars pushed ahead to prepare two other lectionaries, for the 1984-1985 and 1985-1986 church years, respectively.

industries. After the war these changing attitudes, combined with the increase in church growth, caused many women to think more seriously of the possibility of ordination. Yet there was not much activity among women to pursue ordination, at least until the maturing of the women's movement in the late 1960s. At the end of the 1960s there were few women in professional roles in the churches, neither were there many studying in seminaries. But that changed in the 1970s. Furthermore, the attitudes of the churches themselves changed in that decade. Some Protestant denominations had ordained women to the ministry for years, but most had not. Some of the latter quietly began to ordain women in the very late 1960s and early 1970s, primarily because women began to insist upon it. During the 1970s there was an increasing pool of women who not only felt the call to ministry, but who qualified themselves for that role. Seminary enrollment figures broken down by sex were not available before 1972, but in that year there were 3,358 women enrolled in schools of theology, 10.2 percent of the total enrollment. In the succeeding years the number increased dramatically until 1980, the last year covered by this book, there were 10,830 female seminary students, 21.8 percent of the total enrollment. That was an increase of 222.5 percent in eight years. In the same years the percent of increase of male students was only 30.7 percent. However, there did seem to be evidence that rate of increase among female students was declining as the 1970s ended. [11]

Even with this increased number of women interested in serving in the ministry, Protestant churches were not unanimously receptive. In 1979 only four percent of all the Christian clergy in America were women. Of the 163 largest denominations, 76 ordained women but 87 did not. The number of women in the total clergy of some representative denominations were: Presbyterian Church (U.S.), 75 out of 5,156; United Methodist Church, 319 out of 35,480; United Presbyterian Church, 295 out of 13,772; Lutheran Church of America, 55 out of 7,695, and Southern Baptist Convention, 20 out of 55,000. Of all female clergy in ten mainstream denominations 52 percent came from the United Church of Christ, the American Baptist Church, and the Chris-

---

[11]Constant H. Jacquet, Jr., ed., *Yearbook of American and Canadian Churches 1981* (Nashville: The Abingdon Press, 1981) 252.

tian Church (Disciples of Christ). Some (certainly not all) conservative denominations had a good record, from the feminist point of view. One-third of all female clergy were in fourteen Pentecostal denominations, another one-third were in the Salvation Army. More than one-half of the clergy in the Salvation Army was female, 3,037 out of 5,095.[12]

Even though interest in women clergy increased during the 1970s, the picture was not bright even in those groups that did ordain women. Many churches simply would not hire women ministers, or, if they did, only for subordinate positions. Many men and a sizable number of women, even in the more "liberal" denominations, simply were not ready for women clergy.

• *Turmoil Among Episcopalians*

That the ordination of women was an issue of some magnitude in American religion was made known to the public most forcefully by the controversies among the Episcopalians, Catholics, and, to a lesser extent, Jews.

In the Episcopal Church there had been discussions about the ordination of women since the late nineteenth century, but with inconclusive results. Intermittently after that some women were ordained as deacons, but not as priests. In 1944 the Bishop of Hong Kong ordained a woman, but she later resigned when the leadership of the church in England did not accept her ordination. From 1945 to 1965 there was not much agitation for the ordination of women, although in 1958 the Episcopal Theological School in Cambridge, Massachusetts, voted to admit women to the same standard theological course that prepared men for ordination. So, by the early 1970s, a group of women had emerged fully qualified by training for ordination.

With the feminist spirit soaring in the land, sentiment arose among many Episcopalians for the ordination of women to the priesthood. The General Assembly of the church in 1970, responding to the report of a committee appointed to study the matter, rejected a recommendation to ordain women to the priesthood, but approved the ordination of women

---

[12]Lareta Haltman Finger, "Women in Pulpits," *The Other Side* 15 (July 1979): 15-16, 19.

to the diaconate, a level of service to the church below priesthood. The bishops also voted to set up another commission to study the matter. In September 1973 the General Assembly again voted against the ordination of women to the priesthood. The bishops called for still another study committee (apparently to pacify the Episcopal Women's Caucus and other women in the church who were sorely disappointed by the course of events). Finally, to break the logjam and force the issue, on 29 July 1974 11 women were ordained to the priesthood by three retired bishops. For the women and those who ordained them, the act was not so much a violation of the will of the convention as it was radical obedience of God's call to them to fulfill a vocation.

The ordination precipitated debate, accusations, recriminations, and threatened schism within the church. In August 1974 the bishops declared the ordinations invalid. Many theologians and others in the church pointed out both administrative and theological flaws in the bishops' resolution. In 1976 the General Assembly voted that the previous ordinations were valid and that henceforth women should be ordained to the priesthood. The bishops did later unilaterally modify that action by declaring a kind of local option rule—that each bishop could either accept or reject women priests and ordinations within his diocese. But the die was cast. Between the time women's ordination was approved in 1976 and a survey in November 1979, 340 Episcopal women were ordained, 160 as deacons and 180 as priests.

What was the principal opposition to priesthood for women? The argument was that a priest is an intercessor between humans and God. Of course, Jesus Christ is the model for the priesthood because he was the one who specifically came to bridge the gap between sinful humanity and God. Jesus was male. Since he was the prototype for all priests, all priests must be male. There were some variations on that theme in the debate that swirled around the issue. Some objected that it would be wrong to have a menstruating woman serving at God's altar, or a pregnant woman, or even a beautiful woman, since she might distract the worshipers from their true purpose in being at worship. Some priests even argued that the worship service is a "seminal mass," in which the priest, as the representative of Christ, engages in a sex act with the bride of Christ, the church. Obviously women could not do that, it was argued (apparently with a straight face), because they would be performing a lesbian act with the church instead, which would be illegitimate. But the principal objection was simply that Christ was male and so all priests should be male.

• *Female Priests in Roman Catholicism*

In the Catholic Church the issue of female priests came up in 1910 when, in Britain, the Saint Joan's International Alliance was formed. Its purpose is suggested in the group's original name: the Catholic Woman's Suffrage Society. It worked behind the scenes on the issue of ordination. When plans for the Second Vatican Council were announced in the late 1950s, Saint Joan's Alliance submitted documents requesting the Council to approve ordination for women. In spite of the group's efforts, the Council did not approve the idea. Undaunted, Saint Joan's Alliance sent petitions for the ordination of women to Rome annually throughout the 1970s. The American affiliate of Saint Joan's Alliance was started in 1965 and thus played a role in this lobbying activity.

Many Catholic women, particularly nuns, caught the spirit of secular feminism in the late 1960s and applied it to their religious situation. In 1974 the Leadership Conference of Women Religious, the representative body for nuns in the United States, passed a resolution:

1. that the LCWR supports the principle that all ministries in the Church be open to women and men as the Spirit calls them: 2. that the LCWR affirms the principle that women have active participation in all decision making bodies in the Church. [13]

In the next year a Conference on Women's Ordination was held in Detroit. The planners of the conference had expected 600 persons to attend, but 1,400 attended and another 600 had to be turned away. Many felt that this attendance demonstrated that there was a greater interest in the ordination of women to the priesthood than even its most ardent supporters had dreamed. At the same event an organization entitled Priests for Equality was formed to support women in their attempts to be ordained. By 1979 it had 2,000 members.

---

[13]Rosemary Ruether, "Entering the Sanctuary: The Roman Catholic Story," in Ruether and McLaughlin, eds., *Women of Spirit*, 375.

These events did not go unnoticed by the Vatican. On 27 January 1977 Pope John Paul II issued the statement, "Declaration on the Question of the Admission of Women to the Ministerial Priesthood." The thrust of the document was that there was no possibility that the church would approve the ordination of women. There were two principal grounds for this rejection: it had never been done, that is, the tradition of the church was against it and, even though the church regards men and women as equal, there is a sacramental bond of Christ, maleness, and the priesthood (essentially the same arguments used by opponents of women's ordination in the Episcopal Church).

The reaction to the papal statement was not what the Vatican had hoped. Although many bishops praised the document as having put the controversy to rest, it did not. Many theologians wrote sharply critical responses to it, saying that it misused tradition and misunderstood theology. Surveys of the Catholic population showed an actual increase in support for the ordination of women after the papal decree. The surveys did not yet indicate that a majority of Catholics were in favor of women priests, but the rates of increase were such that pollsters predicted that early in the 1980s a majority of Catholics would support the concept. In November 1978 2,000 persons gathered for a second Women's Ordination Conference. Many felt that the meeting itself and certainly its large attendance was a direct result of the Vatican statement. The bishops of the church failed either to endorse or to understand the conference. The conference organizers summed up their frustration over lack of progress toward ordination in a biting statement.

> The bishops are always telling us what the roles of women are in the church. But we claim the same role as the women who were present at the crucifixion and resurrection of Jesus the Christ. . . .There were no bishops there then. It is our observation that the bishops are like the apostles. They always arrive late—a little out of breath. [14]

The 1970s ended with no official approval for the ordination of women in the Roman Catholic Church. But the issue was still a topic of interest and debate. Some observers, especially some supporters of the idea, felt that eventually the church would ordain women, not so much

---

[14]Finger, "Women in Pulpits," 25.

because it would have a change of heart theologically, but because of the practical need for more priests. Between the end of Vatican II and late 1979, some 10,000 American priests had left the ministry. The number of seminarians declined from 49,000 in 1965 to 11,200 in 1978. In the same period the number of nuns declined from 181,421 to around 131,000. Conditions were even worse in Latin America. It was worth speculating that many of those nuns would not have left their vocations and there would not have been a shortage of priests if women had had the opportunity to serve in the priesthood.[15]

• *Women as Rabbis*

Historically Judaism has been a male-dominated religion, patriarchal in the strictest sense of the word as feminists use it. Judaism has always claimed to idealize women and to treat them as equals with men. In a sense, that is correct, but in an odd sense. Women have been highly regarded so long as they stayed in their proper roles as wife and mother. Historically the Jewish home was under the control of the man and the woman had well-defined functions. That her principal roles were to be mother and helpmate is illustrated by the fact that Judaism even relieved women from some of the ritual requirements of the religion and from the study of Scripture so they might give their full attention to rearing children and serving the well-being of their husbands. Women's subservience to men was comprehensive. In legal matters of marriage, divorce, and inheritance, their rights were severely restricted. In worship, they were segregated from men, did not count in the number of adults required to make up a congregation, and could not read from the Scriptures in public. There was even a traditional prayer for men in which they thanked God that they had not been born a woman. In this kind of second-class status in home and synagogue, it is not surprising that psychologically women did not think of themselves as leaders.

---

[15]"John Paul's U.S. Triumph," *Newsweek* 94 (15 October 1979): 40-45. See also Dolly Pomerleau, Maureen Fielder, and William Callahan, "Women Priests: A Research Report," *America* 141 (17 November 1979): 299-300, and "Women's Ordination: The Future of Equality,"*America* 136 (12 February 1977): 118.

Indeed, women did not serve as rabbis. Traditionally rabbis were scholars of Scripture, teachers and interpreters of Jewish law. Although women could become scholars, they could do so only through independent study, since they were denied access to the rabbinical education made available to men. It was unthinkable that a woman should become a rabbi, although there are a few recorded instances where women did achieve, on their own initiative, the requisite scholarship to function as a rabbi. But no Jewish congregation would allow those rare women to teach publicly the knowledge they had gained.

In the late eighteenth and early nineteenth centuries, particularly in Western Europe, Judaism began to change. It divided into three groups, distinguished by distinct attitudes toward observance of the Jewish tradition. The Orthodox party was the most traditionalist, believing that it was entirely possible to practice religion in the modern world as religion had always been practiced. The Reform party was modernist in attitude, believing that if Judaism were practiced in modern times as it had always been practiced, it would be so irrelevant that it would soon be obsolete. So Reform was willing to make modifications in the tradition in order to adjust to contemporary society. Between these two was a party that called itself Conservative. These folk were willing to change in order for religion to survive in new and different times, but they were not willing to make wholesale modifications. They were willing to adapt the tradition to its environment only when it was absolutely necessary. Given these attitudes, it is not surprising that when the question of the ordination of women to the position of rabbi was first seriously discussed, it was primarily within Reform Judaism.

In this country, the Central Council of American (Reform) Rabbis declared themselves to be in favor of ordaining women to the rabbinate as early as 1921, but the implementation of that decision was repeatedly delayed because it was felt that even Reform congregations were not ready for such a radical break with tradition. After World War II there were some women who qualified themselves educationally for the position, since the Reform seminary allowed women to enroll in the rabbinical program, but there was still some hedging on actual ordination. In the meantime many Jewish women caught the spirit of the revived feminist movement and began to press even harder for ordination. Finally, in 1972, Sally Priesand was ordained, the first American woman and perhaps only the second or third in all of Jewish history to have become a rabbi. By 1980 a few others had been ordained by the Reform branch.

Reconstructionism, a branch of Judaism that originated in this century and that is even more willing to adapt to modern culture than Reform, declared itself to be in favor of the ordination of women at least as early as 1968, when it opened its theological seminary. In 1974 Reconstructionism ordained its first woman rabbi and, by 1978, two others had been ordained. In that same year 25 percent of those studying to be Reconstructionist rabbis were women. In spite of these advances in both the Reform and Reconstructionist branches, women rabbis still had problems. Most synagogues were not willing to hire women rabbis and, if they did, it was usually as a staff person, rather than as senior or sole rabbi.

Orthodox Judaism ended the 1970s adamantly opposed to the ordination of women, just as it always had been. Orthodoxy continued to see women in terms of the traditional gender-role stereotype. However, there were Orthodox women who were active in the Jewish Feminist Organization, which was founded in 1974 "to struggle for the liberation of Jewish women." They were trying to agitate for more participation in synagogue ritual, to break out of the home with more ease in order to pursue career goals, and to relax some of the male-favoring marriage and divorce laws of Judaism.

Conservative Judaism, consistent with its heritage, was more willing to bend in its attitude toward feminism than Orthodoxy, but less willing than Reform. In 1973 the United Synagogues of America, an arm of Conservatism, adopted a three-part resolution on feminism: (1) that women should have equal opportunity to assume leadership and authority in synagogue activities; (2) that women should participate in ritual; (3) that women should be admitted to the Rabbinical School of the Jewish Theological Seminary of America.[16] Those were accomplished. The seminary then appointed a panel of Conservative experts in Jewish law to study the question of the ordination of women to the rabbinate. In 1979 the commission recommended the ordination of women and asked the seminary to install procedures leading to that goal. However,

---

[16]Anne Lapidus Lerner, "'Who Hast Not Made Me a Man': The Movement for Equal Rights for Women in American Jewry," *American Jewish Year Book* 1977 3-38.

the faculty of the seminary refused to implement the recommendation. Consequently, as the 1970s ended Conservative Judaism was at a stalemate on the question of the ordination of women.

Although, as noted above, there were some evangelicals who were feminists, there were also many who were not. Those even further to the right on the theological spectrum were opposed to feminism, even in its reformist variety. Many fundamentalists were vociferous in their opposition to feminism because they believed it to be a serious challenge to traditional moral values, to Scripture, and ultimately an affront to God. In the battle throughout most of the 1970s over whether the Equal Rights Amendment should be added to the Constitution and in the highly emotional discussion over abortion, fundamentalists and secular conservatives claimed that feminism was pro-abortion and anti-family. Feminism was seen to take the position that each individual woman was virtually a deity unto herself, that she believed that her will was nearly absolute. Consequently, if she wanted to have an abortion, that was nobody's business but her own; it she wanted to abandon her family or radically reorder its structure, that was certainly her right. Thus these conservatives opposed feminism and all it stood for, at least in part because they had distorted what it did stand for. During the election of 1980 these positions were forcefully articulated in opposition to the ERA and because the conservatives wanted to elect only those people who stood for the old "tried and true" values. One of the principal spokespersons for this view was Phyllis Schlafly.

Another conservative viewpoint regarding feminism might be described as nonfeminism, rather than anti-feminism, since it did not speak out against the movement. This was the view popularized by Marabel Morgan in her book *The Total Woman*. The book and the classes that were frequently taught were only for women who were married. One even got the impression that the author felt that the marriage/home context was the only proper one for women, although she did not explicitly say that. The book was devoted to describing ways that women could make their husbands happy. The assumption was that by submitting to him and serving his every emotional and physical need, the home would be happy, their marriage would be secure, and consequently the woman would be happy, too. The total woman was to maintain the traditional sex-role model and to go to extremes to make sure that her husband was the head of the household. The woman's role was to be *helpmate*. This kind of relationship was that which was commanded by God in the Bible. But Morgan saw a "helpmate" as a consummate manipulator of male ego.

> Have you ever wondered why your husband doesn't just melt when you tell him how much you love him? But try saying, "I admire you," and see what happens. If you want to free him to express his thoughts and emotions, begin by filling up his empty cup with admiration. He must be filled first, for he has nothing to give until this need is met. And when his cup runs over, guess who lives in the overflow? Why, the very one who has been filling up the cup—you!
>
> Love your husband and hold him in reverence, it says in the Bible. That means admire him. *Reverence*, according to the dictionary, means "To respect, honor, esteem, adore, praise, enjoy, and admire."[17]

Morgan did not hold the partnership view of marriage espoused by most feminists.

• *Women and Others*

Finally, the feminist movement was often criticized, sometimes even by its supporters, for being an elitist movement. That is, the charge was sometimes made that feminists were women who dashed in fancy cars to meetings held in middle- or upper-class homes of other feminists so that they could complain about how badly they were oppressed. The charge was occasionally made that the women were actually out of touch with the real social issues of the times. Some of those in the movement acknowledged that there was some validity to the accusation. But if they granted the accuracy of the charge at all, they also did something to correct it.

Toward the end of the 1970s feminist theology gave more attention to the contribution it could make to some of the grinding social problems of poverty, hunger, and racism in this country and around the world. The point was frequently made, for example, that black women

---

[17]Marabel Morgan, *The Total Woman* (Old Tappan NJ: Fleming H. Revell Co., 1973) 58.

suffered from a double oppression—being both black and female. Indeed, many of them suffered from a third oppression, poverty. The movement became more sensitive to the plight of women around the world. In most countries women had suffered not only from patriarchy, but also from economic conditions and, frequently, racism. What was to be done?

Many feminist theologians made sure that their work was not couched in narrow feminist terms. Whether of the Goddess-worhiping revolutionary type or the reformist type which remained loyal to the Judaeo-Christian tradition, they took care to demonstrate that all people should benefit from the themes of equality and fairness. Rosemary Ruether, for example, argued that all dualisms, all attitudes of "us versus them," should be overcome. She pointed out that the same theme of liberation and equality that demands that men should not be dominant over women also demands that no race should lord over another, that no nationality or political system should be oppressive of human beings. Ruether contended that women have a key role to play in bringing about better relationships of all people and classes because they have a long history of being oppressed and thus have great insights out of which to articulate a holistic, life-affirming ethic and theology. But, she maintained, women could play this leavening role only if they were willing to identify with the struggles of other groups.

Consequently, many of the feminist theologians, particularly the reformers, read black theology, Latin American liberation theology, and the reports of oppression from around the world and tried to make a contribution to the alleviation of suffering. Because neither black theology nor Latin American liberation theology, in their formative stages, were especially conscious of the double jeopardy under which women of color or poverty lived, feminists tried to sensitize the other theologians to take seriously the special plight of women. They argued that even the most liberationist of theologies could still think in terms of "man" in the generic sense and overlook the particular needs of women. They attempted to enter into dialogue with others who were particularly interested in the oppressed and added another dimension, arguing powerfully for egalitarian rather than hierarchical relationships in the human community.

• *Suggestions for Further Reading*
for Context and Perspective

A Guide to Inclusive Church Language, 2d ed. The Task Force on Women: Presbytery of the Twin Cities Area, June 1979.

Adler, Margot. *Drawing Down the Moon: Witches, Druids, Goddess-Worshippers, and Other Pagans in America Today*. Boston: Beacon Press, 1979.

Christ, Carol P. and Judith Plaskow, eds. *Womanspirit Rising: A Feminist Reader in Religion*. San Francisco: Harper and Row, 1979.

Daly, Mary. *Beyond God the Father: Toward A Philosophy of Women's Liberation*. Boston: Beacon Press, 1973.

_____. *The Church and the Second Sex*. New York: Harper and Row, 1968, 1975.

Hageman, Alice L., ed. *Sexist Religion and Women in the Church: No More Silence!* New York: Association Press, 1974.

James, Janet Wilson, ed. *Women in American Religion*. University of Pennsylvania Press, 1980.

Jewett, Paul K. *Man as Male and Female*. Grand Rapids MI: Wm. B. Eerdmans Co., 1975.

Morgan, Marabel. *The Total Woman*. Old Tappan NJ: Fleming H. Revell Co., 1973.

Ohanneson, Joan, ed. *Woman: Survivor in the Church*. Minneapolis: Winston Press, 1980.

O'Neill, Lois Decker, ed. *The Women's Book of World Records and Achievements*. Garden City NY: Doubleday Anchor Book, 1979, chapter nine.

Ruether, Rosemary Radford, ed. *Religion and Sexism: Images of Women in the Jewish and Christian Traditions*. New York: Simon and Schuster, 1974.

_____and Rosemary Skinner Keller, eds. *Women and Religion in America: A Documentary History*. Vol. 1: The Nineteenth Century. San Francisco: Harper and Row, 1981.

_____and Eleanor McLaughlin, eds. *Women of Spirit: Female Leadership in the Jewish and Christian Traditions*. New York: Simon and Schuster, 1979.

Scanzoni, Letha and Nancy Hardesty. *All We're Meant to Be: A Biblical Approach to Women's Liberation*. Waco TX: Word Books, 1974.

Spretnak, Charlene, ed. *The Politics of Women's Spirituality: Essays on the Rise of Spiritual Power Within the Feminist Movement*. Garden City NY: Doubleday Anchor Book, 1982.

EPILOGUE

By early 1984, when this book was going to press, the conservative religion of the 1970s was still very much alive. Its high priests were the ministers of the "electronic church" and its principal cheerleader was the President of the United States, Ronald Reagan.

The search for something to give meaning to life continued unabated, for good reasons. The arms race between the United States and Russia galloped madly ahead and humanity contemplated nuclear incineration. An economic recession and its accompanying unemployment brought suffering to many and uneasiness to most. Society was becoming ever more technocratic and dehumanized. Many observers believed that throughout the 1980s and beyond (provided humans allowed themselves to live that long) people would be interested in values and in trying to find some meaning for their lives.

It is difficult to predict future trends in religion. Who, in 1959, could have predicted the remarkable events of the next two decades? But it is reasonable to expect that the religion of the rest of the twentieth century will have been influenced by what happened in the 1960s and 1970s. If that should be the case, then it will be well to to know and understand the major events and trends of those decades. I hope that this book may have provided that service to its readers.

INDEX

Abington Township School District v. Schempp, 14, 143, 144, 145, 146
Abolitionist Movement, 202
Abortion, 123-24, 127, 169, 226
Acts chapter 2, 61, 62
Adam, 103
Altizer, Thomas J. J., 19
American Academy of Religion, 214
American Baptist Church, 218
American Council of Christian Churches, 35-36
American Society of Church History, 214
Amish, Old Order, theory of education, 159
Amos 5:24, 190
Angley, Ernest, 165
Anti-Saloon League, 203
Anti-Semitism, 25, 26
Assassination of national leaders, 13-14
Assemblies of God Churches, 40, 41, 80, 90
Astounding Science Fiction, 96
Astrology, 92
Authority as a defense against modernity, 126-27, 134

Automation and human labor, 121-22
Azusa street revival, 64, 65, 72
Bainbridge, William, 87, 92, 95
Baker v. Carr, 14
Baker, John and Joan, 73
Bakker, Jim and Tammy Fay, 166
Baptism of the Holy Spirit, 63-64, 65, 131; *see also* Classical Pentecostalism, Pentecostalism, Neo-Pentecostalism, Tongues
Basic Bible Church, 151
Bennett, Dennis, 72-74
Berrigan, Daniel and Philip, 25
Beyond God the Father: Toward a Philosophy of Women's Liberation (Mary Daly), 210
Bible, interpretation of, 32, 33, 34, 44, 46, 126-27; feminist interpretation of, 212-13; feminist translation of, 204, 216-17; in conservative theology, 41-42; liberation themes, 212-13; patriarchal themes, 214; *see also* Conservatism, Evangelicalism, Liberalism, Fundamentalism
Bill of Rights, 140, 145
Birmingham AL, 7, 182-84, 185

Black church, 179, 180, 181-82, 185-87, 189, 194-95
"Black Manifesto" (James Foreman), 186
Black power, 11, 184-87, 192
Black theology, 212, 228; and black churches, 194-95; attitude toward violence, 192; nature of, 187-91; racism in, 191; sources of, 189-90; theme of reconciliation, 191; use of Marxist categories, 192-93; varieties of, 191-95
Black Theology Project, 194
Bob Jones University, 45, 148-49, 149n
Bonhoeffer, Dietrich, 15-16, 19
Brainwashing, 86, 94, 107, 108, 161-62; *see also* Cults, Deprogramming
Braunfeld v. Brown, 142n
Brennan, William, 171
Bright, Bill, 50
Brown, Antoinette, 203
Brown, H. Rap, 184
Brown v. Board of Education, 4, 5, 178
Bryan, William Jennings, 35
Budapest, Zsuzsanna, 209

Campus Crusade for Christ, 50, 51, 52
Carmichael, Stokely, 184
Carter, Jimmy, 31, 36, 57
Cathedral of Tomorrow (Akron OH), 166
Central Council of American (Reform) Rabbis, 224
Charismatic Movement, 71, 74
Chicago Call: An Appeal to Evangelicals, 42
Children of God, The (The Love Family), 49, 50, 93-95
Christ, Carol P., 208, 209
Christian Broadcasting Network, 167
Christian Church (Disciples of Christ), 40, 88, 218-19
Christian Echoes National Ministry v. United States, 150, 172
Christian Foundation of Tony and Susan Alamo, 49
Christian Voice, 170
The Christian World Liberation Front (Berkeley Christian Coalition), 51

Church and State, *see* Separation of church and state, First Amendment
Church and the Second Sex, The (Mary Daly), 205, 209
Church attendance trends, 3, 37-39, 48, 118
Church construction costs, 38, 39-40
Church membership, after 1965, 38; decline in liberal denominations, 116-18; from 1940 to 1965, 37; growth in conservative churches, 117-18; trends, 36-39
Church of Jesus Christ of Latter-day Saints (Mormons), 40
Church-related colleges and universities, government aid to, 156-57
Churches of Christ, 40, 41
Civil disobedience, 183-84
Civil Rights Act of 1964, 7, 15, 148, 158n
Civil Rights Movement, 5-8, 9, 48, 185, 186, 192, 194; background of, 177-79; white support for, 185
Classical Pentecostalism, 65, 74, 75, 81, 90, 131, 219; emotionalism, 69; justification, 63; nineteenth-century background, 63; origin of, 64-65; sanctification, 63; sociological characteristics, 69-71; socio-economic progress, 71, 80; *see also* Neo-Pentecostalism, Pentecostalism, Tongues
Collins, Sheila, 209
Committee for Public Education and Religious Liberty v. Nyquist, 157
Communism, 2-3, 8, 10, 102, 105, 106, 122, 169, 193; Chinese, 122
Computers, 119, 121
Cone, James, 191, 192-93
Conference of Charismatic Renewal in the Christian Churches, 81
Congregational Church, 203
Congress of National Black Churches, 195
Congress of Racial Equality, 181

Congress, United States, 8, 9, 145, 148, 152, 157, 169, 170

Connor, Eugene "Bull", 182

Conscientious objection, selective objection to war, 152; based on unconventional religious belief, 151-52

Conservatism, 20-21, 31, 34-36, 48, 49, 53, 117, 126, 132-35, 214; and electronic church, 168; and separation of church and state, 171-74; compared with Liberalism, 41; defined, 32, 41-42; deemphasizes social action, 43; diversity in, 44-53; evangelism, 129-30; growth of, 40-43, 133-36; political action, 169, 170; rejected secular theology, 20; social action, 53-57; supplies authority, 126-28; supplies eschatology, 128-30; supplies healing, 130-34; the Jesus movement, 21

Constitution of the United States, 123, 140, 144, 145, 172, 173; Article III, 145; Article VI, 140, 172-73; Fourteenth Amendment, 140; Eighteenth Amendment, 203-204; Nineteenth Amendment, 204; *see also* First Amendment

1 Corinthians 12-14, 61, 62, 67

Cornell University, 12

Cox, Harvey, 16, 19

Cross and the Switchblade, The (David Wilkerson), 75

Crystal Cathedral (Garden Grove CA), 165

Cults, 50, 51, 86-87, 90-96, 109, 160-64; audience, 92, 95; client, 92-93, 95; cult movements, 93-96; importation, 91-92; individual-transforming, 95, 96-102; innovation, 91; world-transforming, 95-96, 102-109; value judgments, 109; *see also* Deprogramming

Cultural traumas of the 1960s and 1970s, 118-19

Dallas Theological Seminary, 45

Daly, Mary, 205-206, 209-11

Darrow, Clarence, 35

Darwin, Charles, 34

Daughters of Sarah, 214

David, Moses (David Berg), 49, 50, 93, 94

"Day of Discovery" (Richard De Haan), 166

Dayton, Donald, 214

Dayton, Lucille Sider, 214

De Haan, Richard, 166

Death of God theology, 18-20; *see also* Secular theology

"A Declaration of Evangelical Social Concern", 56

"Declaration on the Question of the Admission of Women to the Ministerial Priesthood" (John Paul II), 222

Deism, 32-33

Democratic National Convention in Chicago (1968), 12

"Depatriarchalizing in Biblical Interpretation" (Phyllis Trible), 213

Deprogramming, 160-64

Detroit MI, 186, 193, 221

Dianetics, 96-97; *see* Scientology; "Dianetics: the Evolution of a Science" (L. Ron Hubbard), 96; *Dianetics: The Modern Science of Mental Health* (L. Ron Hubbard), 96

Dispensationalism, 46, 54

Divine Principle (Unification Church), 103

Doe v. Bolton, 169

Drugs, 4, 127

Du Plesis, David, 74-75

Duquesne University, 75, 76

Eisenhower, Dwight D., 4, 178

Election of 1980, 171, 173; and conservative social action, 57

Electronic church, 164-70; audience of, 167; effect on local churches, 168; financial support of, 167; political involvement, 168

Emotionalism, 131, 132

Engel v. Vitale, 14, 143, 144

Environment, the, 120, 121, 208-209

Episcopal Church, 38, 40, 73, 74, 81, 88; General Assembly, 219-20; ordination of women, 219-21; Episcopal Theological School in Cambridge MA, 219; Episcopal Women's Caucus, 220

Equal Rights Amendment, 169, 205, 226

Eschatology, 128-29, 134

Escobedo v. Illinois, 14

Establishment, the, 11, 12, 48; church as part of, 17, 43

Establishment Clause, 140-43, 160, 163, 171-72; excessive entanglement test, 146, 147, 154, 155, 156; primary effect test, 144, 146, 154, 155, 156; secular purpose test, 144, 146; *see also* First Amendment, Separation of church and state

Evangelical feminist scholars, 214

Evangelical Women's Caucus, 214

Evangelicalism, 31, 41, 43, 54, 74, 133, 134, 171, 226; and Christian action, 56-57

Evangelicalism, Establishment, 46, 48, 50, 126, 214; interpretation of the Bible, 46

Evangelicalism, New, 46-48, 51, 78, 168, 214; and social action, 47, 56; interpretation of the Bible, 46-47; *see also* Conservatism

Evolution, 34, 35, 47, 54, 55

Eve, 103, 208

Existential questions, 115, 132

Exodus of Israel from Egypt, 190, 211

Falwell, Jerry, 45, 165, 170, 174

Family, the, 123, 127

Faubus, Orval, 178

Fellowship of Christian Athletes, 51, 52

Fellowship of Witness (Episcopal Church), 41

Feminine Mystique, The (Betty Friedan), 204

Feminism, historical background, 202-207

Feminist theology, 123, 193, 202; the Bible in, 204, 212-13, 214; Bible translation, 216-17; criticism of, 227-28; historical studies in, 213-15; inclusive language, 215-17; modern, 204-207; opposition to, 226-27; post-Christian, 210-11; reformist, 206, 211-17, 226, 228; revolutionary, 206, 207-11, 228; social action in, 228-29; sources for, 206-207; *see also* Patriarchy, Women

Finney, Charles G., 33

Fiorenza, Elisabeth Schüssler, 214

First Amendment, 140-41, 147, 149, 150, 163, 173, 174; incorporated into the Fourteenth, 140; *see also* Establishment clause, Free exercise clause, Separation of church and state

Flast v. Cohen, 146, 154

Food and Drug Administration, 101

Foreman, James, 186

Founding Church of Scientology, 97, 100

Free exercise clause, 141, 142, 158-60, 171; test for deciding cases, 158-59, 160; *see also* First Amendment, Separation of church and state

Freedom rides, 6, 181

Friedan, Betty, 204, 205

Full Gospel Business Men's Fellowship International, 72, 81

Full Gospel Business Men's Voice, 72

Fundamentalism, 34-36, 41, 43, 49, 50, 54, 57, 74, 126-27, 133, 134, 148, 150, 171, 226; defined, 35; media ministries, 164-65, 168; open, 45, 47, 48; Separatist, 44-45, 47, 49

Fundamentals, The, 34

Galatians 3:28, 207

Gallup, George, Jr., 31

Gay rights movement, 169

Ghana Consultation on Black/African Theology, 193

Gideon v. Wainwright, 14

Gillette v. United States, 152

Ginsberg, Allen, 4

God, as a source of patriarchy, 216; working in history, 134-35
Goddess(es), 207-11; as personification of nature, 207-209; witchcraft (wicca), 208-209; *see also* Feminist theology
Goldenberg, Naomi, 209
Goldstein, Valerie Saiving, 205
Good News (United Methodist Church), 41
Gorder, Paul Van, 166
Government interference in church affairs, 147-49, 150, 151; *see also* Separation of church and state
Grace Cathedral (Akron OH), 165
Graham, Billy, 20, 46
Great Society, 9
Grimké, Angelina, 202
Grimké, Sarah, 202, 204
Gulf of Tonkin, 8
Gyn/Ecology: The Metaethics of Radical Feminism (Mary Daly), 210

Ha, Hak Jan, 104
Hamilton, William, 19
Hardesty, Nancy, 214
Hare Krishna, 92
Hargis, Billy James, 150
Healing, as a defense against modernity, 134
Hebrew prophets, 190
Helms, Jesse, 145
His (Inter-Varsity Christian Fellowship), 52
Hitler, Adolf, 15, 26
Holocaust, The, 25, 26, 178, 213
Holy Spirit Association for the Unification of World Christianity (Unification Church), 102-109
"Hour of Power" (Robert Schuller), 165
House of Representatives, United States, 145
Hubbard, LaFayette Ronald, 96, 97, 98, 101, 102, 102n; *see also* Scientology
Hubbard Research Foundation, 96, 97
Human abilities, confidence in, 120
Humanae Vitae (Pope Paul VI), 24

Humbard, Rex and Maud Aimee, 166, 167

Inclusive language; *see* Language, Nonsexist
Inclusive language lectionary, 217
Inflation and recession, 122
Influence of religion on American life, 39
Internal Revenue Code, Section 501(c)(3), 149-51
Internal Revenue Service, 147, 149, 151
Inter-Varsity Christian Fellowship, 51-52
Isaiah 6:1, 210
Israel, Six-day war, 26

James 5:14-15, 131
Jehovah's Witnesses, 40
Jesus Movement, the, 21, 48-53
Jewett, Paul, 214
Jewish Feminist Organization, 225
Jewish Theological Seminary of America, 225
Jim Crow laws, 5, 186, 189
Jimmy Swaggart Evangelistic Association, 166
John XXIII, Pope, 22, 77, 222
Johnson, Lyndon B., 8, 9, 12
Jones, Jim, 86
Jones, Major J., 191
Judaism, 4, 25-27, 39, 178; and secular theology, 25; and social struggles, 25; ordination of women, 223-26; ordination of women in Conservative, 225-26; ordination of women in Orthodox, 225; ordination of women in Reconstructionist, 225; ordination of women in Reform, 224-25; Orthodox, 142; Orthodox women, 201; reaction to 1960s, 26-27

Kelley, Dean M., 113-18, 125, 126, 130, 134, 135
Kennedy, John F., 13, 21-22
Kennedy, Robert, 13
Kent State University, 27
Kerouac, Jack, 4
Khomeini, Ayatollah, 174

King, Martin Luther, Jr., 4, 6, 10, 13, 179-85, 187, 191, 192

Korea, 102, 104, 105

Language, nonsexist, 215, 217

Late Great Planet Earth, The, (Hal Lindsey), 45

"Letter from Birmingham Jail" (Martin L. King, Jr.), 182-84, 192-93

Liberalism, 34, 43, 55, 75, 113, 117, 129, 131-35, 169; and the electronic church, 168; compared with Conservatism, 41; decline of, 40-41; defined, 32; media ministries, 164-65; social action, 53-54

Liberation, of the oppressed, 189-90, 191, 228; *see also* Black theology, Feminist theology

Liberation theology: African, 193; South American, 192, 193, 194, 228

Life Science Church, 151

Lincoln, C. Eric, 186, 187, 188

Lindsey, Hal, 45

Little Rock AR, 4, 5, 178, 179

Lutherans, 74, 81

Lutheran Church in America, 218

Lutheran Church (Missouri Synod), 41

McAteer, Ed, 170

McCarthy, Joseph, 2

McDaniel v. Paty, 159, 171

McGowan v. Maryland, 141n

McIntire, Carl, 35, 45

McLaughlin, Eleanor, 214

McLuhan, Marshall, 124-25, 131, 132

Mail-order ministry: vow of poverty, 151

Male theology, 201-12

"Man come of age," 16, 19

"Man for others," 19; Jesus as, 16

Manson, Charles, 86

Manson "Family," the, 109

Mark 13:7-8, 129

Marxism, 47

Matthew 28:19-20, 54

Meaning in life, 124, 125, 126-34, 136; need for, 113-19; relation to church growth and decline, 116

Media, the, 7, 48, 52, 82, 109, 124, 125, 132, 134, 167, 182; ministries, 41, 164-70; *see also* Electronic church, Television

Medical technology, 119

Melodyland Christian Center, 78

Mennonite Church, 40

Messianic Jews, 81

Methodists, 38, 81

Military draft, 9

Military service, religious objections to, 151-52

Miranda v. Arizona, 14

"Mo Letters" (Moses David), 94

Mollenkott, Virginia Ramey, 214

Montgomery AL, 5, 179; bus boycott, 4, 179-81

Moon, Sun Myung, 102, 103, 104, 107, 108

Moral majority, 122, 170, 171, 172

Morgan, Marabel, 226-27

Mormonism (Church of Jesus Christ of Latter-day Saints), 91

Moynihan, Daniel Patrick, 157

Murray v. Curlett, 143n

National Association of Evangelicals, 36, 46

National Christian Action Coalition, 170

National Committee of Black Churchmen, 186, 195

National Council of Churches of Christ in the United States, 35-36, 46, 217

National Labor Relations Act, 148

National Labor Relations Board, 147-48

National Labor Relations Board v. Catholic Bishop of Chicago, 148

National Organization for Women, 205

Nazi Germany, 4, 15, 25, 178

Neo-Pentecostalism, 128, 131; as left-wing conservatism, 79; characteristics of, 77-82; in congregations, 78; ecumenical dimension, 80-81; evangelism, 81; hostility towards, 79-80; origins of, 71-77; spiritual elitism, 79; *see also*

Classical Pentecostalism, Pentecostalism, Tongues
Neoorthodoxy, 3
New Morality, 17-18
Newsweek, 31
1960s and 1970s, technological developments, 119-21; social/political trends, 121-26
Nixon, Richard, 14
Nonviolent resistance, 7, 180, 182, 183-84, 185, 192
Notre Dame University, 76
Nuclear war, 3
Nuclear weapons, 2, 120-21

Office of Economic Opportunity, 148
O'Hair, Madalyn Murray, 139, 143n
"Old-Time Gospel Hour, The" (Jerry Falwell), 165
"Oral Roberts and You," 166
Oral Roberts University, 166
Origin of the Species (Charles Darwin), 34
Other Side, The, 47, 57
Ozman, Agnes, 64

Packwood, Robert, 157
Pan-African Conference of Third World Theologians, 194
Parham, Charles Fox, 64
Parks, Rosa, 179
Parochial Schools, government aid to, 152-57; and the NLRB, 148; court decisions, controversy, 157
Patriarchy, 203, 207, 208, 228; female stereotypes, 199-200; God as a source of, 200-201, 210; in the Bible, 212-13; Judaeo-Christian tradition, 200-201; male stereotypes, 199-200; result of dualism, 211; *see also* Feminist theology
Patrick, Ted, 162
Paul, 66, 67, 68, 77, 207
Paul VI, Pope, 24, 77
Pentecostalism, emotionalism, 77; gifts of the Spirit, 68, 77; New Testament origins, 61; Roman Catholic, 75-77; *see also* Classical Pentecostalism, Neo-Pentecostalism, Tongues

People's Temple, 86, 109
Plessy v. Ferguson, 178
Pluralism, religious, 105, 109, 174
Political leadership, corrupt, 122
Popular piety, 3, 43
Population growth, 121
Pornography, 169
Prayer and/or Bible reading in public schools, 142-45, 169
Premillennialism, 54
Presbyterian Church in the United States, 40, 88, 218
Presbyterian Lay Committee (Presbyterian Church in the USA), 41
Presbyterians, 38, 74, 81
Presbyterians United for Biblical Concerns (Presbyterian Church in the USA), 41
Priesand, Sally, 224
"PTL Club" (Jim Bakker), 166
Public schools, prayer in, 142-45, 169; teaching religion, 144; *see also* Separation of church and state

Quebedeaux, Richard, 44

Racial and ethnic prejudice, 4, 7
Radical religion, 36, 48; *see* Secular theology
Randolph, A. Philip, 10
Reagan, Ronald, 145n, 157n, 170, 171
Religion as social activism, 16-18
Religionless Christianity, 15-16, 17
Revivalism, 33, 63
Right On! (Christian World Liberation Front), 51
Roberts, Oral, 165, 166, 167
Robertson, Pat, 167, 170
Robison, James, 45, 170, 174
Roe v. Wade, 169
Roman Catholicism, 21-25, 62, 75, 81, 88, 148, 153, 169, 192; and secular theology, 24-25; Conference on Women's Ordination, 221, 222; Leadership Conference of Women Religious, 222; opposition to women's ordination, 222; ordination of women, 221-23; Pentecos-

talism, 75-77; Priests for Equality, 221; women, 201, 205-206, 209-10; *see also* Vatican Council II

Roundtable, the, 170

Ruether, Rosemary, 211-12, 228

Russell, Letty, 214

Rustin, Bayard, 10

Sabbatarians, 142, 158

Saint Joan's International Alliance, 221

Saint Luke's Episcopal Church (Seattle WA), 73

Saint Mark's Episcopal Church (Van Nuys CA), 72

Salvation Army, 40, 219

1 Samuel 28:3-20, 93

Satan, 103

Scanzoni, Letha, 214

Schlafly, Phyllis, 226

Schuller, Robert, 165, 167

Science, impact on religion, 34, 47

Scientology, 96-102, 106, 108; the analytical mind, 98, 99; auditing, 99; clear, 99, 100, 101; E-meter, 99, 101; engrams, 98-99; opposition to, 97, 100-102; the reactive mind, 98; reply to criticisms, 101-102; Thetan, 98

Scopes, John Thomas, 35

Scopes trial, 35, 55-56

Sect to church progression, 90

Sects, 89-90, 109

Secular City, The (Harvey Cox), 17

Secular humanism, 169

Secular right wing, 169

Secular theology, 15-20, 41, 46, 118

Secularism, 54, 55

Seminary students, 42-43

Senate, United States, 145

Separation of church and state, 105, 163, 171-74; background, 139-41; *see also* Establishment clause, First Amendment, Free exercise clause

"700 Club" (Pat Robertson), 166-67

Seventh-Day Adventist, 40

Sexual mores, 4

Sexual relationships, 123, 124, 127

Seymour, William I., 64

Shakarian, Demos, 72

Sherbert v. Verner, 158

Sherrill, John, 76

Sit-ins, 5-6, 10, 181-82

Situation ethics, 17-18

Social activism, 168-71; *see also* Evangelicalism, New; Fundamentalism, Liberalism

Social Gospel, the, 53-54, 55

Society for the Study of Black Religions, 193

Society of Biblical Literature, 204, 214

Sociology of religion, 86-87; *see also* Churches, Sects, Cults

Sojourners, 47, 57

Southeast Asia, 8, 10

Southern Baptist Convention, 40, 41, 218

Southern Christian Leadership Conference, 181, 182

Soviet Union, 2, 121

Space exploration, 119

Spiritualism, 93

Spretnak, Charlene, 209

Sputnik I, 3, 119

Stanton, Elizabeth Cady, 204

Starhawk, 209

Stark, Rodney, 87, 92, 95

Stendahl, Krister, 214

Stone, Merlin, 209

Student Nonviolent Coordinating Committee, 10, 184

Students for a Democratic Society, 12

Sunday closing laws, 141-42

Sunday schools, 3, 37-38

Supreme Court, 4, 14, 123, 141, 143, 145-48, 151-53, 155-60, 169, 173, 178; *see also* Establishment clause, First Amendment, Free exercise clause

Swaggart, Jimmy, 166, 167

"TV children," 124-25, 131-32; and church growth, 132

TWA v. Hardison, 158n

Tax exemption, and government policy on race relations, 148-49; and mail-order ministries, 150-51; and political activity, 149-50

Tax Reform Act of 1969, 147

Taxation of religious institutions, 146-51

Taxpayer suits, standing in, 146-47

Television, 20, 124-25, 131, 164, 168, 169

Television ministries, 165-67

Tennessee, legal restrictions on ministries, 159-60

Theology in the Americas, 193-94

They Speak With Other Tongues (John Sherrill), 76

Third World, the, 121

Thomas Road Baptist Church (Lynchburg VA), 165

Time, 20

Torcaso v. Watkins, 142, 173

Tongues, as intelligible languages, 62, 66; prayer and devotion, 66; as unintelligible languages, 62, 66; in private devotions, 67; interpretation of, 62, 67; nature and value of, 65-69

Total Woman, The (Marabel Morgan), 226

Tremmel, William C., 114, 115, 125

Trible, Phyllis, 213

Trinity, the, 33

Unchurched, the, 135

Understanding Church Growth and Decline 1950-1978 (Dean Hoge), 117

Unification Church, 92, 102-109; criticism, 106-108; opposition to Communism, 105; origin, 102-103; recruitment, 106-107; response to criticism, 107; theology, 103-106

Unitarianism, 32, 33

United Church of Christ, 40, 81, 218

United Methodist Church, 40, 63, 88, 218

United Presbyterian Church in the USA, 40, 41, 218

United States v. Seeger, 152

United Synagogues of America, 225

Universal Life Church, 151

Vahanian, Gabriel, 19

Van Buren, Paul, 19

Vatican Council II, 22, 75, 153, 209-10, 221; implications for nuns and priests, 23-24; practical results, 23-25

Vietnam war, 8-10, 48, 151, 152

Vietnam, benefits to American industry, 9; civil rights movement arguments, 9

View of history, 128-29, 130

Violence as a tool of social change, 184, 185

Voter registration, 6

Voting Rights Act of 1965, 7, 15

Wallace, George Corley, 14

Wallis, Jim, 57

Walz v. Tax Commission of the City of New York, 146

Warren, Chief Justice Earl, 14

Way, The, 50

Wesley, John, 63

Where Have All Our People Gone? (Carl Dudley), 117

White theology, 188-89, 191, 201

Why Conservative Churches Are Growing (Dean Kelley), 113

Wierwille, Victor Paul, 50

Wilkerson, David, 75

Willard, Frances, 203

Winthrop, John, 33

Wisconsin v. Yoder, 159

Woman's Bible, The, 204

Women, and Roman Catholicism, 205-206; anti-alcohol crusade, 203; body experiences of, 206, 207-208, 209; ordination to ministry, 203, 217-26; *see also* Feminist theology

Women's Christian Temperance Union, 203

World Council of Churches, 74

World War II, 1, 4-5, 15, 71, 75, 117, 118, 177, 217, 224

Youth, 39, 48-53, 117, 135; alienation from American life, 4, 11; and the civil rights movement, 10-11; antiwar activities, 10, 11; drop out of establishment society, 12-13, 48; try to recreate the society, 12

Youth for Christ International, 52

Young Evangelicals, The (Richard Quebedeaux), 44

Young Life Campaign, The, 52

Zickmund, Barbara Brown, 214